AF895088

Europe's Postwar Growth

Written under the auspices of
The Center for International Affairs
Harvard University

Europe's Postwar Growth

THE ROLE OF LABOR SUPPLY

by CHARLES P. KINDLEBERGER

HARVARD UNIVERSITY PRESS

CAMBRIDGE, MASSACHUSETTS 1967

© Copyright 1967 by the President and Fellows of Harvard College

Distributed in Great Britain by Oxford University Press, London

All rights reserved

Library of Congress Catalog Card Number 67-14342

Printed in the United States of America

To P.M.F. and R.J.F.

ACKNOWLEDGMENTS

The Center for International Affairs at Harvard University financed the research on which this book is based, including a trip to Europe in the summer of 1964 for the purpose of interviewing academic economists and officials in Belgium, the Netherlands, Germany, Austria, Switzerland, Italy, and France. I am grateful for the Center's support and for the generous welcome which I was given in Europe. I should like to list all who helped, but their numbers are too great. Research assistance at home base at M.I.T. was provided in 1963–64 by T. Paul Schultz and in 1964–65 by Militades Chacholiades. Robert J. Gordon both compiled Table VI-2 and reviewed the first draft with great care and penetration. Suggestions for changes were also received from William Diebold, Jr., and John Cornwall. I am grateful to all of them for their assistance. Mrs. Carolyn Washburne was helpful in preparing the manuscript. An earlier version of Chapter V was published in the Banca Nazionale del Lavoro *Quarterly Review* for September 1965.

The book suffers from the fact that it was written without my having seen the manuscript of the impressive book by Edward F. Denison, with the assistance of Jean-Pierre Poullier, *Why Growth Rates Differ, Postwar Experience in Nine Western Countries,* to be published by the Brookings Institution in 1967. Denison's meticulous and detailed quantitative estimates of the ingredients of growth partly confirm and partly contradict my more intuitive and impressionistic analysis.

Noneconomists have permission to skip the first 13 pages of Chapter I, which describe the Lewis model of growth in somewhat technical terms, and to start the chapter on page 18, which indicates how useful this model is in explaining the course of growth in Britain and the United States in the nineteenth century, before going on to postwar Europe in Chapter II. Two noneconomists, the Rev. Dr. and Mrs. Rollin J. Fairbanks, have permission to skip the whole work, although it is dedicated to them in friendship.

Charles P. Kindleberger

Massachusetts Institute of Technology
September 1966

CONTENTS

TABLES

FIGURES

Europe's Postwar Growth

INTRODUCTION

In a previous book, I concluded that economic history suffered from the availability of too many models of economic relationships, all of a certain plausibility but none demonstrably more useful as an explanation of the past than others.[1] After finishing that work, however, I came to think that one model of economic analysis — W. Arthur Lewis' model of growth with unlimited supplies of labor, with its strong affinities to the Marxian system — had much more explanatory power in history than I had allowed. It is helpful in accounting both for the growth of Britain during the Industrial Revolution and for the rise of real income of labor after the slowing down of the rate of growth in the second half of the nineteenth century; it is relevant to the growth of the United States from 1880 to 1913; and in particular, as I seek to demonstrate here, it is useful to explain the very high rates of growth of some countries of Europe in the period since World War II — rates which are higher than can normally be sustained over long periods and are therefore entitled to be called supergrowth.

The Lewis model does not account for all the divergences in growth in Europe from country to country or from industry to industry. Specific national exceptions are described below. Other instances where the data do not conform to the model may have been glossed over somewhat in the enthusiasm of pointing out the strengths of the model. I am even ready to admit that despite its explanatory power in recent European growth labor elasticity cannot account for all deviations from normal growth paths, nor does there seem to be any single model which can. Nevertheless, the case for applying the Lewis model to Europe remains strong.

A recent claim has been made that "modern growth theory" accounts for the facts of European experience and permits projections better than any of the standard Harrod-Domar models

1. *Economic Growth in France and Britain, 1851–1950* (Cambridge, Mass.: Harvard University Press, 1964).

used by, say, Alexander Lamfalussy or Angus Maddison.[2] It is hard to judge this claim in detail since the experience of various European countries over recent years is presented as a smooth curve without the separate points on the scatter diagram. But modern growth theory, as set forth in the article in which the claim is made, implies that rates of growth, other things being equal, will taper off slowly.[3] I predict, on the contrary, that European growth rates cannot be sustained at the high rates achieved from 1950 to 1961 or 1962 and that supergrowth at rates of 6, 7, or 8 percent per annum per capita must give way to more normal rates of 2, 3, or 4 percent. The main concern is with supergrowth and not with the factors which go to explain normal increases in productivity.

This book had its proximate origin in a remark of Robert Mundell at an international trade seminar at M.I.T. in 1962. He stated that an increase in the share of income going to labor in a country would worsen that country's balance of payments. Since I was taking part in an interdisciplinary seminar on Western Europe at the Harvard Center for International Affairs — a group composed largely of political scientists, sociologists, and even lawyers, along with economists — I was led to broaden the scope of the investigation beyond the confines of the impact of income distribution on the balance of payments, widening the field of vision, on the one hand, to include economic growth along with the balance of payments and, on the other, going behind income distribution to the labor supply and in particular to the striking current phenomenon of European labor migration with its political and social as well as economic impact.

It has been suggested by a reader of the manuscript that I have been led to write not one but two books, or even two and a half books: one on the Lewis model as it applies to the separate countries of Europe; one on the migration of labor from the Mediterranean countries to northern Europe, especially to Switzerland, Germany, France, and Belgium; and a fragment at the

2. Jerome L. Stein, "Economic Growth in the West," *Economica*, XXXII (February 1965), 74–87.

3. "The rate of growth of productivity is positively related to the rate at which organizational improvements are taking place, and negatively related to the level of productivity, the rate of growth of the labor force, the rate of depreciation and the rate of interest" (*ibid.*, p. 85).

end to relate these issues to a variety of considerations from the United States balance of payments to social justice. This is not far wrong.

The thesis of the book is that the major factor shaping the remarkable economic growth which most of Europe has experienced since 1950 has been the availability of a large supply of labor. The labor has come from a high rate of natural increase (the Netherlands), from transfers from agriculture to services and industry (Germany, France, Italy), from the immigration of refugees (Germany), and from the immigration of unemployed and underemployed workers from the Mediterranean countries (France, Germany, and Switzerland). Those countries with no substantial increase in the labor supply — Britain, Belgium, and the Scandinavian nations — on the whole have grown more slowly than the others.

With the exhaustion of Europe's excess supplies of labor, in the early 1960's, the high rates of economic growth of the 1950's are slowing down, and their character is changing. Not only is the upward trend in income less steep; interruptions are more frequent and longer, and balance-of-payments surpluses give way on occasion to deficits. The virtuous circle of exports leading to higher incomes, profits, and investment, which in turn lower prices and stimulate exports once again, is replaced by the classical negative-feedback mechanism in which increased exports are followed by higher prices, which cut off exports and attract additional imports.

The expansion of the 1950's has, as mentioned above, followed what W. Arthur Lewis calls the model of "growth with unlimited supplies of labor." Lewis and others, such as Ragnar Nurkse and John Fei and Gustav Ranis, have sought to apply the model to less developed countries.[4] The model's most striking relevance, however, has been among the developed countries of Europe. Not every rapidly growing developed country in Europe has

4. See W. Arthur Lewis, "Development with Unlimited Supplies of Labor," *The Manchester School,* XXII (May 1954), 139–191; Ragnar Nurkse, *Problems of Capital Formation in Underdeveloped Areas* (New York: Oxford University Press, 1953); John C. H. Fei and Gustav Ranis, *Development of the Labor Surplus Economy: Theory and Policy* (Homewood, Ill.: Richard D. Irwin, 1964); Gustav Ranis and John C. H. Fei, "A Theory of Economic Development," *American Economic Review,* LI (September 1961), 533–565.

followed this pattern. French and Austrian growth at high levels occurred in the face of tight labor markets. Moreover, the Mediterranean rim of less developed countries — Portugal, Spain and Greece, and southern Italy — has benefited in growth from the loss of labor (a different though in some ways complementary model).

Abundant labor can sustain a growth process; it cannot initiate it. Most writing on European postwar growth — especially by the British writers — has concentrated on the maintenance of demand. Many economists assume a Keynesian model of growth in which demand creates its own supply, in contrast to the classical or Say's law model in which supply creates its own demand. In my view, it makes little difference whether the initial lead is taken by demand, through increased consumption, investment, exports, or government spending, or taken by supply stemming from technical change. It is crucial only that demand leading to supply or supply leading to demand does not run up against rising wages which cut profits, investment, productivity increases, and hence slow down the growth process. Once the dynamic process has started, that is, it depends upon supply, the steady expansion of capital and labor, and the absence of bottlenecks which would throw the expansion process either into reverse or, more typically, into a slower forward gear.

Moreover, the availability of excess labor does not determine the levels at which growth will be maintained, such levels being a function of the availability of better technology and better methods of organizing production and distribution. An elastic labor supply supports high rates of investment — with more rather than less embodied technological change — and ensures that these can be sustained rather than reversed. But the labor supply, so long as it lasts, is a permissive rather than an initiating or even a determining factor.

What has caused Europe to run out of labor and thus throttle down from the unusual growth rates of about 6 percent per annum during the 1950's in the faster-growing countries to more normal rates of about 3 percent? Among the contributing factors must be mentioned the raising of the Berlin Wall in August 1961, the growing nationalism that has led Switzerland to halt immigration and Greece to slow down emigration, and the difficulty that immigrants typically do not provide the appropriate mix of skills needed for the labor force. A number of countries have tried to substitute control of wage rates, or "incomes policy," for the assistance to growth furnished by unlimited supplies of labor. It seems unlikely that they will succeed.

These are the themes of the book. It starts with a chapter on the Lewis model and that model's great power for explaining British and American growth in the nineteenth century. There follow four chapters on postwar growth in European countries: one on the countries of expanding labor supply — Germany, Italy, the Netherlands, and Switzerland; a second on Austria and France, which departed from the model and grew rapidly; a third on the countries of unchanged labor supply — Scandinavian, and Belgium and the United Kingdom, which were slow growers; and a fourth on the countries of emigration.

Next comes a chapter on demand — covering especially exports, consumption, investment, and government expenditure — and one on supply, apart from labor, with emphasis on technological change and the efficiency of investment. The bulk of the rest of the book is devoted to labor markets in Europe and to intra-European migration, winding up with a discussion of manpower policy, on the one hand, and incomes policy, on the other. Final chapters address the implications of the change from the Lewis model to more usual forms of growth for the economic and financial relations between Europe and the United States, and relations between growth and social justice.

The method employed is analytical rather than statistical or econometric. Tables are used, but little attempt has been made to produce new or even newly arranged data.

CHAPTER I

The Lewis Model of Growth with Unlimited Supplies of Labor

The Model

The Lewis model of economic growth is disaggregated; that is, it has more than one sector. It also has more than one factor. In its simplest version, applied to a closed economy, it has two sectors, industry and agriculture, and two factors in each sector (three in all): capital and labor in industry, labor and land in agriculture. Labor is redundant in agriculture. There is so much labor attached to the land that its marginal product is zero. To remove one unit of labor from the sector would leave total output virtually unaffected. Since this labor is paid a wage, presumably at a subsistence level, and its marginal product is zero, labor income is in effect contributed out of the marginal product of land, or out of rent. To the extent that the economy involved is a peasant society, with farms owned by the peasant and family labor employed, the marginal product of labor is zero but the family lives off the rental share. Where there are landlords and landless workers, wages are higher than marginal product, though at the subsistence level. The difference must come out of the landlord's rental.

In industry, employment is determined by the demand for labor, which is a function of technology, the availability of capital, and the demand for industrial products. Income distribution proceeds through competitive factor markets. Wages are determined, however, not by the demand for labor but by the infinitely elastic supply at a price that may be somewhat above the subsistence level in agriculture to compensate for the higher costs of town over rural life.

Suppose that some disturbance occurs in the industrial sector

— an increase in the demand for its product, a technical change which increases industrial efficiency, or new capital made available from outside the system. This disturbance increases the demand for labor. Under ordinary conditions, wages would rise, as a shift of the demand curve to the right met an upward sloping supply curve for labor, a curve which might be completely inelastic or even backward-bending. But with redundant labor available and ready to move in from agriculture, the increased demand for labor results in higher profits and no change in the wage rate. Figure I-1 shows the impact on wage rates and total

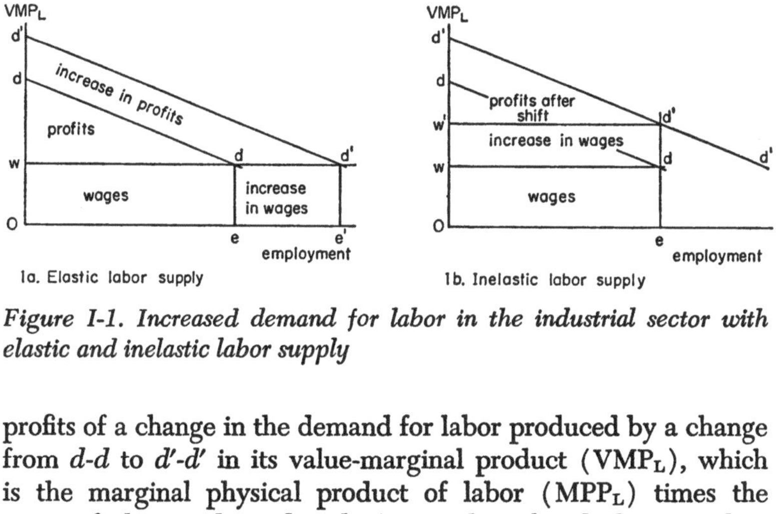

Figure I-1. Increased demand for labor in the industrial sector with elastic and inelastic labor supply

profits of a change in the demand for labor produced by a change from *d-d* to *d′-d′* in its value-marginal product (VMP_L), which is the marginal physical product of labor (MPP_L) times the price of the good produced. (Note that the declining value-marginal product curve is a demand curve for labor and that the area under it represents total value product, which can be divided between wages — the quantity of labor times its product — and the remainder, the latter going to the other factor in a two-factor model — in this case profits.) In the left-hand portion of Figure I-1, with an infinitely elastic supply of labor at the wage *o-w*, profits rise after an increase in the VMP_L of labor, from *w-d-d* to *w-d′-d′*. In the right-hand half of the figure, where employment is unchanged because of zero elasticity in the labor supply, the wage rate rises from *o-w* to *o-w′*, the wages bill from *o-w-d-e* to *o-w′-d′-e′*, and profits are changed from *w-d-d* to *w′-d′-d′*. They are unchanged, smaller, or somewhat increased, depending on the nature of the demand shift.[1]

With unlimited supplies of labor, the initial disturbance in the industrial sector leads to increased employment of labor and increased profits. Wages are spent on consumption, but profits are saved and reinvested. In the next period, therefore, the demand for labor increases again, and profits rise further. So long as labor continues redundant, the growth process continues through higher profits, reinvestment, increased productivity for labor but a constant wage. This is the model of growth that Marx identified and regarded as highly exploitive of labor. It can continue, however, only so long as there is an elastic supply of labor, redundant in the agricultural sector and available to the industrial sector.

Constant wage rates and rising profits seem to imply that wages decline as a percentage of national (or sector) income. Not necessarily, however, since the wages bill grows with increased employment. In Europe after 1950, wages rose *pari passu* with profits during the stage of unlimited supplies of labor, and wages remained a constant share of national income.

Once the supply of labor runs out, increased capital formation in industry results in higher wages and possibly in lower profits. Wages rise as a share of income. Continuous increases in profits and investment come to a halt, which ends the continuous upward shift of the demand for labor. The character of the growth process alters.

In agriculture, the growth process differs from that in industry. As labor leaves the sector, changes occur in the marginal product of labor, on the one hand, and in income distribution and expenditure, on the other. Initially the marginal product of labor is zero. As labor leaves, the marginal product of the remaining labor is initially unaffected and then begins to rise. The movement out of agriculture will continue so long as the conventional or subsistence wage in agriculture is above the marginal product, but after a time the marginal product rises to the subsistence

1. John C. H. Fei and Gustav Ranis discuss the impact on income distribution of the character of technical change, and especially whether such change is labor-saving or capital-saving, labor-using or capital-using (*Development of the Labor Surplus Economy: Theory and Policy,* Homewood, Ill.: Richard D. Irwin, 1964, chap. 3).

wage. At this stage, any increased demand for labor from agriculture by the industrial sector will raise the marginal product of labor and agricultural wages, leading to rising wages in industry.

Before this happens, however, changes will have taken place in income distribution in the agricultural sector. The initial losses of labor without a reduction in output will have raised incomes per capita of those remaining behind. Fei and Ranis make much of this increase, believing that it is likely to be saved by the landowners to whom it accrues and that the savings will be made available for investment in industry through a capital market, which joins the two sectors much as the labor market does. At times, they seem to think that this source of capital formation is more significant for the Lewis model than the increased profits of the industrial sector. But two steps supervene. In the first place, it is necessary that the increased income be saved. This assumes a high marginal propensity to save in agriculture, which strikes most observers as unlikely. In countries with peasant cultivators, many income recipients in agriculture are hungry and show a high marginal propensity to consume first food and then industrial consumers goods if they have a chance. In the second place, assuming that the increase in income is saved, it seems unlikely that the savings would be made available to the industrial sector rather than used for improvements in agriculture, for better housing in agriculture, or even invested abroad, the choice made by the French peasants in the late nineteenth century. Capital markets are unlikely to be effective in a peasant economy, for one thing; for another, once wage rates in agriculture rise because the marginal product of labor has reached the level of the subsistence wage, new incentives for investment in agriculture come into play. So long as labor is paid a wage above its marginal product, its cost can be regarded as sunk, with a marginal cost or a shadow price of zero. Labor will be used in place of capital wherever it can be physically substituted. But once income distribution shifts to the competitive model where factors are paid their marginal products, it becomes worthwhile to substitute capital for labor in agriculture as savings increase and the relative cost of capital falls. The rise of marginal productivity of labor in agriculture to the going wage leads agriculture out of stagnation into positive growth.

Not only is it unlikely that the agricultural sector will provide capital for investment in the industrial sector; the workers who leave agriculture for industry may well choose to send home remittances saved out of their wages, which can be invested in the sector from which they have come and to which they think they may one day return. This is particularly the case where the two sectors are in reality two countries and the transfer of workers is in reality international migration. Capital formation is stimulated in each sector independently, and some savings may be transferred from one to the other. In the European case, however, what occurs is not a transfer of savings from the sector or country losing the labor but the opposite.

In a closed economy the change in income distribution and spending may pose a serious problem for intersectoral relations. As Nurkse first pointed out, the higher income in agriculture may be spent on food, whereas the labor leaving agriculture for the city will leave its food behind and will need to be fed. The attempt of the new industrial labor to buy food in the industrial sector—possibly more than before, now that its money income has increased—will meet with a reduced supply, and the terms of trade will turn against industry and in favor of agriculture. The problem will not exist if the food left behind is marketed by the agricultural sector (and no more is demanded by the industrial recruits). The marketing will be undertaken if the rise in income per capita in agriculture is spent not on food but on industrial consumers goods, is invested in industrial equipment for the agricultural sector, or is saved and invested in the industrial sector. Still another possibility is for government to tax away the increase in income in agriculture, as happened in Japan. In the long run, the problem may be met in a closed economy by increased productivity in the agricultural sector, which ensures that the full bill of food requirements of the industrial sector is met through increased marketing.

Europe of course is an open economy, not a closed one. In this circumstance, the food requirements of the new industrial recruits can be met by exporting industrial products and importing food from abroad, should the domestic agricultural sector fail to provide. We can accordingly dismiss the terms of trade between agriculture and industry. If anything, especially in

France and because of rapidly increased agricultural productivity, Europe's problem was one of too much food made available for the city from the country.

Obviously the Lewis model postulates very different types of growth in the industrial sector and in the agricultural sector. For industry, growth continues as a positive-feedback process, once it gets a start. The initial increase in the marginal product of labor when the supply is elastic and wages are constant raises profits which are reinvested. The reinvestment leads to further increases in the marginal product of labor.

In agriculture, in contrast, the initial improvement comes from eliminating redundant labor. This raises the marginal productivity of labor to the going wage and eventually stimulates replacement of men by machines. The labor supply of the industrial sector grows. That of agriculture declines.

Income Per Capita?

Thus far the question remains open as to whether economic growth here means the rate of expansion of total income or that of income per capita. This is a complex question in the disaggregated Lewis model. Increased labor in the industrial sector may mean that total growth proceeds there faster than the increase in income per capita. At the limit, all investment may be merely capital-widening, with the rate of overall growth equal to the rate of increase of the capital stock and the labor supply, and no change in the capital/labor ratio or in income per head. In the agricultural sector, however, the loss of labor means an increase in income per capita, even without investment. Such investment as takes place is by definition capital-deepening, since capital is substituted for labor.

The net of the two sectors, assuming no change in the total labor force, is necessarily an increase in the capital/labor ratio and an increase in income per capita, even if there is no rise in income per capita in the industrial sector. The outcome is of course strongly affected by the initial relative size of the two sectors.

Where there is a large technological gap in industry between existing and best practice, the capital-widening process made possible by the elastic labor supply (though initiated otherwise) may in fact lead to capital-deepening, as modern equipment is added to less efficient capacity of an earlier vintage. In actuality, capital-widening and capital-deepening are very difficult to distinguish: every extension of capacity under present circumstances implies some considerable improvement in efficiency, and most attempts at increased efficiency involve some enlargement of capacity. In the case at issue, a considerable contribution to the especially high rates of growth after World War II was made by capital investment embodying technological advances, which went a long way toward closing the technological gap between European standards and those in the United States. Apart from a superficial discussion in Chapter VII, this embodied technological progress is not treated here.

Supplies of Labor

Thus far the Lewis model has been discussed as though the European economy consisted of only two sectors in the single countries, with each country's economy closed. But the elastic supply of labor available for the industrial sector, where the growth process is assumed to start, need not come exclusively from national agriculture. There are at least five sources:

1. Transfers from inefficient sectors in the economy, including (in addition to agriculture) distribution, handicrafts or artisan manufactures, and even within sectors and industries, from small-scale inefficient enterprises to larger and more efficient ones.
2. Increased participation in the labor force by the population, especially by women, young people, and those previously retired.
3. Open unemployment.
4. A high rate of natural population increase.
5. Immigration.

The source of the elastic supply of labor complicates the question of whether growth should be measured overall or per capita. When the national population is constant, as under the first three sources of additional labor for industry, increased growth in the industrial sector leads to increased growth per capita, even without embodied technological progress, as income per capita increases in agriculture (or other sectors where inefficient units of labor are leaving) or as increased employment out of a given population gives increased income per capita even if there is no gain in income per worker employed in industry.

Under the last two sources, however, the numerator of the fraction, total output, may grow as before, but the denominator has also increased, with more people contributing to output. There need be no increase in efficiency in any sector. Where the gain in employment comes from a strong rate of natural increase (after a lag), as in the Netherlands and lately in France, growth will be very different measured overall or per capita. In the case of immigration, however, one could argue that the nation is not the proper unit for measuring growth. Paul Rosenstein-Rodan has suggested that the less developed countries are the agricultural sector of the developed countries, which constitute the industrial sector. If one were to measure the income of the developed country plus that of the residents of the less developed countries who ultimately migrate to the former, the total population would be stable — apart from any natural increase — and the rates of growth overall and per capita would be identical, as in the first three sources of additional labor.

Timing

The turning points come at different times in the two sectors. In agriculture, the incentive to substitute capital for labor is felt as soon as the marginal product of labor turns from zero to positive and before wages start to rise. This is because the opportunity cost of labor changes, and with the change some investments become feasible. So long as the marginal product of labor in agriculture remains below the subsistence wage in that sector, however, continued transfers will occur into industry, if demand for labor keeps rising there, and industrial wages will hold steady. It is when pressure on labor supplies in agriculture raises farm wages, and industrial wages in turn must rise to attract further labor into industry, that the industrial turning point is reached. Fei and Ranis call this "take-off" in Rostovian terminology, implying that development has been uncertain to that point but that thereafter it is self-sustaining and continuous. In the present view, however, this turning point is altogether otherwise. So long as excess labor is available, economic growth can proceed at very high levels. When the economy runs out of the extra labor or labor of the right skills, economic growth slows down. This is not the point where the economy leaves the ground, so much as that where its flight levels out from a rapid rate of climb. Thereafter savings lack the extra buoyancy given them by super profits and will from time to time decline as wage increases cut profits. Technical change will presumably continue as before, but investment, having leaped up, now settles back.

The Lewis model is a dynamic one. For excess supplies of labor to produce a growth in income per capita is paradoxical in static terms, where increments of labor presumably lower the marginal product of labor and reduce its income. The paradox is seen perhaps more clearly when the labor moves not between sectors but between countries. Immigration into a country raises income per capita, not only of other factors — owners of capital, owners of land, entrepreneurs, noncompeting groups of labor — but also of competing labor. In the short run, by the nature of the model which relies on constant wages, the incomes of all other factors and noncompeting labor are raised but not that of labor. But the growth process which the extra profits, savings, and investment produce ultimately raises wages and income per capita of all factors.

Demand or Supply

Excess labor in the Lewis model, as indicated before, is permissive rather than initiating. Once growth is started, the extra labor at constant wages sustains growth at a high level. In the discussion above, the model was set in motion by an increase in the demand for labor in the industrial sector, which can arise from any autonomous change, either in the demand for goods or in the techniques for making them. The process of growth needs to be started. Thereafter the model generates demand for goods and cranks out supply by itself.

Despite the fact that the initiating mechanism can arise either from the demand or the supply side, this is a supply model of growth. Higher rates of growth, or supergrowth, continue so long as the supply of labor remains elastic and helps contribute to the supply of capital. There are no bottlenecks. Supergrowth comes to a halt when the supply of labor reaches a limit and the extra demand generated by the system encounters a less than infinitely elastic supply of labor. At that point, wages and prices rise, profits, investment, and so on are reduced, so that the growth rate slows down and becomes irregular.

Most theories of economic growth applied to Europe today focus more narrowly either on demand for, or on the supply of, goods. British writers in particular — Angus Maddison, F. T. Blackaby, and to a lesser extent J. R. C. Dow — assume that demand creates its own supply (a Keynesian assumption) and that if demand can be sustained, economic growth can be sustained.[2] The balance of payments in an open economy creates problems for the maintenance of demand, as will be seen below. It is necessary for exports to grow as fast as income and imports, assuming an income elasticity of demand of one, or the balance of payments will turn adverse and require slower growth. The foreign-trade aspects of these models resemble those of Raul Prebisch as applied to the less developed countries.

Conversely, a number of models of European growth — those of the Economic Commission for Europe, for example, and of the IFO-Institut für Wirtschaftsforschung of Munich — focus on supply. They assume that anything that can be produced can be sold and that the problem of growth lies in the technical relationships between inputs and outputs and the nature of the expansion of inputs.[3]

The Lewis model, while simple, is more complex than these. If we leave aside the foreign-trade aspects for a moment, growth can get a start from either demand or supply in goods markets.

2. Angus Maddison, *Economic Growth in the West: Comparative Experience in Europe and North America* (New York: Twentieth Century Fund, 1964); F. T. Blackaby, "The Recent Performance of the British Economy," *Advancement of Science,* XIX (March 1963), 489–498; J. R. C. Dow, *The Management of the British Economy, 1945–60* (Cambridge: Cambridge University Press, 1964).

3. Economic Commission for Europe (ECE), *Economic Survey of Europe in 1961,* Pt. 2: *Some Factors in Economic Growth in Europe during the 1950's* (United Nations: Geneva, 1964), chap. 2. The ECE set out an analysis along the lines of the Lewis model in its *Economic Survey of Europe in 1958* (United Nations: Geneva, 1959), prior to the large-scale migration.

For an example of the work at the IFO-Institut, see Karl Christian Kühlo, "Bases for an Analysis of Growth," *German Economic Review,* II (1964), 289–297.

Thereafter attention shifts to factor markets where the availability of labor at a constant price is central. Demand is assumed to be generated by payments to factors — a Say's law model — and factors other than capital and labor (that is, entrepreneurship and land) are assumed to be in elastic supply. Given the availability of labor, the model explains the growth of capital and of goods supply.

When the Lewis model does not apply because of limited supplies of labor, as in postwar Britain, the trouble lies not with inadequate demand but with inelasticity of goods supply at constant prices. When adequate demand is provided, the supply of goods expands for 15 or 18 months before running into a bottleneck — a lack of labor. That lack raises wages and prices, reduces profits, slows down investment, and turns the balance of payments adverse.

The Balance of Payments

Lewis put his model mostly in terms of a closed economy. When the economy is opened, there is need to take account of the balance of payments. If growth in the industrial sector starts off in domestic commodities, the development of profits from an elastic labor supply can worsen the balance of payments, as growth of income spills over into imports. There is need, therefore, for some mechanism for keeping foreign payments and receipts in equilibrium. One means is for the initial stimulus to come from foreign demand — a *deus ex machina,* so to speak, which gives the economy initially a favorable balance of payments and therefore room in which to grow for a time free of foreign-currency constraints. Another is competition in industries producing for export, competition which, with constant wages and some productivity increase, lowers export prices. Add elastic demand abroad for the export commodities, and the balance of payments is taken care of in a regular fashion. Profits are not so high in export commodities, but volume grows faster than price declines. Or add a strong dose of technological advance in export lines, and (given constant wages, high profits, and high investment) somewhat lower prices with elastic demands expand export sales and keep the balance of payments in line.

After the turning point in industry, however, the balance of payments does not function so effectively. The virtuous circle in which more exports lead to more growth which leads to lower export prices, higher export sales, and still more growth is broken; more exports lead to higher wage rates and higher prices, to reverse the balance-of-payments mechanism, as in the classic price-specie-flow mechanism or in the more modern income-multiplier version in which incomes rather than prices do the trick.[4] There is no dynamic increase in investment which sustains export growth.[5]

There is more to the process than this. Since wages are spent and profits are saved in marked degree, the rise of wages after the turning point adversely affects the balance of payments through lowering of the average propensity to save. This is Mundell's point referred to in the Introduction,[6] and it assumes that investment is unchanged. But investment may be affected by the change in profitability. With a Keynesian investment function, the decline of profits will lead to a decline in investment that will offset some of the adverse change in the balance of payments; with Schumpeterian investment motivation, the reduction of profits stimulates attempts at cost reduction and may even increase investment. Since profits have fallen, this means an appeal to the capital market and possibly borrowing abroad. Higher investment and reduced savings by themselves worsen the balance of payments in the short run but may improve it in the long. An inflow of capital may improve it. Here is a complex set of relationships about which prediction is difficult. But it is pos-

4. Alexander Lamfalussy, *The United Kingdom and the Six: An Essay on Economic Growth in Western Europe* (Homewood, Ill.: Richard D. Irwin, 1963).

5. See the discussion of export-led growth by W. Beckerman and Bela Balassa, in which Balassa held that it was necessary to feed continuous supplies of labor into the model, and Beckerman disagreed. On our showing, Balassa has the better of the argument. W. Beckerman, "Projecting Europe's Growth," *Economic Journal,* LXXXII (December 1962), 912–925; B. Balassa, "Some Observations on Mr. Beckerman's 'Export-Propelled' Growth Model," *ibid.,* LXXIII (December 1963), 784–785; Beckerman, "Reply," *ibid.,* pp. 785–787; Balassa, "Rejoinder," *ibid.,* LXXIV (March 1964), 240–242.

6. See also Jørgen H. Gelting, "The Supply of Labour and the Foreign Balance," in Hugo Hegeland (ed.), *Money, Growth and Methodology: Essays in Honor of Johan Akerman* (Lund: C. W. K. Gleerup, 1961), pp. 393–394.

sible with the Lewis model that the balance of payments stays favorable up to the turning point and worsens thereafter.

The difference between the Keynesian and the Schumpeterian investment functions is not discussed in the typical Lewis model but is needed for relevance to the position of postwar Europe. In the usual version of the Lewis model, investment in the industrial sector is almost entirely capital-widening rather than deepening. More demand for output with a constant wage leads to higher profits, more savings, and more investment. This is capital-widening, although embodied technological progress can be invoked to produce the cost reduction needed for stimulating exports. Where the Schumpeterian investment function obtains, with investment designed to substitute capital for labor and lower costs, and responding not to higher profits but to higher costs and lower profits, the Lewis model for the industrial sector does not really apply. This is the model of behavior in the agricultural sector, where investment responds to rising costs.

In the real world, however, it can happen that the industrial sector, or the highly developed industrialized country, behaves in the way which we reserve for agriculture. This is the problem of general equilibrium — anything can happen: rising wages can harm investment or stimulate it. Some observers in Germany for example object to inward migration because it holds down wages and therefore postpones automation, capital-deepening investment par excellence.[7] J. R. Sargent is baffled that rising wages in Britain do not lead to capital-deepening investment, as in theory they should or at least might.[8]

There is something clearly arbitrary about the Lewis model in that there are different investment responses in the two sectors. And they can run the other way. But in general, investment responds to higher profits in industry and higher costs in agriculture.

A Historical Illustration of the Lewis Model: Britain and the United States in the Nineteenth Century

The economic development of England and the United States during the nineteenth century may be said to have been deter-

7. Interview, IFO-Institut für Wirtschaftsforschung, Munich, July 1964.

8. J. R. Sargent, *Out of Stagnation: A Policy for Growth,* Fabian Tract No. 343 (London: Fabian Society, 1963).

mined by the application in each country, and in each country for half the century, of different aspects of the Lewis model. In England during the first half of the century and in the United States during the second (especially in the last quarter), growth proceeded by the mechanism of the industrial sector of the Lewis model: unlimited supplies of labor, high profits, and high investment of a capital-widening variety. In England during the second half of the century and in the United States during the first, labor was limited and profits scarce. In the United States, the response to the high wages was rapid technological progress of a labor-saving kind. In Britain, on the other hand, the response took the form of capital exports.

This is the theme, though perhaps not quite so succinctly put, of H. J. Habakkuk in his book on British and American technology in the nineteenth century. A classic historical controversy has raged in Britain between the Hammonds, Marx, Hobsbawm — who maintained that the level of living of the working classes fell during the period to 1850 — and Ashton, Clapham, Hartwell, *et al.* — who insisted that it rose.[9] On this issue, Habakkuk implies that if there is difficulty in determining whether real wages rose or fell to the 1850's, they probably did not change much in either direction.[10] Profits were high in the industrial sector and also investment. In agriculture there was unemployment and underemployment as far back as the demobilization after 1815 when 400,000 returning soldiers were unceremoniously dumped on the labor market. The demand for labor for railroad construction began to give rise to shortages in the 1840's, especially at haying time and harvest, and after emigration received a fillip from the gold discoveries of 1849 and 1851.[11] This shortage stimulated a renewal of interest in improvements in agriculture, culminating in High Farming, or rapid technical progress in machinery, drainage, and fertilizer. But the level of wages did not rise until the exhaustion of the excess supplies of labor,

9. See, for example, T. S. Ashton, "The Treatment of Capitalism by Historians," in F. A. Hayek (ed.), *Capitalism and the Historians* (Chicago: University of Chicago Press, 1954), pp. 31–61.

10. H. J. Habakkuk, *American and British Technology in the 19th Century* (Cambridge: Cambridge University Press, 1962), pp. 138–139.

11. See E. L. Jones, "The Agricultural Labour Market in England, 1793–1872," *Economic History Review,* XVII (December 1964), 322–338.

in the 1850's. The major improvement came later during the Great Depression, when rising real wages and minimal profits combined to produce the puzzling "profitless prosperity."

From the vantage point of mid-century, Marx and Engels were correct in their analysis of capitalism. Capital was formed by drawing more and more labor into the market at subsistence wages. But they were hardly very imaginative about the range of possibilities after the reserve army of the unemployed was exhausted. Marx believed that continued investment would drive down the rate of profit to zero, leading to the collapse of the system. The shift of investment from the domestic market to overseas operations, making possible capital-widening in space with other labor, was one means of postponing the crisis. Another factor was technological progress, which permitted capital-deepening and maintained the profitability of investment. And Marx and Engels altogether failed to see that the use of the last of the unemployed, even without foreign lending or technological progress, could raise wages positively above the subsistence level, as the Malthusian barrier was burst through, with a possible steady state of low profits, moderate growth, and rising real wages.

In the United States, growth in the first half of the nineteenth century proceeded on the basis of a model relying upon "unlimited supplies of land." "Natural resources were cheaper and their supply more elastic in the U.S.A. than in England to an extent which offset the effects of its dearer labor." [12] Labor was dear because a factory owner had to pay his workers what they could earn in farming on virtually free land. But the high price of labor stimulated technical innovation and the substitution of capital for labor in a way that is reserved in the Lewis model for the agricultural sector after the turning point has been reached.

In mid-century all this changed. First came waves of immigration from northern and western Europe, then exhaustion of free fertile land, and finally, in the 1880's and 1890's, mass immigration from southern and eastern Europe. There was a shift to the other aspect of the Lewis model, growth with unlimited supplies

12. Habakkuk, *American and British Technology in the 19th Century*, p. 45.

of labor in the industrial sector.[13] Technological progress of a labor-saving character had already been set in motion and continued through inertia. But wage rates for common labor were held down, profits were maintained, and growth through high rates of investment proceeded.

Habakkuk's principal thesis is that abundant labor in England and abundant land in the United States shaped the character of innovations in the two countries and that the general superiority of labor-saving innovations like movable parts as compared to resource-saving inventions like the steam engine and iron ships gave the United States an advantage in the growth process. This may be so, but the greater economy of labor-saving over resource-saving inventions is not self-evident. What emerges from his discussion is the importance of unlimited supplies of labor to Britain in the first half of the century and to the United States in the second. The rise of real wages in Britain after 1850 — that is, following completion of the move from the countryside to the town — is most significant.

The impact of immigration on real wages raises one question for the United States which will recur in postwar Europe. Melvin Reder observes that immigration to the United States was favorable per capita to the native population, when one might have expected it to lower real wages.[14] In part, income was probably supported by growth, along the lines of the Lewis model, but the phenomenon may also be partly explained by the fact that unskilled foreign labor was a noncompeting group. In a static model, an added factor lowers the marginal product of substitute factors and raises that of complements. If native labor is not in competition with the immigrants, which was true for the later immigration from southern and eastern Europe after 1880, if not for the earlier movement from Britain, Germany, and Scan-

13. John R. Commons said that "unregulated immigration is America's reserve army of the unemployed" (*Races and Immigrants in America*, 3d ed., New York: Macmillan, 1924, p. xxvi).

14. Melvin W. Reder, "The Economic Consequences of Increased Immigration," *Review of Economics and Statistics*, XLV (August 1963), 221–230. See also Professors Lindahl's and Edding's discussion of the paper by J. J. Spengler, "Effects Produced in Receiving Countries by Pre-1939 Immigration," in Brinley Thomas (ed.), *Economics of International Migration: Proceedings of a Conference held [in 1955] by the International Economic Association* (London: Macmillan, 1958), pp. 394–395.

dinavia, wage differentials would be expected to widen, and native wages to increase rather than be lowered or maintained at a constant level.[15]

The Delayed Industrial Revolution

The Lewis model of growth thus explains the Industrial Revolution in Britain in the first half of the nineteenth century and of the United States in the second half. What has happened in Europe since World War II is in reality the same process. This is stated explicitly by E. Tosco in describing Italian economic expansion:

> The large numbers of unemployed and of underemployed and the division of the workers organizations kept the power of the unions

15. The foregoing potted history, along with the earlier analysis, must not convey the impression that the Lewis model is applicable only to developed countries and not the less developed for which it was devised. After working through the material for this book, I learned of the penetrating attempt to apply the Lewis model to British Central Africa by William Barber. The similarities and differences as compared to European experience are striking.

With regard to similarities, the basic wage rate was maintained virtually unchanged from 1930 to 1950, for employment of Negro unskilled workers expanded as they moved off the reservations and immigrated into Southern Rhodesia from Nyasaland. This elastic labor supply enabled noncompetitive European colonial wages to rise. The Native Commissioners originally set a limit of half the able-bodied males as the number who would be allowed to leave the reservations, retaining the others so as to maintain the viability of native agriculture. When the pressure of demand drew off more, the Native Land Husbandry Act of 1951, converting communal land to freeholds, permitted a reorganization of agriculture, like the enclosures of nineteenth-century England or the *rémembrement* of France today. In Southern Rhodesia, housing was provided mainly for single males, since the municipality made money from housing them and lost in trying to accommodate families. (William J. Barber, *The Economy of British Central Africa. A Case Study of Economic Development in a Dualistic Economy*, London: Oxford University Press, 1961, esp. pp. 39, 186, 246, 260.)

Among the differences between events in Africa and events in Europe may be noted the lack at any attempt at assimilation in the Rhodesian case. To give another example, the target sought by migrant workers in Kampala, Uganda, tended to include bride price, to enable the male to acquire a wife, whereas in Europe many of the Mediterranean men and some women were saving for a dowry to facilitate the acquisition of an appropriate husband in the family. (Walter Elkan, *Migrants and Proletarians: Urban Labour in the Economic Development of Uganda*, London: Oxford University Press, 1960, pp. 42, 131. This book makes a distinction between migrants, who maintain a foothold in agriculture though they move between it and the city, and proletarians who move permanently to the city.)

weak and resulted therefore in a lag between increases in productivity and increases in wages. The high profit margins of enterprises, due to this enforced saving by workers constituted the principal factor in the "Italian miracle." In its general lines, this process is no different to that experienced in the industrial revolution in other countries.[16]

The same explanation is offered implicitly by John Knapp and Kenneth Lomax in stating why Britain was at the bottom of the "League tables" of economic growth: it did not need what the Continental countries did — a lot of catching up.[17] And even in Germany, there is the thesis that despite the rapid industrialization in three waves in the nineteenth century — the 1850's, the 1870's, and the 1890's — there had never been the full social and economic experience with industrialization known elsewhere.[18]

If this explanation is accepted, it is evident why Britain and even Belgium have not grown so rapidly as the rest of Europe and thus why the rapid pace of expansion of the 1950's and early 1960's cannot be sustained.

16. E. Tosco, "Economic Policy in Italy," in *Economic Policy in Our Time,* vol. III: *Country Studies* (Chicago: Rand McNally, 1964), p. 161.

17. John Knapp and Kenneth Lomax, "Britain's Growth Performance: The Enigma of the 1950's," *Lloyds Bank Review,* No. 7 (October 1964), pp. 1–24.

18. Ralf Dahrendorf, "The New Germanies," *Encounter,* XXII (April 1964), 50–58.

CHAPTER II

Fast-Growing Developed Economies with Expanding Labor Supply: Germany, Italy, Switzerland, and the Netherlands

Country Groupings

The next four chapters sketch briefly the course of postwar economic growth of 15 European countries and the forces which have given shape to it. The division of countries is based on data compiled from the Economic Commission for Europe's *Some Factors in Economic Growth in Europe during the 1950's*, contained in Table II-1.[1] The first group consists of those countries — Germany, Italy, Switzerland, and the Netherlands — which were the fastest growers among the developed countries of Europe. These are the subject of the present chapter. The following chapter treats the two exceptions to the Lewis model — Austria and France. Chapter IV focuses on the slow-growing developed economies of Scandinavia, Belgium, and the United Kingdom. Chapter V deals with the underdeveloped countries of the Mediterranean northern coast, Greece, Turkey, Spain, and Portugal.[2]

The division follows the broad statistical breakdown of Table II-1, except for the treatment of Austria with France rather than with the fast growers with relatively high rates of labor input. The reason for this is that the Austrian labor figures used by

1. Geneva: United Nations, 1964.
2. The Economic Commission for Europe typically analyzes growth in 22 countries of western Europe, rather than 15. Omitted here are Canada and the United States, to which a different model applies, and the 5 rather atypical or very small "western European" countries: Finland, Luxemburg, Iceland, Ireland, and Yugoslavia.

TABLE II-1

Growth of output, labor force and labor productivity, average gross investment ratio, and incremental capital/output ratio in selected European countries, 1949–1959

Country	Gross domestic product trend (compound	GDP per capita annual	Active labor force percentage	Labor productivity rates)	Average gross investment ratio (percentage)	Average incremental capital/output ratio (ICOR) (coefficient)
A.						
Germany	7.4	6.3	1.6	5.7	24.2	3.3
Italy	5.9	5.4	1.1	4.8	22.0	3.7
Switzerland	5.2	3.8	1.5	3.7	23.7	4.5
Netherlands	4.8	3.5	1.2	3.6	24.3	5.2
B.						
Austria	6.0	5.8	1.1[a]	4.8	23.2	3.9
France	4.5	3.6	0.1	4.3	20.1	4.6
C.						
Norway	3.4	2.5	0.3	3.1	31.3	9.5
Sweden	3.4	2.8	0.5	2.9	21.3	6.3
Denmark	3.2	2.4	1.0	2.2	17.6	5.5
Belgium	3.0	2.4	0.3	2.7	17.6	5.6
United Kingdom	2.4	2.0	0.6	1.8	16.3	6.7
D.						
Greece	5.9	5.0	1.5	4.3	16.5	3.0
Turkey	5.9	2.9	2.4	3.4	15.0	2.6
Spain	5.2	4.3	0.8	4.3	16.3	3.1
Portugal	4.1	3.4	0.6	3.5	16.0	4.0

Source: Economic Commission for Europe, *Some Factors in Economic Growth in Europe during the 1950's* (Geneva: United Nations, 1964), chap. 2, Table 1 (p. 1), Table 4 (p. 12), and Table 16 (p. 31).

[a] This figure is subject to considerable doubt.

the Economic Commission are of dubious quality, and one would have a hard time making the case that Austria follows the Lewis model of growth. It is therefore better to treat it as an exception. Another exceptional number stands out in the table: the gross investment ratio for Norway, which with a relatively slow rate of growth produces a very high incremental capital/output ratio (ICOR). Again, the Danish rate of growth of the labor supply is uncomfortably high for my thesis. With these exceptions, however, the developed countries divide fairly readily into Group A — with high rates of growth, relatively high rates of labor input, and high gross investment ratios — and Group C, including the Scandinavian nations, Belgium, and the United Kingdom — with considerably lower rates of economic growth, both overall and per capita, and lower rates of growth in the active labor force and investment (apart from the Norwegian case, and not much lower in the instance of Sweden). The Mediterranean countries differ sharply from Groups A and C in that their high rates of growth are associated with high increases in the labor force but relatively low rates of capital formation. The result, of course, is low ICOR's.

Processed data for 1959 to 1963 are available for only 8 of the 15 countries, and, because of changes in the price index used to deflate current values to real quantities, they are not on an identical basis. Table II-2 presents the ECE data for 1959–1963 with comparable figures for 1954–1959 on GDP, the gross investment ratio, and ICOR. These figures show that increases in rates of growth of output are associated with increases in active labor force and that decreases in output growth are associated with decreases in labor force — in every instance but Italy.

Tables oversimplify, to be sure. The rate of increase in the active labor force is not the best indication of the elasticity of the labor supply. Germany had substantial unemployment up to 1954, and Italy's unemployment began to melt only after 1959. Moreover, the Netherlands and Denmark, with relatively high rates of growth of the active labor force, and Belgium and the United Kingdom, with low rates, were alike in having long since exhausted their underemployed reserves of labor in agriculture. Further reserves of labor have been found in some countries in inefficient self-employed retail establishments and among artisans and handicraft workers — in France and Germany, to mention the most conspicuous.

But the ECE data show a "marked, though by no means perfect association between high (or low) rates of growth of domestic product and high (or low) rates of growth of the active

TABLE II-2

Growth of Table II-1 factors in selected European countries, 1959–1963 compared with 1954–1959

Country	Gross domestic product		Active labor force (compound annual percentage rates)		Labor productivity		Gross investment ratio (percentage)		ICOR (coefficient)	
	1954–1959	1959–1963	1949–1959	1959–1963	1949–1959	1959–1963	1954–1959	1959–1963	1954–1959	1959–1963
Germany	6.9	5.4	1.6	0.8	5.7	4.6	21.7	23.9	3.1	4.4
Italy	5.7	6.2	1.1	0.1	4.8	6.1	23.0	26.1	4.0	4.2
Netherlands	3.7	5.2	1.2	1.4	3.6	3.7	24.4	26.1	6.6	5.0
Austria	5.7	5.2	1.1	—	4.8	5.2	24.1	25.6	4.2	4.9
France	4.6	5.8	0.1	0.7	4.3	5.1	20.2	21.7	4.4	3.7
Sweden	3.1	3.8	0.5	1.2	2.9	2.6	22.2	24.3	7.1	6.5
Belgium	2.0	3.8	0.3	0.5	2.7	3.3	18.0	19.1	9.0	5.0
United Kingdom	2.0	2.6	0.6	0.9	1.8	1.7	16.7	19.3	8.6	7.4

Source: ECE, *Some Factors in Economic Growth in Europe during the 1950's*, chap. 7, p. 13.

labor force in western countries during the 1950's."[3] There is "practically no correlation between rates of expansion of domestic product and rates of capital input for these (22) countries," and the close association of rates of growth of output "with rates of input of labor and capital in combination appears to be attributable almost entirely to the influence of the labor input."[4]

But we deal with the countries singly, and in groups by chapter.

Germany

The relationship between the rate of economic growth and the expansion of the labor supply is shown with great clarity in a chart produced by what might be termed in English the German Council of Experts to Advise on Economic Growth in its first report, *Stable Money, Steady Growth,* and reproduced as Figure II-1.[5] The top and two bottom curves show GDP, the increase in the labor force and in labor productivity per hour of work, all in annual percentage rates of growth; the second and third curves portray the investment ratio and ICOR as a percent of gross domestic product and as a coefficient, respectively. The thin line represents the annual figures (except for the ICOR), the thick line a five-year moving average to suggest trend. The annual figures are strongly correlated for the rate of growth, the investment ratio, and the rate of growth of the labor input, but similarity of trend is limited to the rate of growth of output and that of the quantity of labor.

These relationships make it very hard to accept the alternative explanations that attribute the brilliance of German economic growth to a combination of luck, Marshall Plan aid, and national character (Henry Wallich); to sound monetary policy (Per Jacobsson and Patrick Boarman), to active fiscal policy (Frederick Reuss); to the maintenance of competition in goods and factor markets (Egon Sohmen); to intense capital formation fostered by government (Karl Roskamp); to government action to manage demand, maintain competitiveness, and foster invest-

3. ECE, *Some Factors in Economic Growth in Europe,* chap. 2, p. 12.
4. *Ibid.,* chap. 2, pp. 18, 30.
5. See Sachverständigenrat zur Begutachtung der gesamtwirtschaftlichen Entwicklung, *Stabiles Geld, Stetiges Wachstum: Jahresgutachten 1964/65* (Stuttgart and Mainz: Kohlhammer, 1965).

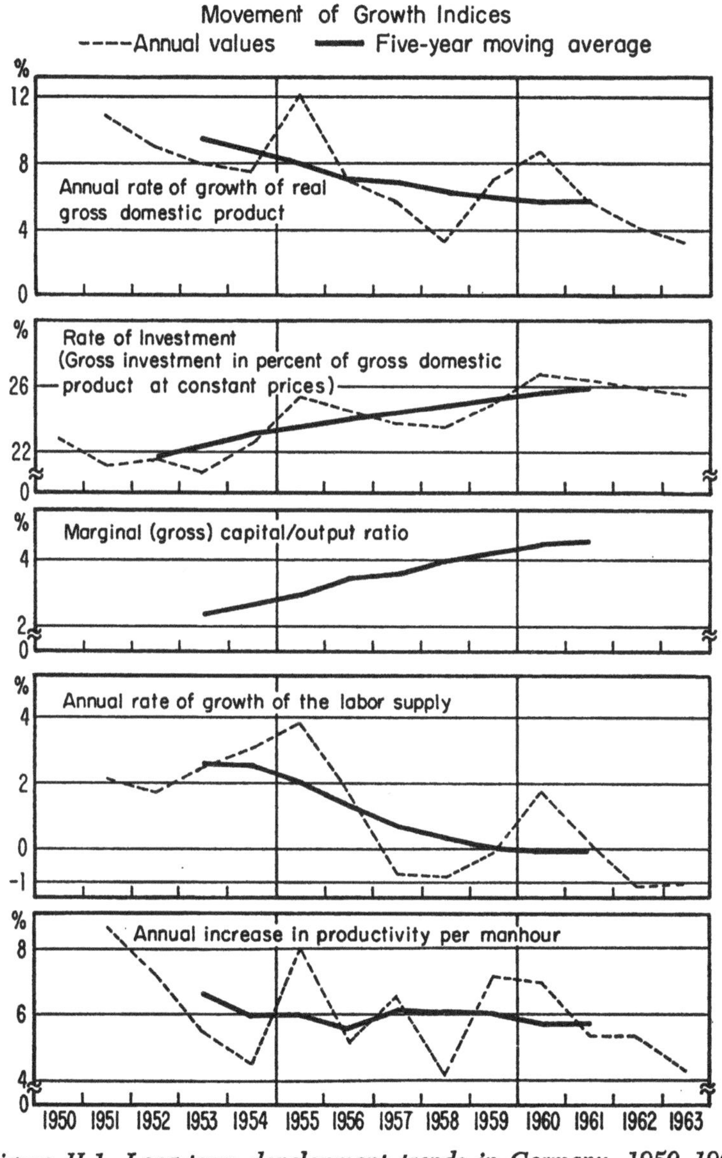

Figure II-1. Long-term development trends in Germany, 1950–1963

Source: Sachverständigenrat zur Begutachtung der gesamtwirtschaftlichen Entwicklung, *Stabiles Geld, Stetiges Wachstum: Jahresgutachten 1964/65*, Stuttgart, 1965 ment (Angus Maddison), and so on.[6] These elements contributed to demand, no doubt, but the *sine qua non* was the elastic labor supply which held down wages and maintained profits and investment.

Some writers, though they do not ignore labor elasticity, object to placing such great emphasis on it. Rolf Krengel, for example, states that the prognosis of labor supply is unimportant for predicting economic growth, since any change in labor can be compensated for by changes in the capital/labor ratio.[7] This is the exact antithesis of the view taken here that the capital/labor ratio in separate sectors is difficult to alter, so that the rate of growth of the labor supply is one of the most important factors making for growth.

The sources of the German labor supply have also been set down concisely by the Council of Experts in a table, given here as Table II-3. In the early years of the 1950's, the biggest sources of supply were the rate of natural increase, unemployed, and refugees. It is impossible to distinguish these separate sources with accuracy, since one day's refugee became the following day's unemployed and the third day's addition to the employed labor force. But from the collapse of fighting on the Russian front to the 1950's, some 9 million refugees entered West Germany from the east — Volksdeutsche, expellees from the territory taken

6. Henry C. Wallich, *Mainsprings of German Revival* (New Haven: Yale University Press, 1955); Per Jacobsson, *Some Monetary Problems, International and National* (London: Oxford University Press, 1958), p. 264; Patrick M. Boarman, *Germany's Economic Dilemma, Inflation and the Balance of Payments* (New Haven: Yale University Press, 1964), esp. chap. 2; Frederick G. Reuss, *Fiscal Policy for Growth without Inflation: The German Experiment* (Baltimore: The Johns Hopkins Press, 1963); Egon Sohmen, "Competition and Growth: The Lesson of West Germany," *American Economic Review*, XLIX (December 1959), 986-1003; Karl W. Roskamp, *Capital Formation in West Germany* (Detroit: Wayne State University Press, 1964); Angus Maddison, *Economic Growth in the West* (New York: Twentieth Century Fund, 1964), p. 102.

In connection with Sohmen's views, see the comments by K. W. Roskamp, A. I. MacBean, and W. G. Shepherd, R. G. Opie, and reply by Egon Sohmen, *American Economic Review*, L (December 1960), 1015–1031. Cf. Egon Sohmen, "The Dollar and the Mark," in S. E. Harris (ed.), *The Dollar in Crisis* (New York: Harcourt, Brace & World, 1961), pp. 183–200.

7. Rolf Krengel, "Attempt at a Prognosis of Output and Factors of Production of Industry in the Federal Republic of Germany, 1965 and 1970," in R. C. Geary (ed.), *Europe's Future in Figures* (Amsterdam: North Holland Publishing Co., 1962), p. 62.

TABLE II-3

Sources of labor supply in Germany[a]

	Changes in yearly average number (thousands)						
	1951	1955	1960	1961	1962	1963	1964[b]
Natural population increase[c]	+255	+375	− 35	− 46	− 90	− 52	− 28
Unemployment reserve	+148	+293	+241	+ 90	+ 26	− 31	+ 14
Refugees	+127	+161	+ 56	+125	+116	+ 49	+ 2
Foreign workers		+ 8	+112	+196	+154	+144	+128
Statistical discrepancy	− 7	− 2	+ 53	− 21	− 14	− 13	+ 5
Employed workers	+523	+835	+427	+344	+192	+ 97	+121
Independent workers and family helpers	− 89	− 37	−109	− 55	−131	−153	−100
Occupied workers	+612	+872	+536	+399	+323	+250	+221

Source: Sachverständigenrat zur Begutachtung der gesamtwirtschaftlichen Entwicklung, *Stabiles Geld, Stetiges Wachstum: Jahresgutachten 1964/5* (Stuttgart and Mainz: Kohlhammer, 1965), Table 26, p. 51.

[a] From 1961 the Federal territory; previously without the Saar or West Berlin.

[b] Including changes in participation rates.

[c] Estimated by the Council of Experts.

over by the Soviet Union and Poland, and refugees from the People's Republic of Germany. From then until the erection of the Wall between the zones in August 1961, another 3 million refugees were added to the population. From these 12 million expellees and refugees, the labor force benefited to the extent of about 7 million. Labor participation rates were relatively low for the earlier expellees (who consisted in unusual proportion of old people, women, and children) and relatively high for the later refugees (who came from the more active strata of the population). Slowly up to 1960, and rapidly thereafter, foreign workers were recruited for work in Germany, and this became the largest single source of additions to the total labor supply in 1961.

The expellees and refugees constituted one of the finest sources of additional labor in all of Europe. They were skilled in much higher proportions than the unemployed, peasants, and foreign workers. To the extent that the regime of the People's Republic was antagonistic to middle-class people, the proportion of professional and managerial personnel among these classes was probably higher than those of West Germany. They were much more assimilable than the foreign workers. Perhaps a little more than the local population of West Germany, they were anxious to reconstitute their fortunes, having left all possessions which survived the war behind. And finally, they were mobile to a degree possessed only by the foreign worker and far in excess of the local population which had managed to come through the war with its housing relatively intact. This large increment in the population — 9 million thrust on top of 38 million already there — was initially thought of as a burden but as early as 1951 came to be thought of as a stimulating challenge, and even "indispensable for the recovery of Western Germany." [8]

The foreign workers, like the refugees, were for the most part hungry for income, hard-working, and mobile. They lacked the capacity for assimilation, on the one hand, and the balance of skills, on the other. The countries of emigration, especially Greece, now complain that the German employers take away their most skilled workers. On the whole, however, the level of skill among the foreign migrant workers is not very high. It is this fact that limits their use in Germany, rather than the social and political problem presented by their absorption, which looms so large in Switzerland. In 1964 there were 950,000 unfilled positions in Germany but requests for only 45,000 foreign workers.[9]

Foreign workers have one advantage over refugees of the same nationality: their numbers can be controlled. At least with respect to admission, their intake can be increased or reduced as a policy measure.[10] West Germany early took measures to promote the mobility of the refugees, particularly the provision of housing in areas where job opportunities existed. But when total

8. Friedrich Edding, *The Refugees as a Burden, a Stimulus and a Challenge to the West Germany Economy,* Research Group for European Migration, Study No. IV (The Hague: Nijhoff, 1951), p. 17.

9. The proportions must not be taken too seriously. Since foreign workers are continuously available, the need for them can be given for the next weeks or months, whereas with the shortage of skilled labor anticipated needs are reckoned in advance.

10. It has been said privately by an individual known for his strongly negative views on Germany that the German government regulated the flow of refugees from the camps into the economy as a whole as a means of holding down wages. I have found no evidence of this calculated a view of the refugee problem, nor has a graduate student who pursued the questions intensively.

employment became overfull, the German government in company with employers went abroad to recruit as early as 1957–58.[11]

This excess supply of labor in the 1950's enabled Germany to maintain a high demand for exports, investment, and consumers goods without inflation. Wage rates rose during the period, but no higher than did other incomes, so that the proportion of wages as a percentage of national income increased only very slightly during the 1950's, as shown in Table II-4. Once the supply of

TABLE II-4

Distribution of German gross national income (percentages)

	From dependent work	From enterprise and property[a]		From dependent work	From enterprise and property[a]
1950	58.6	41.4	1958	60.5	39.5
1951	58.7	41.3	1959	60.2	39.8
1952	57.4	42.6	1960	60.6	39.4
1953	58.7	41.3	1961	60.8	39.2
1954	59.4	40.6	1962	62.5	37.5
1955	58.8	41.2	1963[b]	63.9	36.1
1956	59.5	40.5	1964[b]	64.8	35.2
1957	59.7	40.3			

Source: *Stabiles Geld, Stetiges Wachstum,* Table 35, p. 70.
[a] Including income of the state from enterprise and property.
[b] Preliminary.

readily available labor in the right skill mix became strained, after 1960, the percentage of income going to wages rose sharply. Part of this increase was statistical and represented the shift of independent workers to paid employment, a trend which picked up in 1962 and 1963, as shown in Table II-3. But most of it reflected pressure of demand against a decreasingly elastic supply.

There is considerable evidence that wages have been held down by weak unions or, in a differing interpretation, by very

11. H. Besters, "Economic Policy in Western Germany, 1949 to 1961," in *Economic Policy in Our Time,* vol. III: *Country Studies* (Chicago: Rand McNally, 1964), pp. 447, 479.

farsighted union leaders who restricted wage demands when exports or price stability were threatened.[12] An early German trade-union leader was called "unforgettable" because he convinced the unions "that they should make do with an income which left industry and commerce enough financial scope."[13] The metal workers in 1964, under the "militant leadership" of Otto Brenner, and after a year in which it was acknowledged by the government that productivity had set a new record, accepted a settlement of approximately 7.3 percent wage increase over a 15-month period and abandoned their claim for a reduction in the working week, to the great surprise of German public opinion.[14] Behind the weak or farsighted unions, however, has been the fact of labor supply.

With the rise in the wage share of national income, the balance of payments should turn adverse. Up to 1965, this has been forestalled by a number of factors: by personal savings on the part of wage earners; by an entrepreneurial shift from capital-widening to capital-deepening — a shift which other countries have found it difficult or impossible to make; and by the 1963 and 1964 inflation in France and Italy, conforming more closely to the model, which spilled over and buoyed up German exports. When the Lewis model is extended to an open economy and enterprise saves but workers do not, the gain of wages at the expense of property income expands consumption, reduces savings, and hurts the balance of payments. But this model did not apply thoroughly to Germany until 1965 and was delayed in application to Switzerland, because of a high marginal propensity to save on the part of labor. Savings of German households increased steadily from 3 percent of disposable income in the early 1950's to 5.5 percent in 1956, 8.5 percent in 1962, and 9.5 percent in 1963. In 1963 disposable income rose by 6.7 percent and savings by 20 percent to yield, with respect to demand for savings, the remarkable income elasticity of 3. The shift from capital-widening to capital-deepening seems to have occurred in

12. See Arthur M. Ross, "Prosperity and Labor Relations in Europe: The Case of West Germany," *Quarterly Journal of Economics,* LXXVI (August 1962), 331–359.

13. "The Deutsche Mark," *Die Welt,* June 20, 1963, summarized in *German Tribune,* July 6, 1963.

14. *Frankfurter Allgemeine Zeitung,* July 8, 1964.

the period after the acute labor shortages of 1960, although Krengel ascribes it to 1955.[15] As shown in Table II-5, labor was

TABLE II-5

Labor shortage in West German industry

		Percentage of responding firms stating that production was hindered by a lack of labor			Percentage of responding firms stating that production was hindered by a lack of labor
1954	October	10	1960	April	56
				July	62
				October	54
1955	July	24	1961	April	50
	October	26		July	52
				October	58
1956	April	21	1962	April	51
	July	20		July	54
	October	18		October	48
1957	April	15	1963	April	38
	July	20		July	46
	October	34		October	48
1958	April	9	1964	April	53
	July	13			
	October	13			
1959	April	18			
	July	42			
	October	50			

Source: Total series kindly communicated by the IFO-Institut für Wirtschaftsforschung, which asks questions of German industry, three times a year inquires about the shortage of labor, and marshals the data in the form of percentage of firms reporting that their output was handicapped by lack of labor.

short consistently from the middle of 1959, but the peaks after July 1960 did not regain the acuteness of that period.[16] And

15. Rolf Krengel, "Some Reasons for the Rapid Economic Growth of the German Federal Republic," Banca Nazionale del Lavoro *Quarterly Review*, No. 64 (March 1963), pp. 134–135.

16. It is of some interest that the percentages in primary-product industries, where perhaps foreign labor can be more readily used, run consistently below those in investment and consumption goods, between which there is no clear difference in pattern.

from 1959 to 1963, exports to the European Economic Community almost doubled, owing in large part to the inflation in France and especially Italy, while those to other countries increased only 22 percent.

The Lewis or Marxian model can be frustrated in another way. The savings to finance the investment stimulated by the falling rate of profit can be furnished not only by workers but also from abroad. Interest rates rise as entrepreneurs react to the fall in both profits and internal funds available for investment by attempting to borrow on the capital market. The rise in domestic rates attracts a capital inflow. Germany has tried to resist this source of surplus in the balance of payments in a number of ways, especially by imposing withholding taxes on foreign owners of German bonds and forbidding banks from paying interest on foreign deposits. These measures have not been completely successful.

The German case, therefore, illustrates the Lewis model only up to the turning point. The rate of growth has slowed down, but investment and growth have remained remarkably high.

Italy

The unification of Italy in 1860 makes it necessary to discuss the vastly different economies of northern and southern Italy as though they were one. It is possible to break down many of the statistics by provinces and to recombine them regionally, but it is an appalling amount of work. If that were done, we should discuss northern Italy in this chapter in connection with the fast-growing Lewis-model developed economies and deal with southern Italy in Chapter V, along with Portugal, Spain, Greece, and Turkey. As it is, we will treat Italy without regard to regional differences, as the convenient statistics require us to do, making such subjective adjustment in the data as seems appropriate.

Italy so treated follows the Lewis model of growth with unlimited supplies of labor, as the quotation in Chapter I makes clear, but, like Germany, with its own national variation.[17] Mrs. Vera Lutz lays great emphasis on the duality of the labor market, which leads her to divide industry into two groups. In Group I,

17. See above, pp. 22–23.

modern industry, wages are held high by monopolistic factors in both industry and labor. Growth is rapid here, but there is little increase in employment. In Group II industries, on the other hand, backward industries of small artisan shops such as food, clothing, and woodworking, the increase in employment has been substantial, but productivity has increased only slightly. Labor moving off the farm and from the south has been offered little in the way of effective employment and has been forced into emigration or unproductive unemployment in handicraft or services.[18]

A corollary of this emphasis on imperfection in the labor market and in the product markets for Group I goods is that wages in modern industry have risen unduly. Mrs. Lutz, and in his turn George Hildebrand, argue that the unions, which many observers characterize as weak, have forced wages up.[19] Other imperfections existed in labor markets — minimum-wage laws, statutory social-security changes and sliding-scale legislation, and the Fascist legislation of 1931 and 1939, forbidding labor to leave its home territory without an assured job. But the rise in wages was below the increase in labor productivity until 1962, as Table II-6 shows, and strongly correlated with the cost of living and unemployment but not with productivity. If the annual percentage change in manufacturing hourly earnings (W^*) is regressed against the annual percentage change in the cost of living (P^*), the annual change in productivity (O^*) and the annual percentage of unemployment according to the Central Institute of Statistics (ISTAT) estimates (UN), the following equation results:

$$W^* = \underset{(.48)}{1.56\,P^*} - \underset{(.32)}{.67\,UN} + \underset{(.62)}{.63\,O^*} + .87 \qquad N = 9 \qquad R^2 = .76.$$

The coefficient for productivity is not significant. If the preliminary figure for 1963 is added, the regression is somewhat improved.

Hildebrand shows a comparable result for the period through

18. Vera Lutz, *Italy: A Study in Economic Development* (London: Oxford University Press, 1962).

19. George H. Hildebrand, *Growth and Structure in the Economy of Modern Italy* (Cambridge, Mass.: Harvard University Press, 1965).

TABLE II-6

Wage, price, productivity, and unemployment trends in Italy

Year	Manufacturing hourly earnings	Manufacturing hourly productivity	Cost-of-living index	Unemployed as percent of labor force
	(in percentage change over preceding year)			(ISTAT data)
1951	9.7	10.7	9.3	—
1952	5.0	3.3	4.3	—
1953	2.4	8.8	2.0	—
1954	3.5	6.9	3.0	8.9
1955	6.2	8.0	2.9	7.6
1956	6.3	7.6	4.7	9.4
1957	4.5	5.7	1.8	8.3
1958	4.8	6.7	4.4	6.5
1959	2.7	9.4	0.0	5.5
1960	4.9	6.9	2.5	4.1
1961	6.8	5.2	3.3	3.4
1962	15.1	8.1	5.6	3.0
1963[a]	14.2	8.7	9.0	2.4

Source: Calculated from Organisation for Economic Cooperation and Development (OECD), *General Statistics* (Paris, September 1964), pp. 107–108.

[a] Preliminary.

1962 with a "one-to-one direct correspondence between changes in the cost of living and changes in wages." He explains that the cost of living rose substantially after rents and utilities were unblocked in pricing, and that the prices of services kept on rising as the wage increase in the high-productivity industries was extended to low-productivity areas. But he still believes that Italy cannot conform to a Lewis model of growth because of rising wages, and thus he relies on an explanation of structural problems, including primarily wage push by noncompetitive forces in the labor market.[20]

Mrs. Lutz's distinction between Group I and Group II com-

20. *Ibid.*, pp. 380, 384. Gustav Schachter attributes the fact that the consumer price index rose much higher than the wholesale index (which actually fell) to the exploitive pricing by retailers (*The Italian South: Economic Development in Mediterranean Europe,* New York: Random House, 1965, p. 148).

bines certain industries with a considerable lag in production technique, like textiles, with the expanding metal-producing and processing industries. From 1951 to 1959, the advance in engineering employment of almost 100,000 persons is canceled out by the decline in textiles of 116,000. But the base of 1950 is a poor one. At that time the larger firms had excess labor on their rolls which they found it expensive to discharge. Considerable underemployment therefore already existed in manufacturing, and expansion of output could take place with increased real employment within the firm but little new hiring. Beyond this, Mrs. Lutz is correct, up to 1959, because the wage structure with relatively low base pay and high social-security payments and discharge penalties made it profitable to work overtime rather than to hire new workers who could not be readily laid off. But she was unfortunate to be writing in 1959. Thereafter to the November 1961 census, as production continued to expand, employment in the engineering industries jumped by 130,000, or more than the total increase in the previous 8 years. In addition, difficulties over the definition of unemployment cast doubt on Mrs. Lutz's conclusion that the gain in output from 1950 to 1959 was achieved without any decrease in unemployment and probably none in underemployment. This may be true on the basis of the Ministry of Labor data, but is dubious in the light of the ISTAT sample surveys. The Ministry of Labor data suffer from the inclusion as unemployed of large groups engaged in occasional work, who are mostly women. These numbers declined sharply between 1957 and 1962. Mrs. Lutz was further unlucky to be writing in 1959 before the sharp increase in emigration from Italy to the rest of Europe from a net of 60,000 in 1959 to 140,000 in 1960, 145,000 in 1961, and 150,000 in 1962.

I am disposed, therefore, to believe that the Lewis model fits the Italian case beautifully, with some of the melting of unemployment and underemployment in industry as well as in agriculture hidden from view. There is no dearth of other explanations: Gardner Ackley, writing about 1962, has constructed an econometric model of Italian growth which puts the emphasis on demand and assumes that supply limitations have played no significant role. Technical change in his model explains 81 percent of the increase in production, and only 19 percent is explained by increased employment. The technical change is a result of heavy fixed investment, some of it induced by demand in a multiplier-accelerator model, some autonomous from the standpoint of current demand but accounted for by the trend of demand and government policy.[21]

Hildebrand attributes the rapid start in Italian recovery to sound monetary policy, inspired by President Einaudi and running counter to the advice of the Rome mission of the Economic Cooperation Administration. Similarly, he ascribes the inflation of 1961 to excesses in policies affecting the money supply, government spending, and wages, which rest at base on the presence of weak government.[22]

The share of wages in national income rose from 1950 to 1956 and then held steady until 1962. This is the Lewis model at work, together with some purely statistical shift as independent farmers, shopkeepers, and artisans transfer to dependent employment. With the further rise in 1963, which produced the remarkable 42 percent increase in wage rates in 2 years, the percentage of wages in national income rose still more, as shown in Table II-7. The response of Italian labor was vastly different from that of German workers. With increased wage income, they saved not more but less. The statement cannot be supported statistically, since savings are not given separately for households and enterprise. But qualitative information suggests that the response to rising wages and prices was to buy more, not less, and to borrow, not save. Costs rose and profits fell, and with the latter stock prices.[23] When the left-of-center government responded to a working-class complaint of inequitable income distribution — a phenomenon which was rapidly correcting itself — by the application of a 15 percent withholding tax on dividends and the nationalization of the electrical industry, capital flowed abroad, to compound balance-of-payments troubles. It was an old-fashioned crisis of the Marxian sort, but one in which government, rather

21. Gardner Ackley, "An Econometric Model of Italian Postwar Growth" (unpublished MS, n.d. [1962 or later]). The polished version of this paper, *Un modello econometrico dello sviluppo italiano net dopoguerra*, SVIMEZ Monograph No. 7 (Rome: Giuffre Editore, 1963), I have not seen.

22. Hildebrand, *Growth and Structure in the Economy of Modern Italy*, p. 14.

23. See Figure XII-1, below, p. 230.

TABLE II-7

Employees' share in Italian net national product, 1950–1963 (percentages)

1950	50.8	1958	56.4
1951	50.1	1959	54.8
1952	52.7	1960	55.1
1953	52.6	1961	55.3 (55.5)[a]
1954	54.3	1962	57.2 (57.4)
1955	54.4	1963	— (62.5)
1956	55.9	1964	— (63.8)
1957	55.9		

Source: G. H. Hildebrand, *Growth and Structure in the Economy of Modern Italy* (Cambridge, Mass.: Harvard University Press, 1965), Table 55, p. 222.

[a] Parenthetical figures taken from *Italian Economic Survey* (May-June 1965), pp. 44, 47, using internal net product at factor cost, according to the "traditional" (not international) schema.

than serving the interests of capitalists, straddled the two groups. The left blamed speculation and wages below those in the rest of Europe, while the right criticized government spending, the rise in wages, and persecution of property owners, instead of both groups recognizing that what had happened was that Italy had run out of its surplus labor and would have to grow in a different pattern.

Switzerland

Switzerland is the classic example of a Lewis model of growth relying exclusively on foreign labor.[24] Its foreignness and the fact that immigration was pushed so far — to virtually one third of the labor force — gives the Swiss case idiosyncratic features that have been analyzed in a penetrating article by Mrs. Lutz.[25]

24. But see the view of a Swiss trade-union leader that Swiss growth was based on three things: Research, promotion of education, and generous depreciation allowances (OECD Manpower and Social Affairs Division, International Trade Union Seminar on Economic and Social Programming, *Supplement to Final Report*, Paris: Organisation for Economic Cooperation and Development, n.d. [presumably 1965], p. 114).

25. Vera Lutz, "Foreign Workers and Domestic Wage Levels, with an Illustration from the Swiss Case," Banca Nazionale del Lavoro *Quarterly Review*, No. 64 (March 1963), pp. 3–68.

She has emphasized the fact that foreign workers have been a noncompeting group which has enabled Swiss workers to climb out of the disadvantaged occupations — agriculture, construction, mining, hotel service, textiles, and metal-working — and to become skilled or semiskilled and middle class.

A further important and interesting discussion has taken place in Switzerland over whether foreign workers retard or stimulate inflation. This question also involves an aspect of imperfect competition, since the foreign workers are originally combined with existing capital, which they enable to be used more effectively, and require little in the way of social overhead capital. After a time, however, with full employment of domestic industrial capital, housing, schooling, hospitals, and so on, additional immigration requires capital expenditure to accompany the additional labor and on this account tends to push up investment and costs rather than hold down costs and prices.

Finally, the Swiss illustration has extra-economic interest as one where the general public — not enterprise or labor, so far as can be judged from press accounts, but the public in its political and social capacity — became disturbed at the *Überfremdung* ("overforeignization") of the country and undertook to bring immigration to a halt and even to roll it back, despite economic costs to various groups of doing so.

Switzerland was highly prosperous from 1950 to 1964. The exact record is difficult to determine because of the inbred Swiss distrust of statistical information about its economy and finances. Industrial activity, for example, is based on indexes which average reports of 50 = poor, 100 = average, and 150 = good. The construction index is limited to dwellings completed. National-income data have been calculated. Limited as the material is, it shows steady growth overall at good rates in the early and middle 1950's, a slowdown in 1957 and setback in 1958, followed by a high rate of growth — close to 8 percent — from 1958 to 1961, and then a distinct slowing down to less than 5 percent in 1962 and 1963.

Switzerland was highly prosperous in the 1960's, prosperous but uneasy. The uneasiness stemmed from the fact that so much of the prosperity depended on foreign factors, workers and capital. The government in 1964 restricted both foreign investment and further recruitment abroad. Both capital and labor are in Switzerland on a short-term basis and therefore likely to leave. Swiss foreign-exchange reserves are large enough to enable her to finance a withdrawal of foreign capital, but an exodus of foreign labor poses questions of how the dirty and servile jobs in the economy, on some of which, like hotel-keeping, the balance of payments depends, can be carried on, if there were to be a sudden departure.

Throughout Europe, the claim is made that foreign workers should be paid identical wages with domestic. But it is difficult to prevent the labor market from dividing into noncompeting groups. Swiss citizens leave agriculture, textiles, construction, mining, service, and so on, and their places are taken, in varying degrees, by foreigners. The very different composition of the domestic and foreign labor force in Switzerland is shown for 1960 in Table II-8. Five sixths of the foreigners are workers, as

TABLE II-8

Percentage of domestic and foreign workers by occupational group in Switzerland, 1960

	Men		Women	
	Swiss	Foreign	Swiss	Foreign
Self-employed	20	3	9	2
Family workers	5	0	7	0
Salaried	23	11	34	13
Workers	44	85	44	84
Apprentices	6	1	6	1
Total	100	100	100	100

Source: Richard Zollinger, "Zur Bevoelkerungs- und Gesellschaftstruktur," *Schweizerische Zeitschrift für Volkswirtschaft und Statistik,* Nos. 1–2 (March-June 1964), p. 34.

contrasted with less than half of the Swiss, and 4 out of 10 of the Swiss workers are skilled or semiskilled.[22] In 1950, foreigners

26. Richard Zollinger, "Zur Bevoelkerungs- und Gesellschaftstruktur," *Schweizerische Zeitschrift für Volkswirtschaft und Statistik,* Nos. 1–2 (March-June 1964), p. 34.

comprised 12.3, 12.1, and 10.5 percent of total employees in clothing, textiles, and clay and stone, respectively, whereas in 1961 they were above 12.8 percent in every branch of factory work except electricity, gas, and water (1.8 percent), and more than a third in clothing (49.2), clay and stone (43.6), textiles (41.3), leather and rubber (39.3), and metal-working (35.0). The third lowest industry, watches and jewelry, had 13.6 percent, and even printing and publishing had 16.4 percent.[27] Between industries, and within industries as between unskilled and semi- and fully skilled jobs, the preference goes to the Swiss, and with it the "wage drift," or the extent to which earnings rise faster than nominal wage rates through overtime and upgrading. On this account the slow rise of the wage index from 90 in 1953 to 100 in 1958 and 105 in 1960, prior to shooting up to 123 in 1963, is not very significant. From 1953 to 1960 while wage rates were rising 16 percent, weekly earnings went up by 27 percent. After about 1960 the labor shortage became so intense that Swiss employers began to recruit foreign workers out of the dirty jobs and into those occupations which had hitherto been reserved for the Swiss. The "noncompeting" groups began much more to compete. From 1960 to 1963, while wage rates rose 17 percent, weekly earnings rose only slightly more, or 20 percent.

Observe one point about the upgrading of the local labor supply. It is true that foreign labor without roots in a country is more mobile than domestic labor. But where the foreign labor takes the low-end jobs and permits domestic labor to move up in the social and economic scale, it helps make that domestic labor more mobile and improves the functioning of the separate labor markets despite the gulf between them.

Up to 1962, according to informants, many Swiss thought that foreign workers held down wages and prices. After the winter of 1962–63, and especially in the spring of 1963, this view was altered, and it was thought that the way to preserve stability was to limit the inflow of labor. The change in opinion turned on whether foreign labor was combined with existing capital or gave rise to the need for new capital outlays.

Some stereotyped numbers will help to illustrate. Suppose that a foreign worker's marginal product is 30,000 to 40,000 Swiss

27. Lutz, "Foreign Workers and Domestic Wage Levels," Table 5, p. 58.

francs (SF) a year. If the capital/labor ratio is SF 50,000 per worker, and the capital/output ratio close to 1½, it will pay to bring in more workers, without capital investment, to use idle capital, and it will be close to worthwhile to invest in plant and equipment for the sake of hiring foreign labor. But this assumes that there is excess capacity in social overhead capital. While the firm may gain from undertaking investment and manning it with foreign labor, the community as a whole may be taking on substantial responsibilities. SF 80,000 to 100,000 of investment in housing and infrastructure may be needed for the single worker, and SF 150,000 to 200,000 for a married worker and his family. It takes 2 to 4 man-years of labor to provide the facilities for an additional worker, once existing housing is fully utilized, if the normal standards of sanitation and comfort for the foreign worker are insisted on.[28]

The Lewis-model type of development in Britain and the United States required the crowding of workers into slums to produce long-sustained growth without inflation. Where business and government make decisions independently, under strong traditions of *laissez faire*, there may be some benefit for business from immigration with housing and infrastructure short, so long as government is willing to continue with investment in infrastructure or the public is willing to tolerate a dual standard in accommodation. But the social utility of such immigration comes into doubt when the public welfare is unable to accept barracks, slums, *bidonvilles*, and overcrowding. With full employment of capital and the maintenance of social standards, Mrs. Lutz claims that there is no reason in principle why it would be more inflationary to let wages in the undesirable occupations rise, to the point where they reattract Swiss workers from the desirable or genteel lines, than to continue with the noncompeting group technique. Short of a very large inflow of workers, however, there is a presumption that the capital requirements for foreign workers at the margin are less than the average, without con-

28. The illustrative figures of this paragraph, and many of the ideas, are based on conversations with Professor Jurg Niehans of the University of Zurich and Dr. F. Aschinger of the *Neue Zürcher Zeitung*. The fact that foreign workers require capital expenditure is mentioned in the Bank for International Settlements, *35th Annual Report, 1st April 1964 to 31st March 1965* (Basle, June 14, 1965), p. 67.

demning them to squalor, so that there is a benefit in dampening inflation with more workers.

It was mainly on social and political grounds that the Swiss finally took steps to stop immigration. Each half-year when the figures of foreign residents were announced, there was an outcry. In the spring of 1964 the Swiss government restricted capital inflow and ordered a cutback in total employment; no factory could recruit additional foreign workers unless its total employment was below 95 percent of a recent base period. Finally in 1964–65 the halt was made more definite. In August 1964 the Swiss government signed an accord liberalizing the regulations under which Italian workers could bring their wives (by reducing the waiting period from 3 years to 18 months) and could become permanent residents (by reducing the waiting period from 10 years to 5).[29] These improvements were required, the Swiss authorities thought, in order to hold their Italian workers in the face of increasing competition from Germany on the one side and Italy on the other. But the general public was opposed, and the Swiss legislature refused to ratify. A proposal was put forward to amend the constitution to limit the number of foreign residents in Switzerland to 10 percent of the total population, and a 5 percent cutback in foreign workers was actually decreed by the government to take effect by June 1965.[30]

What seems to have been the issue, more than the economic question of whether foreign workers held back or contributed to inflation and growth, was the threat to Swiss "Swissness" that a large Catholic, Italian-speaking, perhaps politically biased element, lacking Swiss traditions, posed for the delicately balanced Swiss society and polity. Assimilation was not desired, but it was thought that unless undue economic risks were to be taken, assimilation was called for. As with the Lewis-model type of development in the case of the United States, one end to it can be immigration restrictions. Swiss industry can adjust by reshifting its investment to capital-deepening. A difficulty with this

29. For an earlier statement on the Swiss regulations governing foreign workers, see "Foreign Workers in Switzerland," *International Labour Review*, LXXXVII (February 1963), 1–23 (in reprint).

30. See "Swiss Vote Backs Economic Curbs," *New York Times*, March 1, 1965. The increase in the number of foreign workers in Switzerland as of August of the 5 years from 1960 to 1964 has been 20, 26, 18, 7, and 6 percent, respectively.

solution, however, is that Switzerland is also fearful of undue dependence on foreign capital, especially short-term capital that the banking community has invested in housing mortgages. Along with the restriction of labor is one on capital inflow. The regulations have been effectively defeated by the repatriation of Swiss investments, which reduces the international liquidity position of the country. But the Swiss public is determined that, whatever the price of restriction in terms of growth, inflation, and liquidity, preservation of its national identity shall come first.

The Netherlands

The Netherlands follows the Lewis model of growth in the postwar period, again with its special features, in this case incomes policy and the particular source of the labor supply. The source of the labor lies in a high rate of natural increase and a decline in emigration. Incomes policy helped to stabilize wage rates, along with an elastic labor supply, until the policy collapsed in the fall of 1963.

An initial large increase in population occurred immediately after the war when roughly 300,000 immigrants, one tenth of them "pure-blooded" Dutchmen and many of them of some Dutch blood, arrived in the Netherlands from the Netherlands East Indies.[31] The rate of increase in the labor force, for example, was 4.5 percent in 1948 and 2.6 percent in 1949.

The Dutch natural rate of increase is among the highest in Europe: 13.7 per thousand compared to a western European average of 7.9 in 1958.[32] Currently, 140,000 people are added each year to a population of 12 million. This rate stems from high fertility, in turn a result of religion, but of Calvinists as well as Catholics. Preoccupied with the limited territory of the country, the Netherlands early after the war adopted a policy of supported emigration directed especially to the British Commonwealth.[33]

31. "Holland: How To Handle Immigrants," *Economist*, CCXIV (March 6, 1965), 1008.

32. J. Frederic Dewhurst *et al.*, *Europe's Needs and Resources* (New York: Twentieth Century Fund, 1961), p. 41.

33. See Willem Steigenga, *Industrialization-Emigration: The Consequences of the Demographic Development of the Netherlands*, Research Group for European Migration, Study No. X (The Hague: Nijhoff, 1955). This book proved to be unduly pessimistic about the absorption of Dutch labor in Holland's own borders.

In terms paralleling the later argument in the case of Switzerland, but in contrast with statements by developing countries to be discussed in Chapter V, Dutch economists claim that it saves capital to promote emigration because the country does not have to provide complementary investment in plant and equipment or in houses and general infrastructure.[34] Gradually, however, as rapid economic growth in the country absorbed more and more of the natural increase of the farm population, as well as pulling down the numbers engaged in agriculture, the emigration policy was allowed to lapse without having been officially reversed. Dutchmen insist that Holland is too small in the long run to absorb the expanding numbers of their countrymen.[35] But until 1963 the ability to divert this stream of emigrants to domestic industry and to maintain an incomes policy held down the share of wages going to labor, as shown in Table II-9.

Several other aspects of the Dutch labor force are of interest. One, connected with the high birth rate, is the low rate of participation of women in the labor force: 28.1 percent in 1957, compared with a high rate of 57.1 percent for Austria (in 1961) and an average rate for Europe of about 42 percent. A greater proportion of Dutch women were employed immediately after the war, but the rate declined largely as a result of the drop in the female participation in agriculture and in unpaid family enterprise of all kinds. This has been the consequence of marriage at an earlier age, of large families, but above all of the rigid social disapproval which attaches to female paid employment.[36] A number of Dutch companies have been experimenting with methods to entice women back into the labor force.[37]

Second is the relative importance in the Netherlands of border workers and emigrants to Germany. Border workers in Germany increased from a few thousand in 1954 to more than 5,000 in

34. F. Hartog, "Economic Policy in the Netherlands," in *Economic Policy in Our Time,* III, 136.

35. "The Netherlands are becoming simply too crowded," wrote E. W. Hofstee in "The Netherlands," in Brinley Thomas (ed.), *Economics of International Migration* (London: Macmillan, 1958), p. 107. This paper was prepared for an International Economic Association conference of 1955.

36. See T. Paul Schultz, "Income Distribution in the Netherlands" (unpublished thesis, Massachusetts Institute of Technology, 1965), p. 144.

37. "Dutch Industries Taking Their Toll of Working Wives," *New York Times,* May 3, 1965.

TABLE II-9

Distribution of Netherlands national income, 1938, 1946–1962 (at factor cost)

	Major factor shares measured in percent of total			
			Enterprise	
	Wages and salaries and social benefits	Farm income	Noncorporate and property	Corporate profits
1938	55.9	—	—	—
1946	60.5	—	—	—
1947	58.8	—	—	—
1948	58.8	—	—	—
1949	55.3	3.5	17.8	11.6
1950	55.0	11.3	17.4	11.6
1951	55.0	10.9	17.8	12.3
1952	54.6	11.8	17.3	11.6
1953	53.9	9.4	19.8	11.7
1954	54.3	9.4	19.6	11.1
1955	53.6	8.8	20.4	11.7
1956	55.3	8.3	20.3	10.9
1957	56.7	8.8	18.0	10.7
1958	57.8	9.0	17.5	9.7
1959	56.7	7.7	18.0	11.0
1960	56.6	8.5	16.9	11.0
1961	58.9	7.8	15.9	10.1
1962	61.4	7.0	14.3	9.5

Sources: 1938 and 1946–47 derived from Netherlands Central Bureau of Statistics, *Statistical Studies*, No. 4 (December 1954), Table 4D, p. 37, and Table 8, p. 40; 1948 from "Het aandeel van de lonen en salarissen, inclusief sociale lasten in het nationale inkomen," *Statistische en encono-metrische onderzoekingen* (3d quarter, 1959), Table III, p. 116; 1949–1962 from *Statistische en econometrische onderzoekingen,* various national-account issues.

1960, more than 15,000 in 1961, and more than 25,000 in 1963. Some 60,000 additional workers live as well as work in Germany. At the same time Dutch industry has gained some 20,000 Belgian workers, largely commuters, who are not counted as foreign under the Benelux agreement.

Third, the Dutch attitude toward foreign workers outside of

Belgium is on the whole negative.[38] It was expressed to me that a country should grow with its own resources; that Holland was already overcrowded and had no room for foreigners. There were foreign workers in the Netherlands in 1962, but only 32,000 men and 5,700 women, as compared with an active population of 3.5 million.

Figure II-2 shows the Netherlands labor pool of registered available workers (unemployed) in conjunction with labor applications by employers and with the balance of payments on current account. Between 1951 and 1960, whenever the curve of applications was below the labor pool, the balance of payments was in surplus, and when applications outran the pool, there was a deficit. In 1960 the relationship between the labor market and the balance of payments changed. The reason is baffling, since it was in this period that incomes policy was collapsing under the pressure of demand for labor, and the 17 percent increase in wages in 1964 served primarily to formalize a level of "black wages" that was very nearly being paid anyhow.[39]

Dutch incomes policy has been described in detail many times.[40] There is a Foundation of Labor representing employers and trade unions; a Board of Mediators which has to approve collective bargaining agreements after consultation with the Foundation of Labor; a Social and Economic Council of labor, employer, and government representatives which consults with the Foundation and advises the government. All groups believe in cooperation, in the necessity for a small country dependent on foreign trade to hold back on price increases, and in industrial peace. In the initial stages, the unions exercised great restraint in the interest of recovery, but with a cost-of-living increment to prevent a decline in real wages. From 1954 on,

38. R. Nolen, "Active Manpower Policy in the Netherlands," in OECD Manpower and Social Affairs Division International Management Seminar on Active Manpower Policy, *Report No. 6* (mimeographed, Paris, 1965), p. 13.

39. "Holland: How To Handle Immigrants," p. 1005.

40. Martin P. Oettinger, "The Industrial Relations System in the Netherlands with Special Emphasis since the End of World War II" (unpublished thesis, Harvard University, 1960); Hartog, "Economic Policy in the Netherlands," pp. 118–129; William Fellner *et al., The Problem of Rising Prices* (Paris: Organisation for European Economic Cooperation, 1961), pp. 359–390.

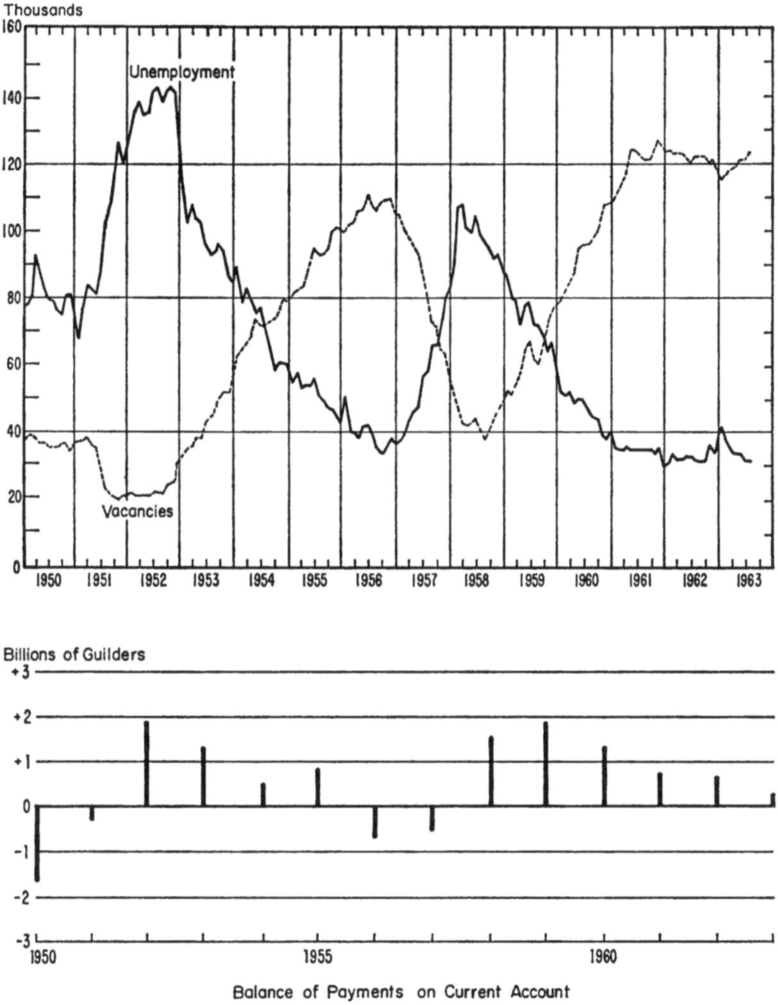

Figure II-2. Registered unemployment and employer vacancies in the Netherlands, compared with balance of payments on current account, 1950–1963

Sources: Unemployment and vacancies: *The Netherlands Budget Memorandum, 1964,* The Hague, 1964 Balance of payments on current account: International Monetary Fund, *Balance of Payments Yearbook,* various issues increases in wages were tied to productivity by sector. In 1962, increases were linked instead to productivity in the economy as a whole. By 1963 the government withdrew from the negotiations. Meanwhile so-called "black wages" in excess of agreed norms started early in the construction industry in the mid-fifties and spread in 1961 and 1962. In October 1963 two shipbuilding companies in Friesland announced that they refused to be bound by the central bargain and made separate agreements with their workers. The Foundation of Labor in an attempt to salvage the system reached an agreement which promised a 10 percent raise in wages plus other benefits — 5 percent overall and another 5 percent subject to negotiation in individual industries. The ultimate rise, including, as already mentioned, the incorporation of wage drift into the standard, amounted to 17 percent. Many firms took advantage of the separately negotiated increases, however, to insist upon changes in work rules that gave a spur to productivity increases. The wage increase negotiated in 1964 for 1965 amounted to 6.8 percent. The standard of the average increase in productivity has been left behind.

The curious aspect of the Dutch position is that the relationship between labor shortage and the balance of payments should alter just as wages began to rise sharply. In part, as in Germany, this was a result of the inflation in France and Italy, which was much faster than that in the Netherlands. The Netherlands did see a deficit in 1964, but it was remarkably limited in terms of the earlier relationships.

The main lesson of the Netherlands experience, however, is that incomes policy, or wages policy as the Dutch more candidly call it, is not a substitute for an elastic labor supply. We return to this theme in Chapter XI.

CHAPTER III

Fast Growth with Limited Labor: Austria and France

Austria

The ECE study referred to at the beginning of Chapter II states that the Austrian labor supply grew at the rate of 1.1 percent a year during the 1950's, which would put the country in the class of those with "unlimited" labor (though at the bottom). This categorization is difficult to accept. The ECE gives Austrian employment as rising from 3,280,000 in 1950 to 3,649,000 in 1959.[1] But the census figures for 1951 and 1961 show a change only from 3,270,000 to 3,372,000; according to the OECD, a compound rise of only 0.3 percent.[2] Still another source sets the later figure at 3,369,000 — virtually no rise at all.[3] The difficulty lies in agriculture, where the ECE figures show little decline but the census indicates a loss of 300,000 workers. The Austrian achievement in scoring a large rise in output with a relatively limited increase in labor input in industry and services is not in doubt. Despite the ECE, it seems likely this was also the case in agriculture. With an adjusted figure for the total labor input, the Austrian score for labor productivity would put it at the top of the list in Table II-1, ahead of, rather than just behind, Germany.

In every other respect than total numbers, the Austrian economy conformed to the industrial sector of the Lewis model. Underemployment existed at the outset of the period. Substantial

1. ECE, *Some Factors in Economic Growth in Europe during the 1950's* (Geneva: United Nations, 1964), p. A-3.
2. OECD, *Manpower Statistics, 1950–1962* (Paris, 1963), p. 21.
3. Kammer für Arbeiter und Angestellte für Wien, *Wachstumperspektiven der Österreichischen Wirtschaft* (Vienna: Österreichischen Gewerkschaftsbundes, 1963), p. 32.

transfer of labor occurred from agriculture to industry and services — almost 200,000 into industry and more than 150,000 into services. The participation rate of women rose from 52 percent to 57 percent, to lead the European League (ex Turkey). Total numbers of independent workers, including family members, declined by 200,000 within the sectoral totals, involving shifts from inefficient to efficient productive units. Economic growth was supported by a considerable reallocation of labor within a constant total. The wage index rose fairly steadily through the 1950's, with a spurt from 1959 to 1962 followed by a return to a pace of 6 to 8 percent a year in 1962 and 1963.

Austrian efficiency is somewhat puzzling. Per Jacobsson once told me that he was delighted with Austrian recovery because it demonstrated the power and significance of monetary policy. When the German economy responded to orthodox monetary policy with a surge of output, cynics scoffed, saying that it was the result of the German love of work. Austria's recovery proved the value of monetary theory, so the story went, because it was well known that Austrians detest work. Another verbal explanation from a non-Austrian economist is that the country acquired the practice of planning, and achieved efficiency by this means, during the days of the Marshall Plan. Planning as a source of efficient allocation has been said to apply to France, to be discussed presently, but if Austria has been allocating resources in conformity with an overall plan, it does so without wide recognition of that fact. Austrian economic literature, for example, treats French planning as something entirely foreign.[4]

During the 1930's, the Austrian economy was weak and stagnant. During the 1950's, it grew at one of the fastest rates in Europe. What happened in between were *Anschluss* with Germany in 1937, the war, and Russian occupation of eastern Austria from 1945 to the treaty in 1955. Germany undertook a substantial amount of investment in Austria before and during the war; the Russian occupation encouraged the Austrian government to start first with reconstruction of infrastructure and cultural monuments — St. Stephen's Cathedral and the Opera House — which left the more productive investment with a low

4. *Ibid.*, pp. 57–58.

ICOR and high labor productivity available for the second half of the decade.

The obvious place to look for German investments is in hydroelectric power. At least ten sites, each of more than 10 million watts capacity, for a total of 687.5 million, were started by the Germans between 1938 and 1942 and completed in whole or in part by the Austrian authorities after the war. Kaprun with 220 million watts capacity and Rodmund with 173 million dominate the list. But it is difficult to find a break in the trend here: hydroelectric power in Austria provided 10.3 percent of energy in coal-equivalent in 1929, 17.8 percent in 1937, 24.1 in 1950, and 32.3 percent in 1958. After 1945 the Austrian authorities began the construction of 15 new installations with a capacity of 1.5 billion watts and at the end of 1959 had 6 more projects under construction with a total capacity of 816 million watts.[5] The German authorities doubtless speeded the planning and construction of electric-power installations, and some of the projects undertaken after the war may have been planned in detail by Germany. But the main thrust of postwar growth was elsewhere.

In iron and steel, aluminum, cement, chemicals, fertilizer, artificial fibers, and transport equipment, Germany laid out and built new plants and rationalized old ones. Russian occupation troops stripped those plants to which they had access, and, finally, Marshall Plan investments, amounting to roughly $1 billion, re-equipped them with modern machinery. In some instances, the Germans planned a project, and the Austrians later carried it through. The outstanding example is the Autobahn: German authorities laid it out, designed the structures, accumulated some of the land, but built only 20 kilometers themselves. Project design, which the International Bank for Reconstruction and Development says is so difficult for the less developed countries to accomplish, makes the subsequent capital investment both easier and of higher productivity per schilling invested.[6] Similar

5. See L. Bauer, "Energiepolitik unter besonderer Berüchsichtigung der Elektrizitäts Wirtschaft," in Anton Tautscher (ed.), *Handbuch der Österreichische Wirtschaftspolitik* (Vienna: Bastei, 1961), pp. 341, 345.

6. It is not without interest that the fastest-growing country in the Far East after the war has been Taiwan, where the Japanese had undertaken a large volume of investment in infrastructure.

starts on investment projects had been made in cement, steel, and aluminum. And it was in nonferrous metals, iron and steel, transport equipment, and electrical energy that the Austrian economy grew the fastest between 1950 and 1960, with decade increases of 300 percent, 235 percent, 195 percent, and 170 percent, respectively.

Austrian growth has further benefited from Germany on a current basis. Austria conforms more closely than any other country in Europe to the export-led growth pattern.[7] Much of the market comes from Germany. Austrian steel mills produce thin steel sheet for German tinplate and automobile manufacture (a highly income-elastic intermediate good), and German tourists flood into the Tyrol (an income-elastic purchase of services). Germany took more than a quarter of Austrian exports in the 1960's (and provided more than two fifths of imports), as compared with 14.9 percent in exports (and 14.2 percent in imports) in 1950.

There are good reasons why Austria could not follow the Lewis model. The rate of natural population increase is low, little more than half the European average and a third of the Dutch rate. Unions are strong, politically entrenched, and have little international solidarity with Mediterranean workers from the south. Moreover, nominal wages are low, with substantial fringe benefits in the form of generous social-security payments and subsidized housing, which makes worker real income higher than is apparent in earnings statistics. Foreign workers prefer cash to income in kind and deferred income. Accordingly, foreign workers who came to work in Austria would probably be immediately drawn on to German jobs, like the 60,000 Austrians working and living in Germany and the 10,000 border workers. Austria suffers something of a brain drain to Germany in its professional and skilled ranks, and its attempts to recruit foreign workers have been limited — 40,000 were authorized under legislation, but only a few thousand were actually recruited — because of union opposition and the widespread feeling that it would produce no lasting result.

7. On a per capita basis, Austrian export growth was the highest in Europe. For more detailed discussion of export-led growth, see Chapter VI below.

Austrian success in expanding investment in the industrial sector without large supplies of each, when other rapidly growing countries of Europe were mostly limited to capital-widening in industry, is attributable only in small part to technological innovation. The oxygen process for reducing iron ore is well known as an Austrian invention, and Austrian industry is also a leader in sintering metallurgy. But on the whole it cannot be said that the country is a technological leader. Most of its processes are of foreign origin and license. Austrian technical progress under German *Gleichshaltung*, Russian removals, and Marshall Plan reconstruction has nonetheless been great. Austria can qualify as a country which developed under a Harrod-Domar or Kaldor investment model, closing a technical gap, with large savings provided from abroad and through company profits.

France

The most striking exception to the Lewis model among the fast growers in Europe is France. I have elsewhere discussed French postwar growth in general, and French planning, so that there is little merit in a full-dress review.[8] In addition the ECE selects France, along with Germany, Norway, and the United Kingdom, for its country analyses, which supplement the general view of European growth in the 1950's.[9] But we may wish to see how that country looks when measured against the Lewis model of infinitely elastic labor supply. The answer is that it did not fit the model during most of the 1950's; it began to about 1956 or 1957; and by 1963, with labor in short supply, it found itself undergoing inflationary pressure and felt the need to slow down. In short, France conforms to the model more or less after about 1957, but the earlier 1950's require explanation.

One explanation is that the figures for the labor supply are wrong. The ECE calls attention to an estimate by A. Sauvy, who puts the growth of the active labor force at 0.4 percent per

8. "The Postwar Resurgence of the French Economy," in Stanley Hoffmann *et al., In Search of France* (Cambridge, Mass.: Harvard University Press, 1963), pp. 118-158; "French Planning," a paper presented at the Universities-National Bureau of Economic Research Conference on Economic Planning, held at Princeton, N.J., November 27–28, 1964.

9. ECE, *Some Factors in Economic Growth in Europe*, chap. 6, pp. 7–15.

year over the 1950's instead of its estimated 0.1 percent.[10] The censuses of 1946 and 1954 are on the whole incomparable, and most sources limit statistical comparison to the period running from the 1954 to the 1962 census. Statistics of the labor force, whether reckoned with and without armed forces, gauged in civilian employment only, or measured in terms of employed and unemployed, all showed annual declines from 1954 to 1957. The cumulative decline amounted to 27,000 for the total labor force, including the military; 310,000 for the civilian labor force, reflecting the expansion of military forces for Indochina and Algiers; and 160,000 for civilian employment. After 1957, however, total numbers expanded, the increase amounting to 450,000 between 1957 and 1962, or 5 percent total and close to 1 percent per annum at a compound rate. These numbers came from the expatriates from Algeria, from immigration, and from release of military conscripts, as well as continued large-scale reallocation among and within sectors. These sources of additions to the labor force are touched upon below. It is probably impossible to unravel what happened to the labor force before 1954.[11] The sources of French growth up to 1957, then, are the issue. After that date expansion required continuous inputs of labor and obtained them until 1963, when inflation set in and growth had to be slowed.

The ECE says that "an analysis of economic growth of France during the fifties could appropriately be subtitled 'a study in the efficient use of scarce productive resources.'" The question is

10. *Ibid.*, p. 7 (n. 29). The reference is to A. Sauvy, "Les perspectives d'accroisement du nombre des emplois en France d'ici 1975," *Population*, No. 2 (April-June 1961).

11. Institut National de la Statistique et des Études Economiques (INSEE), *Annuaire Statistique de la France, 1961* (Paris: Imprimerie Nationale, 1962), gives the numbers engaged in agriculture in France in 1954 based on old and new definitions as 6,371,000, and 5,196,000, respectively. All but a quarter of a million of the difference is due to the way the membership of women in the labor force is defined. On the basis of the old definition, the loss of labor in agriculture from 1946 to 1954 amounted to 1,100,000, which would be on top of the further loss of 1,342,000 between 1954 and 1962. But the first loss cannot be added to the second because of the incomparability of the figures.

Unfortunately, too, it is impossible to check the ECE's figures for sectoral changes in employment, since actual figures are not presented (ECE, *Some Factors in Economic Growth in Europe*, chap. 3, Table 23, and Appendix A).

why, and the obvious explanation is French planning. Efficient direction of labor and capital to particular sectors and branches, in this view, would produce high gains in labor productivity, low ICOR's, and low ICOR/L's (representing the investment ratio divided by the increase in labor productivity).

The exact nature of French planning is in some dispute among the students of the subject: whether it is a substitute for inadequate macroeconomic policy, a technique for inducing consistent governmental policies where only muddle had previously prevailed; whether it provided overall market research for French businessmen who ordinarily underestimated the opportunities for investment for lack of information; whether it primarily evangelized among businessmen to convert them from restrictionist to expansionist attitudes; or whether, finally, it furnished a substitute for the price system which was an inefficient allocator of resources.[12] My own view tends to the next to last, which regards the Plan as basically changing the psychological outlook of business. The relevant alternative, that French planning replaced an inefficient price system with an allocation mechanism of much greater efficiency, seems to me, with two important exceptions, not to stand up in the history of the successive Plans.

The record of the Plans' indications to the economy of what to produce at what rates is not impressive. The First Plan underestimated the growth of demand in electricity, which above other fields should lend itself to accurate forecasting. The Second, using more refined methods such as linear programming, was excessively timid: the 4-year targets were reached in 2 years. At the same time the Plan tried to repress expansion in steel. The nationalized coal industry overestimated the demand for coal, along with the rest of the European authorities, and the Plan underestimated demand and the appropriate rate of investment in automobiles, projections which the industry ignored. The

12. For a rapidly dating bibliography, see my paper on "French Planning." Outstanding items in that bibliography are Pierre Bauchet, *Economic Planning: The French Experience* (New York: Frederick A. Praeger, 1964); John Hackett and Anne-Marie Hackett, *Economic Planning in France* (Cambridge, Mass.: Harvard University Press, 1963); John Sheahan, *Promotion and Control of Industry in Postwar France* (Cambridge, Mass.: Harvard University Press, 1963).

Third Plan provided for correction of the balance of payments in 6 years, a result achieved with devaluation in 9 months. All Plans underestimated the reduction of labor in agriculture and overestimated the requirement in manufacturing. While the Plan points the way for private industry, rather than issues commands, it is also true that nationalized industry and even government departments are not wholly submissive to the Plan's advice, adding new programs like the *force de frappe* or rejecting specific advice on construction projects. French planning did not substitute for monetary and fiscal policy on macroeconomic questions, for such questions continued to be the province of the Ministry of Finance and the Bank of France, not always effectively coordinated with the views of the Commissariat du Plan.

French planning has paradoxically amounted to empiricism, laying out the broad directions in which the economy could and should travel but intervening in *ad hoc* fashion in business decisions as proximate circumstances rendered intervention appropriate. Not its projections of resource allocation so much as its continued emphasis on improved technology and larger productive units has been the cause of great French efficiency during the fifties. French postwar growth has had a high technocratic content which has benefited from the efforts of productivity missions under the Marshall Plan and the Commissariat's insistance on efficient techniques but which has its major source in the Saint-Simon tradition of technical capacity. Though often repressed or diverted to the military services, French technical drive has brilliantly emerged in the postwar period in nationalized industry, especially the Electricité de France, Renault, the railroads and the aircraft companies, and in many private industries. Far more than most of Europe, and somewhat more than Italy, French economic recovery has had not only a broad content of technological catching up with the leaders but also a strong element of independent invention. French planning has cultivated and fostered this trend, but it did not create it.

Where the Plan has been responsible for the great efficiency of postwar growth has been in its policy, applied empirically rather than by general directives, of fostering larger and in general more efficient productive units. In the First Plan, expansion in the steel industry was sparked by a series of mergers suggested by the Commissariat and made a condition of access to capital under governmental control. Some considerable portion of the rationalization into more efficient units was a consequence of joining the Common Market and the resultant competition of imports, strongly felt by the smaller inefficient units. But even in retailing, not subject to international competition, concentration into larger units took place, with the disappearance of thousands of small marginal businesses. French inefficiency in distribution has long been exaggerated, and adequate measurement of the disappearance of family retail establishments and artisan and handicraft workshops is hindered by the incomparability of the 1954 census of firms with those earlier and by the shortness of the time before the next one, in 1958.[13] But separate studies made of the food, hotel, drink, and tobacco trades, on the one hand, and textile, clothing, and leather manufacture, on the other, emphasize the concentration of these industries into larger units, through elimination of the small inefficient units, mergers, and growth of the more efficient.[14] In all industry, the numbers of self-employed skilled workers dropped 24 percent, representing 22 percent of men and 33 percent of women. In textiles, hides and skins, and clothing, the proportions reached 33 to 38 percent.[15]

For all sectors of France, independent workers declined by 1,250,000 between the census of 1954 and that of 1962. Table III-1 divides the economy into expanding and contracting branches by sector and within sectors by independent operators (*non salariés*) and employees. It is evident that within a stable total, and for a period which leaves off 5 years of the 1950's and

13. INSEE, *Les Établissements industriels et commerciaux* (Paris: Imprimerie Nationale, 1953); INSEE, *Les Établissements industriels, artisanaux et commerciaux en France en 1958* (Paris: Imprimerie Nationale,

14. Association Française pour la Croissance de la Productivité (AFAP), Group d'études et de mesures de la productivité, *L'Évolution des résultats de productivité du travail dans l'hôtellerie, la restauration, les débits de boisson et de tabac, au cours de la période 1950–1960* (Paris, 1959), as cited by ECE, *Some Factors in Economic Growth in Europe,* chap. 6, p. 11 (n. 54); L. A. Vincent, "La Productivité en France dans les industries textiles, de habillement et du cuir (1949–61)," *Études et Conjuncture,* XVIII (March 1963), 237–258.

15. See Claude Vimont, "Occupational Mobility of Manpower," in OECD Joint International Seminar on Geographical and Occupational Mobility of Manpower (Castelfusano), *Supplement to Final Report* (Paris, 1963).

TABLE III-1

Sectoral changes in French work force, 1954–1962
(thousands of persons)

	Expanding branches		Contracting branches		
	Independent	Employees	Independent	Employees	Net
Agriculture	—	—	– 956	–316	–1,272
Industry	+4	+ 885	– 137	–253	+ 499
Services	+2	+1,032	– 165	– 82	+ 787
Total	+6	+1,917	–1,258	–651	+ 14

Source: "La Population active par branche entre 1954 et 1962," *Études et Conjuncture,* XIX (March 1964), 11.

adds 3 of the 1960's, total labor did not shift, but there were substantial changes by branch and in the elimination of independent workers. In commerce and "other services," employees went up 299,000 and 260,000, respectively, and independent workers fell by 72,000 and 74,000, respectively, suggesting the movement within branches which contributed heavily to efficiency.

For distribution, the ECE makes a point which is related to the "agricultural sector" in the two-sector Lewis model but applies to services as well in the real world. Labor productivity in services grew rapidly in France and Austria (but slowly in Germany and Italy) as a consequence of limited unemployment and high wages. Services in France and Austria had had underemployment and low wages. Facing rising wages, they utilized existing labor more effectively, by itself and in combination with capital. In Germany and Italy, on the other hand, with substantial unemployment during the first part of the 1950's, labor productivity in services gained slowly as wages remained low and employment rose.[16] The distinction between these two pairs of countries does not apply, however, to agriculture, where the rate of increase in labor productivity was great in all four. Possibly the movement out of farming had social as well as economic causes; at any rate, the result was a scarcity of farm labor along

16. ECE, *Some Factors in Economic Growth in Europe,* chap. 6, p. 11 (esp. n. 57).

with underemployment in services.[17] In Italy there were two sharply differentiated sectors within industry: one efficient, one using a much lower capital/labor ratio and existing only by virtue of ignoring social security. In France, the inefficiency at the end of the war was much more widely spread, with underemployment existing throughout industry as well as in services and agriculture. The result was that rapid growth occurred through improved utilization of labor within the separate sectors as wages rose — at least until 1957 or so. This is a variant in which all sectors behave as agriculture does under the Lewis model.[18]

The behavior of the French balance of payments to 1958 is interesting. It is also important because of the example it may furnish for Britain of a country which ignored its balance-of-payments constraint, got to the brink of disaster, but recovered following a change of governmental institutions. Growth was rapid in 1953 and 1954, but a rapid rise in wages and prices led the balance of payments to turn seriously adverse. This did not inhibit the Mollet Socialist government or the successor Radical groups. J. Benard calls this a deliberately placed bet that rising output would ultimately restore the balance of payments which the expansionary policy entailed, and he adds that in the first months of 1957 the bet looked like a losing one.[19] A partial devaluation took place in the summer of 1957, but there was no halt to the expansionary policy until the second quarter of 1958, under the Fifth Republic. A thoroughgoing devaluation in De-

17. The ECE study shows high rates of labor productivity in agriculture for Germany, France, and Italy: 5.5 percent per year, 4.9, and 4.7, respectively — but only 1.8 percent in Austria (*ibid.*, chap. 3, Table 19, p. 28). But this last figure is too low because of underestimation of the exodus from agriculture in that country, discussed above.

18. Edward F. Denison measured the contribution of improved allocation to economic growth in Europe between 1950 and 1962, amounting to fully half a percentage point of the difference between annual growth rates per man in the United States and those in France, Germany, and Italy. This shows France in the lead for squeezing out nonfarm, self-employed, and unpaid family workers ("Improved Allocation of Labor as a Source of Higher European Growth Rates," in Michael J. Brennan, ed., *Patterns of Market Behavior: Essays in Honor of Philip Taft,* Providence: Brown University Press, 1965, pp. 65–88, esp. Table 3, p. 73).

19. J. Benard, "Economic Policy in France," in *Economic Policy in Our Time,* vol. III: *Country Studies* (Chicago: Rand McNally, 1964), p. 337.

cember 1958, plus new taxes and reductions in spending, lower interest rates, and a restoration of convertibility, led to a return flow of capital and restored the balance of payments on current account. There is debate whether the Rueff Plan carried through by Pinay as minister of finance actually produced the subsequent renewal of growth or succeeded simply because of the underlying strength of the economy which had been allowed to grow with inflation. British economists have suggested that full steam ahead without regard to the balance of payments is sound long-run therapy which will both stimulate fast growth and ultimately correct the balance by greater output. The Labour government in fact embraced this policy in the fall of 1964, but the pressure of an adverse balance was so great that it had to be abandoned.

Whatever the success of the French economy prior to 1957, the manpower squeeze became an increasing concern thereafter. The year 1957 was the turning point, according to Benard, with expansion and increased hostilities in Algeria. Prior to that date the French government had not made great use of immigration because of the open hostility of the trade unions. Afterwards, the immigration valve was turned wide open.[20] The big increase in immigration begins in 1956, when gross total immigration, including workers and dependents, rose from the level of the 50,000's to 120,000 in 1956, 178,000 in 1957, to 220,000 in 1961, and 260,000 in 1963.[21]

The other big source of manpower after 1958 was Algeria, where the character of the settlement in 1961 produced three streams of additions to the labor force. First, there were the Algerians themselves, who on balance ceased to return to their country after 1958 but whose immigration into France revived as early as 1959 and was picking up so rapidly that it became necessary to "organize" it in July 1964, with controls on both

20. *Ibid.*, p. 309.

21. P. Bideberry, "Some Features of Immigration in France and in Europe," *International Migration*, II (December 1964), 277–278. These numbers do not include Algerians, who are not regarded as aliens in France and whose numbers varied between a high of net inward migration of 54,700 in 1951 to a net outward movement of 10,300 in the only year of loss, 1958. For the most part the figures run about 20,000 a year in gain for France (La Documentation Française, "Les Travailleurs étrangers en France," *Notes et Études Documentaires*, No. 3057, January 23, 1964, p. 13).

immigration in France and emigration in Algeria. Second, 850,000 of the 1,000,000 Pieds Noirs, or European (largely French) residents of Algeria, arrived in France, contributing some 200,000 additional persons for the work force. Third, the military, relieved from infantry service in Algeria, was scheduled to decline from 1,200,000 in 1956 to 600,000 in 1965.

The quality of these labor sources is evidently different. Algerians serve in construction, public works, metallurgy — the so-called dirty jobs. The Pieds Noirs in the labor force in Algeria were an unbalanced group by French standards: about 10 percent of them were farmers and farm hands, 25 percent industrial workers, 10 percent in commerce, and 30 percent functionaries (including business management). The reduction in the military call-up releases young agriculturalists primarily, since men in this sector undertook their military service early, plus a broad spectrum of youth of varying stages of education but limited experience.

More than that, the early 1960's reflect the postwar pickup in the birth rate, an increase which began in 1946 and, unlike that in other countries of Europe, maintained a new high level rather than sinking back to low levels after reacting to wartime disruption. French births reached more than 800,000 in 1946, against an average of 636,000 in 1934–1938, and stayed above that level even though they later declined somewhat from the 1948 peak of 868,000.[22]

Despite the increase in the labor force, actual and prospective, wage rates and wage costs rose even after the devaluation and at an accelerating pace after 1960. Hours of work per week have held at the remarkably high level of just under 46 per week, but a third week of vacation was granted by law in March 1956, and a fourth week was won by collective bargaining, despite the opposition of the Commissariat, by the Renault workers (and quickly extended beyond them) in 1963. Prices rose to the point where the balance of payments was threatened. Then in September 1963 a stabilization plan of fiscal and monetary contraction was announced, and it was applied in November of the same

22. La Documentation Française, Haut Comité Consultatif de la Population et de la Famille, *Les Besoins en emplois nouveaux en France par département jusqu'en 1970* (Paris: Presses de l'Édition Artistique, 1961).

year. The spurt of very rapid growth was over. Thereafter France found herself in the position of countries which experienced recessions and deficits in their balance of payments on current account from time to time, instead of continuous rapid growth and export surpluses.

No sharp break occurs in the distribution of income between wages and other incomes over the period, although the proportion of income paid to employees rises continuously, as shown in Table III-2. In part this trend is a function of the switch from

TABLE III-2

Employee compensation as a percentage of French national income, 1950–1962

1950	55.1	1957	58.6
1951	56.1	1958	58.3
1952	57.3	1959	59.5
1953	57.5	1960	58.3
1954	58.9	1961	60.5
1955	58.2	1962	60.6
1956	58.3	1963	62.4

Source: *Études et Conjuncture,* XIX (May 1964), 335.

independent enterprises to paid employment — a statistical adjustment rather than income redistribution. But in the course of events, one would have expected a more substantial redistribution, owing to the devaluation of 1958, on the one hand, and the subsequent inflation, on the other.

With full employment, devaluation succeeds only insofar as it succeeds in expanding income through more effective allocation of resources or in reducing what Alexander calls "absorption," that is, expenditure. One means of reducing absorption is to effect a redistribution of income: to raise the prices of internationally traded goods relative to domestic costs, including wages, and thereby to increase profits in exports and in import-competing industry and to cut real income of wage earners. The fact that the share of wages declined in 1960 may reflect this redistribution, which improved the balance of payments. Moreover, corporate savings rose from 5.6 percent of national income in 1958 to 7.2 percent in 1959 and 9.8 in 1960. With the resumption of the rise in the wages share, however, and the leveling off of corporate savings, and presumably corporate profits as a whole, this source of capital formation declined relatively and made enterprise turn increasingly to external sources of capital formation.

This is an area where French planning has not had much success, in part because it does not know what its objective ought to be. To achieve equity, a greater share of income should be received by wage earners. All the literature on French planning points to a need for planning the distribution of income, almost entirely with a view to achieving easy relations between classes.[23] At the same time, various industries and the Commissariat itself believe in the need for planning an increase in profits for the sake of increasing (from 60 to 70 percent) the percentage of internal financing which French business can undertake.[24] It is generally recognized that the supply of labor has a good deal to do with the rate of growth, and that the Evian Agreement over Algeria and the return of the European settlers made possible a higher rate of growth under the Fourth Plan than had thitherto been contemplated. But the impact of labor supply on income distribution, internal savings, and the investment ratio seems to have been ignored in the model of French growth, and, indeed, taking that impact specifically into account would probably render the Plan overdetermined.

The stabilization actions of 1963 required by rising wages and falling profits have been complicated by a poorly organized capital market in France. With declining internal funds for investment (profits), French industry would normally turn to external borrowing. But the French savers' insistence on liquidity plus the absence of financial intermediaries have kept long-term rates high and long-term money scarce. The Caisse des Depôts et Consignation, which collects savings-bank funds and makes them available to governmental bodies and in limited amount to in-

23. See Bauchet, *Economic Planning: The French Experience,* Pt. III, chap. 2; Hackett and Hackett, *Economic Planning in France,* pp. 309–323.

24. See *New York Times,* November 25, 1964; "Aims of French Enterprise," *France Actuelle,* XIV (July 15, 1965), 7. On the problems of the steel industry, where indebtedness amounts to 70 percent of annual sales, see *Le Monde,* June 24, 1965, p. 19.

dustry, has sought to expand its industrial lending. Government itself entered the market for funds for industry. But the French economy found itself in the same paradoxical situation as much of Europe, with high international reserves, providing international liquidity, but a deficiency of means internally for providing simultaneously for the liquidity desires of savers and the need for industrial borrowers to fund their debts. It was this lack in France, in Italy, and perhaps in other countries which meant that the end of the period of growth with unlimited supplies of labor, with its high profits and high corporate savings, was followed by extended stagnation, rather than by a simple shift from internal to external sources of funds.

CHAPTER IV

The Slow Growers with Limited Supplies of Labor: Scandinavia, Belgium, and the United Kingdom

This chapter is mainly about Great Britain. The treatment of Scandinavia (almost entirely Sweden) and Belgium is even more sketchy than that of some of the other countries already dealt with. For lack of acquaintance with the Scandinavian countries, particularly, I run the risk of making drastic mistakes. But there is some merit in showing how the Lewis model of growth with unlimited supplies of labor can be frustrated in various ways, and from a superficial vantage point the Scandinavian countries seem to offer evidence worth noting.

Two preliminary generalizations may be offered: first, that Britain and the Scandinavian countries have politically shown among the tripartite goals of full employment, stability, and growth a strong preference for full employment over price stability; second, that Britain and Belgium among the countries of Europe have had far less room to transfer labor from agriculture to other sectors because they have long since done so (see Table IV-1).[1]

Scandinavia

The Norwegian enigma is how such a high ratio of investment to national income produces such a small rate of growth. The ECE has gone into this question at some length without pro-

1. See Anne Romanis, "Economic Program and Recent Financial Policies in Belgium," *Staff Papers*, XI (March 1964), 20–58.

TABLE IV-1

Percentage share of agriculture in total employment in selected European countries, 1949 and 1959

	1949	1959
Germany	25	16
Italy	41	33
Netherlands	14	10
Austria	34	29
France	29	24
Sweden (1950–1960)	21	15
Denmark (1950–1960)	27	21
Norway	31	24
Belgium	11	8
United Kingdom	6	4
Greece (1951)	48	n.a.
Portugal (1950–1958)	48	48
Spain (1950–1958)	48	43
Turkey (1955)	81	

Source: ECE, *Some Factors in Economic Growth in Europe during the 1950's* (Geneva: United Nations, 1964), chap. 3, Table 19, p. 28.

ducing a satisfactory answer.[2] No attempt is made here to probe deeper into the question. Norwegian exports have grown at about the average rates of the rest of Europe — 6 percent a year over the decade of the 1950's — but imports grew at roughly the same pace, perhaps stimulated by a high income elasticity of demand for merchandise imports in a highly specialized country that did not produce its own consumer durables. One of the weaknesses of the Norwegian economy was the strong specialization in oil transportation — a service which was in high demand with good prices through the Korean boom and again briefly at the time of Suez but which has otherwise been relatively depressed.

But the simple fact is that apart from the mystery of high investment, ordinary growth, and a resulting very high ICOR, Norwegian growth was remarkable only by being rather normal,

2. ECE, *Some Factors in Economic Growth in Europe during the 1950's* (Geneva: United Nations, 1964), chap. 6, pp. 14–22.

which meant well below that of the Continent. The overall labor force rose very slowly, from 1,464,000 in 1950 to 1,517,000 in 1962, although there was a considerable movement out of agriculture. Unemployment was exiguous. Wages rose steadily faster than productivity, virtually doubling between 1953 and 1963 in money terms, while the cost of living rose from 85 to 114 over the same period. There were problems of inflation and balance of payments, but none of them very serious. Norwegian economic planning seemed to produce no striking effects, unless perhaps it was responsible for the high ICOR.[3]

Denmark's growth was a shade lower than Norway's, but her rate of growth of labor supply was higher, 1.0 percent per year as contrasted with 0.3, and her investment ratio virtually half. Of these scores Denmark is even more normal than Norway. Exports grew at a substantial pace — 8 percent per year during the 1950's — but imports kept pace. The Korean boom hurt the balance of payments because of a sharply adverse turn in the terms of trade, but this corrected itself later in the decade, and it is hard to see that the structure of Danish trade and its significant exports of bacon, butter, cheese, and eggs did much to shape the growth pattern. Employment in agriculture declined sharply, to release 6 percent of the labor force for employment in other sectors. But by and large, it is hard to characterize Danish experience as other than normal. Planning was not outstanding, nor was incomes policy. Danish labor practices have been singled out by conservative opinion as an example of what can go wrong when labor unions dominate political life: an apprentice system which inhibits mobility, demarcation disputes rife, and restrictive practices.[4] Denmark had no interest in foreign labor. The view of the Economic Board of the Labor Movement, which made national policy on the matter, was that manpower requirements should be met with labor from Denmark and other Nordic countries.[5]

3. B. J. Bjerve, *Planning in Norway, 1947–56* (Amsterdam: North Holland Publishing Co., 1959); Alice Bourneuf, *Norway: The Planned Revival* (Cambridge, Mass.: Harvard University Press, 1958).

4. F. W. Paish and Josselyn Hennessy, *Policy for Incomes?*, Hobart Paper No. 29 (London: London Institute of Economic Affairs, 1964), p. 59.

5. OECD Manpower and Social Affairs Division, "Adjustment of Rural Manpower to Industry: Practical Policies and Programs" (papers for a working party meeting of November 1964), interview on Denmark.

Finally, the most important in Scandinavia in numbers, is Sweden, a country with a good rate of growth, 3.4 percent, a fairly high rate of investment and a high ICOR, a small increase in labor input, and considerable inflation and wage drift. The country seeks growth through full employment, automation, and incentive systems of taxes and wages. It is sometimes said to have a significant percentage of foreigners in the labor force — 130,000 out of 3,900,000, or 3 percent — but these turn out to consist of some Hungarian refugees from 1956, a handful of Italians and Greeks, and mainly immigrants from other Nordic countries, which are members of the Scandinavian Common Market for Labor. The Swedish authorities have adopted positive policies for manpower adjustment, which are handicapped in practice by the tight position in housing and the unwillingness of unions, whose recommendations are followed on entry permits for non-Scandinavians, to accede to substantial immigration.[6]

In the clash between full employment and price inflation, the Swedes favor full employment and so state in document after document. The result has been an inflation of 3 percent a year and, as shown in Table IV-2, a wage drift close to that level. Active work-force policy has been used to combat wage drift. This included training for women and grants to finance transfers, going so far as the purchase of farms given up by men transferring to urban work. The Swedish authorities have pioneered in fiscal devices to even out employment — a shift from direct to indirect taxation, anticycle investment-reserve funds, and substantial unemployment insurance and cash assistance. On the whole, economic growth has been satisfactory but not in the class with the Continental rapid growers.

In 1962 the OECD undertook the first of a series of reviews of manpower and social policies. In these reviews, national offi-

6. See I. Svennilson, "Liberalization de la politique suédoise d'immigration dans l'après-guerre," in M. Byé *et al.*, *Demain l'Europe sans frontières* (Paris: Plon, 1958), esp. pp. 147–148. See also OECD, "Adjustment of Rural Manpower to Industry," interview on Sweden, pp. 13, 22; Gunnar Lindström, "Active Manpower Policy in Sweden," in OECD Manpower and Social Affairs Division, *International Management Seminar on Active Manpower Policy* (Brussels, 1964), Report No. 8, p. 6. The crucial role of the unions is not explicit in OECD Manpower and Social Affairs Division, *Labour Market Policy in Sweden* (Paris, 1963), which discusses immigration policies at some length.

TABLE IV-2

Wage drift and employment in Swedish mining and manufacturing 1952–1960

	Wage drift		Unfilled vacancies 2d quarter each year (index: 2d quarter 1952–1960 = 100)	
Period[a]	Percent	Index 1952–1960 = 100	All sectors	Mining and manufacturing
1952–53	2.5	81	94	95
1953–54	3.2	103	119	133
1954–55	3.5	113	125	147
1955–56	3.7	119	108	109
1956–57	2.8	90	86	81
1957–58	2.0	65	73	51
1958–59	2.6	84	80	65
1959–60	4.3	139	115	119

Source: "The Labour Market, 1953–61," *Swedish Economy* (May 1961), p. 29.

[a] From November to November in the calendar years specified.

cials set out the outlines of their manpower policies, which were then commented upon and criticized by two foreign experts, in the case of Sweden a Dane and a Dutchman. Despite the fact that these men came from countries which themselves do not welcome foreign labor, apart from the limited Scandinavian Common Market in Labor, the external critics observed that Swedish immigration is "rather restrictive except for the Nordic countries" and stated gently that "it seems that certain problems could be more easily solved by immigration than by internal migration." [7]

There is nothing wrong with Swedish and other Scandinavian growth. A rate of 3 to 3.5 percent affords a country a respectable place in the League standings. More demand, despite wage policies, leads to rising costs and prices and to balance-of-payments stringency. Therefore, even with good rates of growth in exports, such a demand pattern requires slowdown. This is the normal expectation, apart from the Norwegian attempt to force invest-

7. See OECD, *Labour Market Policy in Sweden*, p. 68.

ment, which failed to speed up growth, and there is no reason to fault it. In fact, it is what the rest of Europe is to come to after exhausting its excess supplies of labor.

Belgium

The Belgian rate of growth during the 1950's at 3 percent was satisfactory in the light of the experience of the last century but low against the standard of the country's neighbors and Common Market partners — France, the Netherlands, Germany, and Italy. From 1959 on, this growth picked up. The Belgian experience has thus been exactly opposite to that of the rest of the European Economic Community: slow at first and then speeding up, as opposed to fast during the major part of the decade and then leveling off to a less spectacular rate.

The best analysis of the Belgian case in the early period is that by Lamfalussy.[8] His explanation has two features: Belgian overspecialization in semifinished products produced in capital-intensive fashion by standard processes and with low or even zero rates of technological progress — soda ash, fertilizer, Bessemer semifinished steel, flat glass, and so on — and Belgian "defensive investment," that is, investment which is required to prevent a firm in a highly competitive industry like textiles from running losses but from which the average rate of profit is very low, on the order of 2 percent.[9]

The complaint that Belgium was overspecialized in the wrong products — having such a large short-run comparative advantage in goods with poor long-run growth prospects owing to both income-inelastic demand and inherently limited external economies in technical change — echoes the arguments of Raul Prebisch and Hla Myint concerning the limited growth possibilities which foreign trade offers the less developed countries. To Prebisch, the less developed countries which export primary products cannot depend on export-led growth because of the

8. Alexander Lamfalussy, *Investment and Growth in Mature Economies: The Case of Belgium* (London: Macmillan, 1961).

9. The marginal rate will of course be higher, since it includes the loss forestalled on the inframarginal units as well as the positive return on new capital.

low income elasticity of demand for their exports.[10] To Myint, certain classes of goods, such as those subject to plantation organization, yield a once-and-for-all change in technique but are then subject to technical "fossilization."[11] Jacques Drèze agrees that Belgium exports standardized products, but he finds the reason not in the accidents of fortune so much as in the small size of the country, which means that it must export according to widely adopted standards if it is to achieve economies of scale.[12]

But to return to Lamfalussy's analysis, labor was available: the rate of unemployment went as high as 6.8 percent in 1952 and 1953 as against an arbitrary level of 3 percent which I would propose as representing reasonably full employment. And the balance of payments was in fair shape, with capital exports taking place, largely in liquid form, especially from 1954 to 1957.

There is merit in Lamfalussy's basic points, but the fact that Belgium grew at faster rates after 1958 casts some doubt on long-run explanations and makes it useful to look for proximate factors. One of these is the behavior of wages, which grew too rapidly in the immediate postwar period, far outstripping productivity and holding down profits. This was partly the result of the Korean boom in raw-material prices, in which Belgian exports did not share, so that the terms-of-trade change from 1948–50 to 1953–1955 adversely affected real national income by 11.5 percent. This was later more than made up, but wage rates had risen 49 percent between 1948 and 1952, and labor costs (wages adjusted for productivity) climbed 28 percent over the same period. In addition to this cost-push inflation, there was deficient demand, both in the home market until 1956 and from 1951 to 1955 in exports.

Until about 1959, therefore, Belgium conformed more or less

10. See Economic Commission for Latin American (ECLA), *The Economic Development of Latin America and Its Principal Problems* (Lake Success, N.Y.: United Nations Department of Economic Affairs, 1950).

11. Hla Myint, "The Gains from International Trade and the Backward Countries," *Review of Economic Studies,* XXII (1954–55), 129–142.

12. Jacques Drèze, "Quelques réflexions sereines sur l'adaptation de l'industrie Belge au Marché Commun," *Comptes Rendus de la Société d'Économie Politique Belgique* (Brussels), No. 275 (1960), pp. 3–37.

perfectly to the diagnosis which the British economists have applied to their own country and to the United States: too little demand and, at the same time, cost-push inflation. Demand picked up in 1954 but ran into balance-of-payments difficulties and a relapse of employment till 1959. Beginning in that year, however, expansion in demand at home and abroad led to substantial growth. Unemployment dwindled rapidly for 4 successive years. Foreign labor was imported by private industry—the government concluded overall arrangements with the suppliers of foreign labor but had no hand in recruitment. Belgian labor transferred out of the coal mines of the Borinage and the Dutch border, leaving these low-grade positions, and housing in the area, to Italian and Turkish immigrants. But even with full employment by 1963, growth continued through a high rate of gain in labor productivity in 1964 and 1965. Wholesale prices kept steady, and with them the cost of living. Growth at higher than 4 percent took place, despite overspecialization and the defensive investment normal in mature economies. It is not entirely clear why.

Some part of the explanation may relate to the establishment of a Programming Bureau for planning in 1959, under the inspiration of the success of French planning. Some of the growth perhaps resulted from the creation of the Common Market and the rising demand for Belgian goods. A third influence may have been the loss of the Belgian Congo and the opportunity it afforded to cut down the drain of manpower and defense expenditure.[13] But the growth phase of the Belgian experience does not fit the Lewis model much more than does the period of slow growth to 1958. On the other hand, Belgium never did achieve rates of growth over 5 percent, like Austria, France, Germany, Italy, and Switzerland. She belongs then with the countries of lower rates of growth, and limited supplies of labor.

The United Kingdom

Perhaps the most fiercely debated postwar experience in economic growth is that of Britain, the lowest in the League standings for reasons which are far from agreed. The controversy

13. The difference between the male labor force including and excluding armed forces declined, however, only from 146,000 in 1954 to 108,000 in 1962.

divides over a variety of issues, and the division of the warring parties is not clear-cut. There is a Keynesian versus anti-Keynesian dispute, between those who think that growth has been hampered by mismanagement of demand which held down investment, on the one hand, and those who believe that the difficulty has lain in overfull employment on the other.[14] Another distinction has been drawn between the neo-leftists, who attribute the slowness to the business, financial, and political establishment because they believe it is in various degrees venial and stupid, and the technocrats, who find fault with business, government, and labor unions and want to substitute planning and incomes policy for a haphazard allocation of resources (at present by government fiat in nationalized industries and by the price system elsewhere).[15] A final and international dimension to the debate cuts across these lines and includes as main schools the rather disparate Little Englanders, who want to get Britain out of the Commonwealth and end sterling as an international reserve currency, and the pro- and anti-Europe and the Common Market warring factions.

In what follows I emphasize the difficulties of supply in a tight labor market, which led to rising prices in periods of expansion like 1951, 1955, 1960, and 1964, after little more than 15 or 18 months of expansion. These rising prices turned the balance of payments adverse and led to tightened monetary and fiscal policy and slower investment and growth.

14. For Keynesian views, see Angus Maddison, *Economic Growth in the West* (New York: Twentieth Century Fund, 1964); J. R. C. Dow, *The Management of the British Economy, 1945–1960* (Cambridge: National Institute of Economic and Social Research, 1964); F. T. Blackaby, "The Recent Performance of the British Economy," *Advancement of Science*, XIX (March 1963), 489–498; Andrew Shonfield, *British Economic Policy since the War* (Harmondsworth: Penguin, 1958). For opposing arguments, see F. W. Paish, *Studies in an Inflationary Economy* (New York: St. Martin's Press, 1962); Paish, "The Management of the British Economy," a review of Dow, *The Management of the British Economy, Lloyds Bank Review*, No. 76 (April 1965), pp. 1–17

15. For a neo-leftist outlook, see Nicholas Davenport, *The Split Society* (London: Gollancz, 1964); Samuel Brittan, *The Treasury under the Tories, 1951–1964* (Harmondsworth: Penguin, 1965). On the technocratic side, see PEP (the Political and Economic Planning organization), *Growth in the British Economy: A Study of Economic Problems and Policies in Contemporary Britain* (London: George Allen & Unwin, 1960); Michael Shanks, *The Stagnant Society* (Harmondsworth: Penguin, 1961).

A fundamental issue here is the extent to which the growth rate in Britain has been determined by governmental policies or by economic circumstances (including business and labor attitudes) which change only slowly and not necessarily in response to government decree. The business cycle, it is widely agreed, is no longer inherent in the economic system, or inevitable, at least in the pre-Keynesian amplitude of its fluctuations. And policy can put its foot wrong in matters of growth. But the issue which requires resolution is whether "wrong thinking about these matters [cost inflation, employment, the balance of payments, debt funding, etc.] was the cause of the United Kingdom having had lower growth than the countries of Continental Europe in the last few years," or whether the lag was attributable to something deeper in the wood like the catching-up process.[16]

The demand school has several subvariants. In one, a simple Keynesian connection between demand and investment is believed to lead to growth. With higher demand, Britain would have had higher investment and higher growth.[17] In another and more popular version, high demand is held to be particularly helpful to growth because the income-elastic commodities, which are stimulated by demand pressure, come from the industries of high and rising productivity, with strong economies of scale.[18] But this simplified version runs into the difficulty that the more demand, the higher will prices rise. The attempt to explain away this barrier produces the theory that small increases in demand produce only small increases in productivity — either factory-by-factory or because they involve goods of limited productivity increase — and wage claims lead straightway to price increases rather than cost reduction, whereas large or steep increases in demand shift demand to the high-productivity industries which are able through economies of scale to raise wages and lower

16. Roy Harrod, *The British Economy* (New York: McGraw Hill, 1963), p. 205; John Knapp and Kenneth Lomax, "Britain's Growth Performance: The Enigma of the 1950's," *Lloyds Bank Review*, No. 74 (October 1964), pp. 1–24.

17. Blackaby, "The Recent Performance of the British Economy," p. 496.

18. Norman Macrae, *Sunshades in October: An Analysis of the Main Mistakes in British Economic Policy since the Mid-Nineteen-Fifties* (London: George Allen & Unwin, 1963).

prices at the same time.[19] More demand means lower prices on this showing, not higher, provided the pressures are kept on high and long.

But the more usual tack is to suggest that the difficulty in Britain has lain not so much with the level of demand but with its instability. Investment is a function not of today's demand but of tomorrow's. Before he undertakes cost-reducing investment which expands capacity, the business executive needs assurance that demand will be sustained. A project which would be undertaken with a steady demand over 4 years might be abandoned in favor of cash if there was a high probability of 1 bad year in the 4. Turning demand off now to meet balance-of-payments deficits and on again for growth after the storm subsides will thus fail to achieve the high level of investment needed. Interruptions rather than inadequacy of demand must bear responsibility for low investment and slow productivity gains.[20] High demand is desirable, to be sure, but it must also be level.[21]

A related view, espoused especially by Roy Harrod but also by Angus Maddison, is that Britain's difficulties arise from having cut demand to restrain cost-push inflation. The proper remedy is incomes policy. Maddison acknowledges that incomes policy calls for "widespread public sympathy and some harmony of social interests" and that the United Kingdom had not found the appropriate mechanism at the time he wrote. He remained convinced, however, that any country which grew at less than 3 percent a year could be convicted of deficient policy and that any country which consistently runs into difficulties which other countries avoid is open to the charge of bad policy.[22]

The anti-Keynesian opposition led by F. W. Paish does not disagree on the importance of policy but claims that demand has been excessive rather than deficient or unstable. It attaches great importance to monetary policy: there is no such thing as cost-push inflation; all inflation comes from excess demand. Income

19. *Ibid.*, p. 47; Blackaby, "The Recent Performance of the British Economy," p. 497.
20. See Maddison, *Economic Growth in the West*, p. 101; Dow, *The Management of the British Economy*, p. 361.
21. See Dow, *The Management of the British Economy*, p. 397.
22. Maddison, *Economic Growth in the West*, pp. 136, 156, 101.

policies are futile or unnecessary. Below 2 percent unemployment, wages will rise as predicted by the Phillips curve. Above 2.25 percent unemployment, wages and prices will be stable. The only possible room for incomes policy would be between 2 and 2.25 percent unemployment.[23] The economic miracles of Germany, France, and Italy would not have been possible with *dirigisme* or widespread government intervention in the economy.[24] Germany furnishes a classic example of the proposition that price stability can be achieved and will coexist with growth, so long as there is a margin of unused resources, particularly labor, beyond the range of the pressure of demand.[25] Evidence against the view that unstable demand depresses investment and holds down labor productivity is found in the rise of labor productivity throughout the decade, not only overall in the British economy but also in manufacturing and in the several manufacturing subsectors.[26]

If demand were managed more adequately, would supply respond? Dow's long book on the management of the British economy, in which he concentrates almost entirely on demand and makes virtually no mention of labor supply, mobility, or even the capital-widening or deepening character of investment, raises the question at the end almost as an afterthought.[27] But there are many who attack government, business, and labor for the failure of supply. Government is all muddle, presided over by the "Treasury knight." [28] On the one hand, "Management inefficiency — the lack of technical and scientific brains at the board

23. Paish and Hennessy, *Policy for Incomes?*, p. 5.

24. Josselyn Hennessy, Vera Lutz, and Guiseppe Scimone, *Economic "Miracles": Studies in the Resurgence of the French, German and Italian Economies since the Second World War* (London: Deutsch, 1964).

25. *Ibid.*, p. 56.

26. F. W. Paish, "Sir Roy Harrod's View of the British Economy," *Economica*, XXXI (February 1964), 1–4; David Willey, "Changes in British and German Manufacturing Productivity, 1951–1962" (preliminary and summary draft of a dissertation presented at the Columbia University International Economic Workshop, 1965), p. 24.

27. Dow, *The Management of the British Economy*, pp. 397–398.

28. Brittan, *The Treasury under the Tories*, *passim*. One should perhaps stay out of the bickering in other nations, but it is difficult to resist the suggestion that blaming the Treasury for British economic difficulties is like blaming the Department of State for the troubles of United States foreign policy — both examples of the fallacy of misplaced concreteness.

room table — was primarily responsible for the rise of our industrial costs."[29] On the other, "the biggest single restrictive practice in industry today is the tea break and the general reluctance of workers to speed up the pace of work."[30] Much of the literature is concerned with analysis, rather than blame, especially the detailed studies of industrial organization, entrepreneurship, innovation, and research.[31] Many writers have proposed remedies, ranging from planning and embracing the stimulating draft of competition by joining the Common Market, to reforming education, sloughing off the Sterling Area and its problems, taking back collective bargaining from the shop stewards and handing it over to a centralized body, and tackling pay, overtime, and production practices afresh at the plant level.[32]

One vital aspect of the British problem is that exports have risen so slowly, at 2.7 percent a year between 1949 and 1959, which is less than half the rate of any other developed country in Europe. This sets balance-of-payments limits to growth in much the same fashion that Prebisch claims is true of the less developed countries. The blame for the slow growth of exports is occasionally assigned to Britain's export structure, and especially the preponderant role played in exports by textiles prior to the war; sometimes to technical backwardness; but in most formulations it is intimately associated with growth itself. Harrod and S. J. Wells, to cite two leading expositors of the view, claim that if growth could be kept going, exports would right themselves through cost reductions in expanding industries.[33] Harrod is not so certain of the outcome that he is unwilling to advise the application of import restrictions to contain the balance of payment in the interim. But majority opinion is inclined to regard

29. Davenport, *The Split Society*, p. 119.

30. Shanks, *The Stagnant Society*, p. 64.

31. See Tibor Barna, *Investment and Growth Policies in British Industrial Firms* (Cambridge: Cambridge University Press, 1962), and the three Oxford University Press (London) volumes by C. F. Carter and B. R. Williams: *Industry and Technical Progress* (1957), *Investment in Innovation* (1958), and *Science in Industry* (1959).

32. On the last point, see Allan Flanders, *The Fawley Productivity Agreements: A Case Study of Management and Collective Bargaining* (London: Faber & Faber, 1964).

33. See Harrod, *The British Economy;* S. J. Wells, *British Export Performance: A Comparative Study* (Cambridge University Press, 1964).

the merchandise aspects of the balance of payments as part of the overall problem of productivity rather than as an exogenous constraint upon its solution.

The number of economists who have addressed the question of labor supply is limited. Blackaby dismisses it because he misunderstands the reasoning in the Lewis models, asserting that an elastic labor supply can account for a rapid rate of growth overall but not a rapid rate of growth per capita.[34] Harrod devotes several pages to labor overall, making a number of important points about the qualitative difference between British emigrants and immigrants and about the gain in productivity from an expanding population when modern machinery is added at the margin to improve the average efficiency of capital per unit of labor without capital-deepening.[35] But these observations are not central to his themes, which rest on demand and cost-push inflation. And the most interesting ideas on labor supply are provided by J. R. Sargent and Michael Lipton.[36]

Over the period from 1949 to 1959 the active labor force grew by 0.6 percent per year, but the increase was greater in women than in men. Net emigration overall amounted to about 300,000 (1946–1957), made up of net emigration of 950,000 to overseas areas, offset in part by net immigration of more than 600,000 from Continental Europe (300,000) and Ireland (300,000).[37] The total numbers were less significant in all likelihood than the qualitative net loss, since many of the emigrants had a secondary education or even university training and advanced degrees (the widely discussed "brain drain"), whereas the immigrants were

34. Blackaby, "The Recent Performance of the British Economy," p. 494. Brittan dismisses the European pools of refugees, unemployed, and underemployed farmers as a cause of the disparity between Britain and European growth performances, citing Blackaby's cursory discussion of the point, but later points to the deeper sociological causes of European export-price advantage in the "refugees in Germany and the southern workers in Italy." He also chides the government for not following a selective immigration policy based on skills to relieve the supply and demand position in overloaded areas (*The Treasury under the Tories*, pp. 137, 290, 271).

35. Harrod, *The British Economy*, pp. 69–75.

36. J. R. Sargent, *Out of Stagnation: A Policy for Growth*, Fabian Tract No. 343 (London: Fabian Society, 1963); Michael Lipton, "Manpower and Growth," *Aspect* (London), No. 11 (December 1963), pp. 38–43.

37. See International Labour Office, *International Migration, 1945–1947* (Geneva, 1959), pp. 142, 169.

partly a return of emigrants who had failed to make an adjustment, partly displaced persons immediately after the war, and finally Commonwealth immigrants.[38] Immigration picked up at the end of the decade, to raise the rates of increase in total population, active population, labor force, and employment after 1959. The social problem created by the influx of increased numbers of colored Commonwealth subjects, however, finally led the Conservative government to interpose obstacles to the traditional freedom of migration in 1962, an action ultimately concurred in by Labour. The argument has been made that the rush to immigrate was partly stimulated by the threat of restrictions, sought by labor to protect itself from the need for mobility.[39] The social pressure for restrictions, at the same time, was caused by the concentration of colored immigrants in industries and localities — textiles in Bradford, rubber in Boothall, transport and hospitals — where British labor refused to go.[40]

Sargent states that "the main cause of our slow growth has been the persistent underlying shortage of labor." [41] He notes the rise in the share of labor in national income from 64.3 percent in 1954 to 67.7 percent in 1960, and especially the fact of labor hoarding by industry. Figure IV-1 is drawn from his study and compares labor employment with capacity of industry in use (as calculated by Paish).[42]

Labor hoarding occurs in periods of shortage because if they

38. See Royal Society, *Emigration of Scientists from the United Kingdom* (London, 1963); J. A. Tannahill, *European Volunteer Workers in Britain* (Manchester: Manchester University Press, 1958). Much has been written about Commonwealth immigrants. Cf. Rashmi Desai, *Indian Immigrants in Britain* (London: Institute of Race Relations, 1963); Clifford S. Hill, *West Indian Migrants and the London Churches* (London: Institute of Race Relations, 1963); G. W. Roberts and D. O. Mills, *Study of External Migration Affecting Jamaica, 1953–55* (Kingston: Institute of Social and Economic Research, 1958).

39. See "Smethwick and After," review of Paul Foot, *Immigration and Race in British Politics*, in *Economist*, CCXVI (August 28, 1965), 787.

40. See "Black Paper," *Economist*, CCXVI (August 7, 1965), 506.

41. Sargent, *Out of Stagnation*, p. 27.

42. See also R. R. Neild's table showing output falling much more than manhours in the recessions of 1951–52, 1955–56, and 1957–58, and with hours falling still less than employment. The result is a decline in output per manhour. The discrepancy between output and manhours narrowed greatly between the first and last period (*Pricing and Employment in the Trade Cycle*, Cambridge: Cambridge University Press, 1963, p. 31).

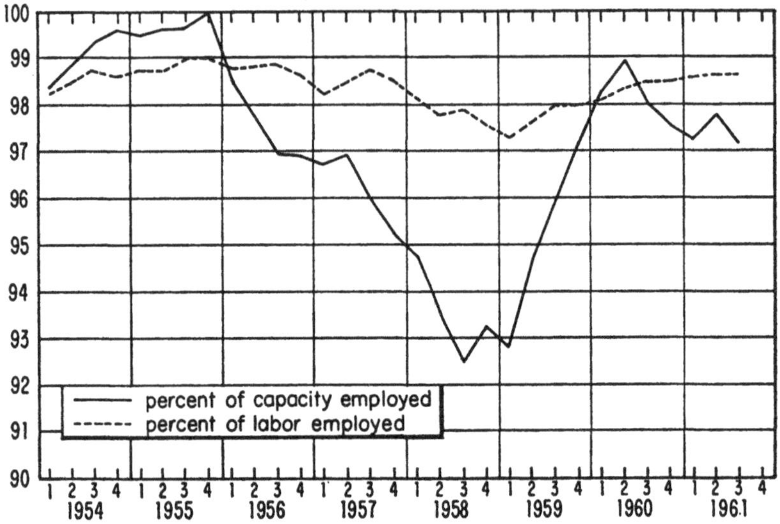

Figure IV-1. United Kingdom capacity utilization compared with employment, 1954–1961

Source: J. R. Sargent, *Out of Stagnation*, The Fabian Society, 1963

dismiss redundant workers, employers are not certain whether they will be able to hire them back during the next upswing. Sargent blames industry for not shifting from capital-widening to capital-deepening investment, responding to the upward trend in wages by substitution of capital for labor. He conjectures that capital may have been difficult to obtain for firms which are not listed upon the security exchanges, and that for these firms borrowing is both expensive and subject to interruption, which discourages ambitious labor-saving investment programs. Sargent does not contemplate the possibility implicit in the Lewis model, that capital-deepening is more difficult to achieve than marginal expansion with improved techniques. He offers suggestions for stimulating a shift in investment in the direction of capital-deficiency, including proposals for a tax on wages, higher compensation for redundancy, stimulation of research and replacement of obsolete machinery, and even repeal of the Commonwealth Immigration Act of 1962, which he terms "revolting."

This view is regarded by Lipton as half-right. There is enough labor, he thinks, but it is badly used, lying about in industries that are really disguised unemployment pools. He singles out the railroads as the biggest waste of labor, with 100,000 to 150,000 of its 500,000 employees redundant. But he has no remedies to suggest to increase the mobility of British labor beyond trade-union cooperation, which would require a policy of equitable income distribution.

The same view is echoed in the *Sunday Times* by William W. Allen, the American production consultant who negotiated the Fawley agreements and who characterized Britain as a "half-time country, getting half-pay for half-work under half-hearted management." [43] In the Fawley refinery of the ESSO Company he had eliminated overtime, raised wage rates 40 percent, redeployed the craftsmen's mates, and cut the total work force of 3,000 by 800 through attrition, without discharging anyone. It is not clear whether these results, which recall the Dutch wage agreements of 1964 (see p. 52 above) could have been achieved through competition in goods markets such as would have resulted from joining the Common Market, from competition in the labor market, from a higher rate of natural increase, or from immigration. The experience of the winter of 1964–65 suggests, however, that they cannot be reached through "incomes policies" or indicative planning.

When J. Kenneth Galbraith reviewed Keynes's *General Theory* on the occasion of its appearance in paperback in 1965, a number of letters commenting upon his review were published.[44] One, by Herbert R. Northrup, chided Galbraith's claims for the Keynesian Revolution by pointing out that the Keynesian analysis could fall into error. Northrup cited the estimate of postwar unemployment in the United States, Hansen's views on secular stagnation, and Walter Heller's advice to the postwar German government (which Galbraith disputed). But the point is well taken. In Chapter II it was made clear that the Keynesian analysis did not apply to the cure of structural employment in Italy, despite the counsel of the United States Economic Cooperation Administra-

43. William W. Allen, "Is Britain a Half-Time Country, Getting Half-Pay for Half-Work, under Half-Hearted Management?" *Sunday Times* (London), March 1, 1964, pp. 15–16.

44. *New York Times Book Review*, July 4, 1965, p. 16.

tion (ECA) mission in Rome. Here we can conclude by suggesting that maintenance of demand does not seem to be the answer for economic growth in Britain.

The difficulty is that maintenance of demand is one trick which economists have learned, as effectively demonstrated in the tax cut of 1964 in the United States, recommended for so long by the Council of Economic Advisers under the chairmanship of Walter Heller. Different problems, different remedies. In the United States demand creates supply. In Britain, demand runs into supply bottlenecks, immobilities of labor in particular, which yield an altogether different result. And the remedies for supply bottlenecks are not understood. One can observe that in the United Kingdom 36,000 persons a year move from localities of high unemployment to places of labor shortage.[45] And one can compare this with a need for 420,000 additional persons in the labor force (an increase of 1.5 percent in order to get an increase of 5.5 percent in output).[46] But it is virtually impossible to raise this rate in the short run. More housing more economically priced, greater unemployment pay, and perhaps, as in Sweden and the Netherlands, financial assistance in moving would help.[47] Immigration raises "many wider issues."[48] But housing and related "social" programs are all long-run measures, of uncertain usefulness. Demand is easy to regulate; increasing peacetime supply has still to be learned.

45. Paish and Hennessy, *Policy for Incomes?*, p. 29.

46. National Institute *Economic Review*, No. 27 (February 1964), p. 7.

47. It is asserted widely that the British workman is attached to his workplace and that occupation of a Council house, below the market for rents, is a more substantial drag on mobility than owning one's own house (Ferdynand Zweig, *The Worker in an Affluent Society: Family Life and Industry*, London: Heinemann, 1961, pp. 125, 129, 205–207).

48. D. J. Robertson, *A Market for Labour* (London: Institute of Economic Affairs, 1961), p. 43.

CHAPTER V

The Underdeveloped Countries of Emigration: Portugal, Spain, Greece, and Turkey

The Agricultural Model

As Table II-1 has shown, economic growth was rapid in the Mediterranean countries of Europe in the 1950's, despite fairly low levels of investment and varying rates of labor input. Moreover, these are countries of emigration rather than immigration. The pattern of growth they followed can be encompassed within the Lewis model, but it is the pattern of the agricultural sector in the model, not that of the industrial sector. Consequently here I treat the less developed countries of Europe like the agricultural sector, despite the fact that these countries have an industrial sector and services, along with agriculture, just as I handled the developed countries of Europe like the industrial sector in the Lewis model. Economic growth can be sustained by emigration and higher wages as well as by unlimited supplies of labor and constant wages. In this chapter, I maintain that this has been the path followed by Portugal, by Spain, by southern Italy (if that could be isolated readily in the statistics from northern Italy), by Greece, and to a limited extent by Turkey.

Unlike the earlier discussion, the argument does not proceed country by country. We do not know the separate cases in sufficient detail to treat them in this fashion. Data on Portugal, Spain, and Turkey are in short supply. The effort would be tiresome for the reader. The account is therefore largely analytical, focused on issues and principles, with an undue proportion of the illustrative material from Greece, where the issue of emigration is sharply drawn by governmental opponents of the movement and where there is a substantial body of material available in English.

The core of the present argument is that growth can proceed in the agricultural sector (or the underdeveloped country as a whole) from rising wages and falling profits that stimulate investment which has hitherto been unprofitable. This is the exact opposite of the industrial sector in developed countries where growth at exceptionally high levels during industrialization, or catching up with the most advanced countries technologically, is assisted by constant or at best slowly rising wages and high profits. The mechanism is somewhat different from that set out by Fei and Ranis.

For Fei and Ranis, industrial profits and the agricultural surplus invested in the industrial sector constitute the main engine of growth. Their discussion of development of the agricultural sector regards productivity changes in agriculture as apparently exogenous or the consequence of some limited investment or innovative activity in agriculture, the reasons for which are not explained.[1] Increases in agricultural productivity make it possible to sustain the period of growth in the industrial sector beyond the point of exhaustion in agriculture of the disguised unemployed whose productivity was zero; in fact, growth can still be sustained at the stage where the underemployed with a marginal product which is positive but lower than the prevailing agricultural wage have begun to transfer to industry. Such increases do this by preventing a decline in the industrial terms of trade. With exogenous or not completely explained increases in agricultural output, the (closed) economy can follow a "balanced-growth path" until the marginal product of labor in agriculture has been brought up to equality or some conventionally determined relationship with the marginal productivity of labor in industry.

But this model is hardly applicable without modification to the situation of southern Europe. The "industrial sector" and the "agricultural sector" are widely separated, and each is connected with the open economies of the rest of the world so that the terms of trade are determined outside the system. The agricultural surplus produced by increasing marginal productivity in

1. John C. H. Fei and Gustav Ranis, *Development of the Labor Surplus Economy: Theory and Policy* (Homewood, Ill.: Richard D. Irwin, 1964), chap. 6.

agriculture without raising wages is available not for investment in the industrial sector (that is, developed Europe) but only in agriculture (or industry) in a Mediterranean country. Moreover, additional capital for the "agricultural sector" can be provided by the savings of those who transfer from agriculture to industry — emigrants' remittances. The Mediterranean countries have been investing these funds, and additional monies received as loans or aid, because of the rise in the marginal productivity of capital as a result of emigration, a result which is built into the mechanism, not an exogenous event.

The movement of labor abroad does not purely and simply stimulate economic growth. There are losses, economic as well as social and political. One possible source is the loss of output, to be set off against the gains in emigrants' remittances and reduced consumption. Emigration has also traditionally been viewed as a capital export thought to be inappropriate for poor countries, for the cost of raising and educating those who become emigrants has been capitalized.

Disguised Unemployment and Underemployment

When the industrial and agricultural sector are in the same country, as in the Fei and Ranis model, it is important to distinguish disguised unemployment (where the marginal product of labor is zero) from underemployment (in which the product is positive but less than in the industrial sector). Withdrawals of labor up to the end of disguised unemployment leave the terms of trade unchanged, so long as the total consumption foregone by the workers who had received their average product in agriculture is sent into the market after them and is saved by the farmers in monetary form or exchanged for industrial products. When the marginal product of labor is positive, however, emigration will lead to a decline in the industrial terms of trade, as total agricultural production declines and with it the amount of food marketed by the agricultural sector. Less than enough food is marketed to feed the emigrants. But this distinction is of limited importance in the present context with the terms of trade of the industrial sector determined outside the system. If one takes, say, Greece as a whole as the agricultural sector and compares it with an "industrial sector" such as Germany, there will be underemployment for a very long time — until Greek income per capita rises to the German level.

But a number of Greek students deny that there is a surplus of labor in Greek agriculture which could be transferred into domestic industry or abroad.[2] In a series of studies, they have attacked the conventional view that as much as a third of the Greek labor force in agriculture — 750,000 out of a total of 2,140,000 — could be removed without hurting output, and they have distinguished the chronic labor surplus, which could be removed for a complete year with only routine reorganization of the work force without leading to a reduction in output, from the labor surpluses at off seasons of the agricultural year, which make a marginal contribution equal to their wage at the planting and harvesting peaks.[3]

The restriction of agricultural reorganization to routine measures is critical. On that basis, Adam Pepelasis may be right that the chronic labor surplus in Greece was eliminated by about 1955 and that since that time there have been important shortages at the seasonal peaks. Some agricultural activities of great seasonality which cannot alone provide a going level of living must be combined with other activities, such as seasonal work in the city, or be abandoned. In others, thoroughgoing reorganization is called for. Pepelasis is aware of the need for modernization of Greek agriculture but believes that mechanization cannot be carried much further in view of land fragmentation.[4] Never-

2. Adam A. Pepelasis and Pan A. Yotopoulos, *Surplus of Labor in Greek Agriculture, 1953–1960* (Athens: Center of Economic Research, 1962); Adam A. Pepelasis, *Labor Shortage in Greek Agriculture, 1963–1973* (Athens: Center of Economic Research, 1963). The conventional view, and an estimate of 400,000 to 700,000 who could have been removed from agriculture with only minor changes in agricultural techniques and practices, put out by the Greek Planning Division of the Ministry of Coordination, is set out in OECD Mediterranean Regional Project, *Greece* (Country Projects, Paris, 1965), p. 102.

3. See also Bent Hansen, *Marginal Productivity Wage Theory and Subsistence Wage Theory in Egyptian Agriculture* (Institute of National Planning Memo No. 547, United Arab Republic, 1965). Another strong objector to the theory of disguised unemployment and underemployment is Theodore W. Schultz, *Transforming Traditional Agriculture* (New Haven: Yale University Press, 1964).

4. See Pepelasis and Yotopoulos, *Surplus of Labor in Greek Agriculture,* and Kenneth Thompson, *Land Fragmentation in Greece,* Research Monograph No. 5 (Athens: Center of Economic Research, 1963).

theless, labor shortage stimulates reorganization of land holdings and the adoption of new methods, when the causation does not run the other way from reorganization and innovation to labor surplus. This is a problem of identification, where it is hard to say whether there is demand pull or supply push. Labor changes in agriculture and technical and organizational change go hand in glove, and it is inappropriate to measure the labor surplus or deficit against a fixed state of the arts.

It is difficult, for example, to say whether the enclosures in England pushed labor off the land, as the Marxists claim, or followed along behind the loss of labor to industrial demand, as a means of employing the remaining and now more expensive labor more effectively. Certainly the enclosures of the nineteenth century which were accompanied by changes in technique under High Farming were of the latter type, and so perhaps were those of the 1740's and 1750's when agriculture productivity increased rapidly along with (or possibly in advance of) the industrial changes which later were termed revolutionary. It is equally difficult today in some countries to say whether agricultural workers have been drawn into the slums of industrial cities or have felt themselves propelled by inability to earn a living on the farm.

Remittances

While Fei and Ranis do not contemplate the possibility of workers transferred from agriculture to industry making savings available for agriculture — in their concentration on the development of an agricultural surplus for investment in industry — there are those who believe that remittances are the major contribution of emigration to economic growth in the country left behind. It is correct that these remittances have been inadequately analyzed from the viewpoint of both the country receiving the workers and that sending them. In the former, immigrants typically work unusually hard [5] — often to the irritation of the

5. This was observed in Europe before World War I by Max Weber: "That the simple fact of a change of residence is among the most effective means of intensifying labor is thoroughly established. The same Polish girl who at home was not to be shaken loose from her traditional laziness by any chance of earning money, however tempting, seems to change her entire nature and become capable of unlimited accomplishment when she is a

native workers insofar as they resent the competition, and send home a large proportion of their wages, which is the equivalent of a high marginal propensity to import. In the early stages of immigration, therefore, before the need to provide the added labor with social overhead capital, immigrants contribute to supply, but not so much to demand for local output, and exert a deflationary effect. In the country from which they depart, however, immigrant remittances represent, first of all, a higher return to labor than can be earned at home, since labor is combined with larger amounts of capital; second, a credit in the balance of payments; and, third, a source of savings. The higher earning capacity of the emigrant abroad requires no explanation. The credit in the balance of payments is statistically complex because of legal distinctions, often of no real significance, between permanent and seasonal emigrants, and their repercussion on the national-income accounts and balance-of-payments bookkeeping.[6] But the remittances constitute a flow of foreign exchange available to the national monetary authorities that is better than exports because it is not preceded by expenditures on labor and

---

migratory worker in a foreign country. The same is true of migratory Italian laborers. That this is by no means entirely explicable in terms of the educative influence of the entrance into a higher cultural environment . . . is shown by the fact that the same thing happens where the type of occupation, as in agricultural labor, is exactly the same at home. Furthermore, accommodation in labor barracks, etc. may involve a degradation to a standard of living which would never be tolerated at home" (*The Protestant Ethic and the Spirit of Capitalism,* New York: Scribners, 1958, p. 191, n. 20).

Note also the comment by William J. Barber on Rhodesia: "When geographically detached from his customary environment, the African will accept tasks which he would decline when closer to home" (*The Economy of British Central Africa: A Case Study of Economic Development in a Dualistic Economy,* London: Oxford University Press, 1961, p. 212). A similar observation has been made about the *overseas* Chinese and Indians by Jagdish Bhagwati (*The Economics of Underdeveloped Countries,* New York: McGraw-Hill, 1966, p. 87).

6. A permanent emigrant contributes to the national income in the country where he works and not the country where he comes from, whereas a seasonal emigrant's labor is regarded as part of the national income of his country of origin, and his expenditures in the foreign land are classed as imports. Remittances are thus income transfers in the first case, and the difference between exports of services and imports of goods in the second. Since the "permanent emigrant" may be in reality temporary, the sharp distinctions of the national accounts are more confusing than helpful.

materials, some part of which may come from abroad or in the case of the expenditure be quickly spent abroad. The remittance multiplier is lower than the export multiplier because the first round of spending does not take place. Furthermore, these remittances have a higher than normal marginal and average propensity to go into savings because so many of them are sent for special purposes. The worker abroad with a family at home has to provide for its subsistence, to be sure, but his purpose in emigrating is often to save for a particular target — to purchase a farm, fishing boat, house, or store — and even if he is working toward savings in general, his family is disposed to live economically, as does he abroad, to await his return. When the family migrates with the worker, remittances are much lower, if they take place at all, and remittances of single workers may be lower than those of married men with wives at home, since the vertical family ties are, or are becoming, looser than those in the nuclear family. By and large, however, emigrant remittances furnish savings and foreign exchange to the developing country, which enable it to undertake domestic capital formation with the import spillover provided for in advance.

When the foreign-exchange rate is seriously overvalued, as was the case in Turkey, the remittances are likely to be forthcoming not in foreign exchange but in kind. Many of the Turks returning from Europe brought back the fruit of their work in the form of large second-hand automobiles, which they used in the *dolmus* business as a cross between a taxi and a bus, plus additional durable consumers goods, which added little to the productive capital of the country. Turkey has recently established a special exchange rate for remittances that are deposited in a mortgage bank and has given the depositor of a given amount access to mortgage loans at 2 percent interest.[7] Reportedly, it has also restricted the importation of second-hand automobiles more than 5 years old.

The savings may, furthermore, be invested in ways which con-

7. S. G. Triantis, *Common Market and Economic Development*, Research Monograph No. 14 (Athens: Center of Planning and Economic Research, 1965), p. 221. The success of this change in raising financial remittances from $250,000 a month to $9 million in January 1965 is indicated in the International Monetary Fund (IMF), *International Financial News*, March 12, 1965, p. 95.

tribute very little to economic growth. This does not refer to the proximate investment by the emigrant in an existing farm, house, or store, since if he purchases an existing asset, what counts is the use made of the funds by the seller. But if new capital is formed in lines of low productivity — house construction as a whole or building new fishing boats in an already overfished area — the contribution of remittances to growth is small.

Table V-1 sets out orders of magnitude of the remittances re-

TABLE V-1

European emigrant remittances, 1963

Received from European emigrants of	Millions of dollars	Paid to European immigrants by	Millions of dollars
Greece	56	France	225
Italy	300	Germany	250
Spain	175–200	Switzerland	335
Portugal	70		

Sources: Greece — Bank of Greece Reports; Italy, Portugal, Spain, Germany, Switzerland — OECD *Economic Surveys;* France — Ministère des Finances, *Statistiques et Études Financières,* XVII (January 1965), Supplements, 22–26.

ceived by the Mediterranean countries, including Italy (and excluding Turkey, for which data are unavailable), and those paid by France, Germany, and Switzerland for a late year, 1963, after European emigration had gotten under way. The Greek figure would be much larger if overseas emigration were included. In all the countries except Turkey, a long tradition of extra-European emigration had existed, but this stream dried up in the second half of the 1950's under the pressure of the European demand for labor.

Remittances then should not be ignored. But it is a mistake, in my judgment, to regard them as the sole or even primary contribution of the loss of labor to economic growth. The demonstration depends only partly on the fact that they are wasted to a considerable extent. Equally indicative is the fact that French agriculture has grown rapidly in productivity in the postwar period with a large exodus of redundant labor, and little of the movement is likely to have involved remittances from town or city employment back to the farm. There is no information, so that it is impossible to be certain. But savings are not likely to be so high when the transfer takes place within the culture: the French migrant to the city will work at the pace of his fellows rather than seek the night shift, weekend work, and overtime, which the foreigner separated from his family and the man with a target for savings will undertake. Secondly, young people in France have little thought of returning to the farm and need their wages to adjust their consumption to urban patterns. Productivity nonetheless advanced in French agriculture with declining employment at a rate of the same order of magnitude as Greek productivity as a whole. It was supported by policies of *rémembrement,* or consolidation of dwarf land holdings. *Rémembrement* had its origin under Vichy and gathered speed with the establishment in 1960 of SAFER (*Société d'Amenagement Fonciers et Établissement Rural*), agencies which were authorized to buy up farm land as it came on the market and consolidate small farms into larger units.[8] Productivity was further assisted by many other innovations in technology, investment, and education. Outside capital played a role in the rural revolution — not always a useful one when the tractor craze left a large heritage of debt. But the relative unimportance of capital as such is attested by the years of French agricultural backwardness when French peasants used their savings to buy successively Czarist bonds, *rentes,* paper money, and gold coin.[9] Remittances are not to be neglected altogether, as in the analysis by Fei and Ranis, but they are not central.

Agricultural Surplus

If the remittances are not critical, neither, in my judgment, is the net saving in consumption which emigration provides and of which Fei and Ranis make so much. In the first place, there must be no decline in production, or the decline in production must be lower than the wages paid to the departing workers or lower

8. Gordon Wright, *Rural Revolution in France: The Peasant in the Twentieth Century* (Stanford: Stanford University Press, 1964), esp. pp. 90, 165.
9. *Ibid.,* p. 145.

than their consumption. Second, the increased income of the remaining workers or landlords, who benefit from sharing the same or only slightly reduced output among fewer income recipients, must be saved in considerable part. In the Fei and Ranis analysis, there is no decline in output for a distance, since the workers are in disguised unemployment, rather than underemployment, and the additional income is entirely saved. The authors concede that these assumptions are extreme and need modification. The question, however, is whether the modification is so substantial as to leave little net savings as a result of the transfer of workers out of the agricultural sector or, in our case, out of the underdeveloped country as a whole.

The first question, whether agricultural labor is in disguised unemployment or merely underemployed, has already been discussed. The more it is fully unemployed, overtly or disguisedly, the higher the increase in income of those left behind. But the question of how much of the increased income of the remaining people will be saved depends on the distribution of income and in turn on the system of land holding. With small land holdings, emigration will increase the incomes of relatively poor peasants and their families, and the increase in income will probably be spent. If, on the other hand, the underemployed persons have been working on latifundia, the chances of a high marginal propensity to save out of increased income are enhanced. Proximate circumstances can alter the result, of course. If the peasants are deeply in debt to moneylenders, the marginal propensity to save is likely to be high, as they attempt to get clear of debt, but once the debt is paid back, it is not likely to remain so. And the combination of industrialization in Italy, which pulled labor off the farm, with land reform, which made the distribution of farm income more rather than less equal, is likely to leave savings limited.

If the increased income per capita is spent, it makes a difference to the total outcome what it is spent on. Mrs. Lutz recommended emigration from southern Italy as a solution to the development problem of the Mezzogiorno because she believes in "balanced growth" and thinks that increasing income per capita of southern Italian farmers is the only way to establish an industrial base in the area, since an outlet for industrial goods among the farmers requires a certain minimum income.[10] Fei and Ranis call for increased income to be saved and invested in the industrial sector. It could be saved and invested in agriculture. Or still a fourth alternative is to have it consumed on home produce — food in an area which has been hungry — which will provide no savings and will in some circumstances hurt exports. But whether saved and invested abroad, saved and invested at home, spent on industrial products, or spent on food, each peseta or drachma of additional income can only be used once. And the suggestion that it will be used exclusively for one of the four possible outlets seems farfetched. I should think that in the ordinary case the marginal propensities to consume food, consume industrial products, save and invest at home, and save and invest in the industrial sector, would be on the order of 0.5, 0.3, 0.2, and zero. If these are the right orders of magnitude, the gains from increased income per capita, arising from consumption declining more than production, will largely be dissipated, although to the extent that they are not, they will help development at home rather than abroad.

There is in fact some doubt in the minds of Greek economists whether incomes at home are increased at all. Not only is it denied that the emigrants come from unemployment or underemployment.[11] It is also claimed that the emigrants are the younger, more skilled, healthy, intelligent and politically reliable in the Greek working population and that their loss pulls down production to a greater extent than their consumption declines. It is easy to agree that this could happen, but hard to see it in the light of the figures for rapid Portuguese, Spanish, Italian, Greek, and Turkish growth. This is the familiar complaint of the agricultural partisans who bewail rural exodus. It is true that population can be depleted below some optimum level and leave villages, regions, and even countries suffering from the diseconomies of too small scale. The contrast can be drawn between southwest France, where rural exodus led to a total decline in

10. Vera Lutz, "Some Structural Aspects of the Southern Problem: The Complementarity of 'Emigration' and Industrialization," Banca Nazionale del Lavoro *Quarterly Review*, No. 39 (December 1961), pp. 367–402.

11. Of course it makes no difference whether the emigrants were actually employed or not, if those who were employed and leave their places filled by unemployed of the same quality.

economic activity, and the rest of the Mediterranean, where, thus far at least, exodus has been stimulating.[12] Since the populations of the Mediterranean countries are still positively growing, though at smaller rates as the more fertile members of the community depart, it is hard to regard this possible danger as imminent or threatening on a wide scale.

Emigration as Capital Export

Another possibility of loss from emigration is embodied in the view that emigrants are a form of capital exports, which is inappropriate in a country that is poor and needs capital in other forms. This question has been debated in Italy since the turn of the century.[13] The first issue is whether the labor was productive in the home country, which has already been discussed, and second comes the question of whether the productivity, assuming it was positive, accrued wholly to the individual or in part to the country as a whole. But even before these questions are addressed, there is doubt whether one should apply capital theory to human beings in developing countries.

If the emigrants were slaves, and raised for the purpose, it would be appropriate to calculate whether it was worthwhile for a poor country to raise slaves for export — a capital-intensive activity in a capital-poor country. The answer would doubtless be "no." But babies are born, and youth raised and educated, without regard to the economic return on the process. It is true that Gary Becker has produced a model of children as a consumption good, a durable consumption good to be sure, which gives off utility over a long time and with heavy depreciation.[14] But this model, used to explain the demographic counterrevolution that increased the birth rate in the United States (and France) after World War II, is appropriate only to a rich country. For the most part, procreation can be regarded as non-

12. See Sergio Barzanti, *The Underdeveloped Areas within the Common Market* (Princeton: Princeton University Press, 1965), pp. 58 ff.

13. See G. Cosmo, "Italian Emigration up to 1940," Banco Nazionale del Lavoro *Quarterly Review,* Nos. 28–39 (January-June 1954), p. 85.

14. Gary S. Becker, "An Economic Analysis of Fertility," in *Demographic and Economic Change in Developed Countries: A Conference of the Universities-National Bureau Committee for Economic Research* (Princeton: Princeton University Press, 1960).

economic, and the increments it brings to the labor force should be considered as exogenous to the production, consumption, and saving decision-making processes.

In this circumstance, labor may be capital, but its costs are "sunk." The question of whether to raise children for emigration is not open. The young people exist, and we need to apply to them not "real-cost" but "opportunity-cost" analysis. What is the most effective use to make of existing labor, to employ it abroad or leave it unemployed at home; or, if there are job opportunities at home, to employ it at home with a small amount of capital or abroad with more?

Immigration can be regarded as an import of capital by the receiving country, even when emigration is costless because the cost of raising young people is a sunk cost for the country of emigration. It was calculated that every refugee arriving in West Germany was a gift of $5,000 capital, because of the costs of raising him.[15] But it can equally be held that, after the point of full employment is reached, immigration requires capital formation, as noted earlier in the discussion of Switzerland, and it can also be argued that emigration is capital-saving. If the worker remained in his native country, it would be necessary to invest in factories and housing for him, as well as schools and general social overhead. If he emigrates, the investment bill reduces to merely schools and the private capital he takes abroad with him.[16]

In addition, there is the important question of income distribution. What difference does it make to the country as a whole whether a worker remains at home or goes abroad: what he is paid goes to him, to dispose of as he likes. His product is not lost to the state because it was never contemplated that it would accrue to the state. He may contribute to the support of his family — possibly to a greater extent from abroad than if he remains home. The state may be said to have lost taxable capacity if he emigrates — a second-order effect — and this will equally be true of the community in which he lives, but he is normally

15. Friedrich Edding, *The Refugees as a Burden, a Stimulus and a Challenge to the West German Economy*, Research Group for European Migration, Study No. IV (The Hague: Nijhoff, 1951), p. 31.

16. F. Hartog, "Economic Policy in the Netherlands," in *Economic Policy in Our Time*, vol. III: *Country Studies* (Chicago: Rand McNally, 1964), p. 136.

free to move from a community even if he does not emigrate. There are second-order effects other than changes in taxable capacity: narrowing of the market for producers, changes in marginal products for other factors, the contribution which his savings may make to capital formation, and so on. But the first-order effect cancels out: his production is lost, but so is his consumption, which is approximately the same. The notion that the country of origin loses an asset and the return on it through emigration is based on faulty analysis.

Training

One hoped-for dynamic gain which applies when the transfer is between countries, though not between sectors in the same country, is the training of industrial workers. The Mediterranean countries hope that most of their emigrants will return and that they will bring back with them skills required for economic development and adjustment to industrial life. The process of conditioning men for factory work has been analyzed in terms of stages of recruitment, commitment, advancement, and maintenance, by which is meant all the steps that go to make a rural hand into a factory worker.[17] Men leave as peasants and return as industrial workers.

This breaks down into two questions. Will they come back, and if so will they have learned anything? On the first issue, it is felt in many European quarters that emigration to Europe is less likely to be permanent than emigration overseas. Possibly. But emigration overseas before World War I from southern Europe was not permanent, despite the fact that it is remembered this way. And many of those who now go abroad for 5 years to acquire a certain capital sum will find themselves settling abroad *ex post,* despite their *ex ante* intentions. It is further clear that those who return do not always come back to the same region or sector from which they departed. Pepelasis estimates that only 10 to 15 percent of the emigrants from Greek rural areas return to their villages, and S. G. Triantis notes that many workers bring back poor ideas as well as skills and even take the trail to Germany for the second time after failing to secure employ-

17. Clark Kerr *et al., Industrialism and Industrial Man* (Cambridge, Mass.: Harvard University Press, 1960).

ment and income commensurate with their training.[18] But it could work out that they do come back.

Italy takes the view that it is up to the individual whether he returns or not. Italian firms have assisted in the process, particularly before the deflationary program of 1964, by advertising for workers in the Swiss and German newspapers. Greece has a program of attempting to encourage return, especially of those of its citizens who go abroad as students and settle down.[19] Turkey limits the validity of its emigrants' passports to two years, hoping to force return. It has been suggested that the Spanish are somewhat fearful of the return of Spanish workers who have been long abroad and acquired a taste for political freedom. But all countries officially desire the ultimate return of their people.

If they return, will they have acquired any skills useful for economic development? In the case of the Greek students just mentioned, most of them will have, but some emigrants, especially the doctors and scientists, are most reluctant to return to work with inadequate hospitals, laboratories, technical assistants, and nurses. There are said, for example, to be 2,500 to 3,000 Turkish doctors abroad, despite the fact that medicine is esteemed in Turkey as the highest profession.[20]

For the mass of workers who have served in European factories and on European farms, there is a substantial question. With emigration to the United States prior to World War I, there was a difference in the experience of the returning Norwegian farmers and Italian laborers. The farmers had made a success in the United States and came back impatient with Norwegian methods and anxious to try new techniques. The *Americani* returning to Italy, on the other hand, were not among the more successful of the emigrants. They lived on their means if they could — without investing in business enterprises — and

18. Adam A. Pepelasis, "Les Problèmes de la Main d'Oeuvre de la Grèce dans le Cadre du Marché Commun," in J. Cuisenier (ed.), *Problèmes du development économique dans les pays meditérranéens* (Paris: Mouton, 1963), p. 322; Triantis, *Common Market and Economic Development,* pp. 220, 222.

19. George C. Haniotis, "An Exercise in Voluntary Repatriation in Greece," *OECD Observer,* No. 11 (August 1964), pp. 12–15.

20. Richard Robinson, "High-Level Manpower in Economic Development: Turkey" (unpublished paper, 1965), pp. 56, 64.

were reluctant to work for wages. Those who bought land had learned nothing of agricultural technique in the United States, where they had been, for the most part, laborers in construction. They dressed differently but within were basically unchanged: their way of life and their social ambitions were still determined by the social conditions of the home country, rather than the United States.[21]

A historical study of emigrants returning from the United States, interviewed in Greece in the early 1950's, produced examples of both sorts — those who had gained skill and the meaning of systematic work from their sojourn abroad and came back to start new industries, and those who "left as a young donkey and returned as an old one." But unfortunately there is no quantitative estimate of how the 40 percent of emigrants who returned divided between the two groups. Of 12 cases studied, only 4 represented successes, but there is no way of knowing whether this was a representative sample.[22]

If the emigrants return and if they have brought back skills which they are content to apply to industry and agriculture, this can contribute to economic development. Here is an opportunity which the Greek government alone among the Mediterranean countries seems to be embracing, despite the difficult problems of readjustment that may be involved.[23] But this is for the future. Training had little or nothing to do with the process of economic growth in the 1950's and early 1960's, growth seemingly stimulated in dynamic fashion by the loss of labor and the subsequent upping of wages.

The possibility exists that the net effect of emigration on skills is negative. Skilled workers are the most sought after by the recruiting agencies of the developed countries, and engineers and doctors find it easy to get away. Wage rates in truck assem-

21. See Ingrid Semmingsen, "Emigration and the Image of America in Europe," in H. S. Commager (ed.), *Immigration and American History* (Minneapolis: University of Minnesota Press, 1961), pp. 42–45, 52.

22. Theodore Saloutas, *They Remember America: The Story of the Repatriated Greek Americans* (Berkeley and Los Angeles: University of California Press, 1956). See also the returned emigrant in Silone's *Bread and Wine*, who was fit for use only as a hired man.

23. See Xenophon Zolotas, *Monetary Equilibrium and Economic Development* (Princeton: Princeton University Press, 1965), chap. 8.

bly in Turkey are said to be close to the west European level, partly as a result of emigration, which slows down growth to the extent that it is dependent on the local supply of skills — at least in the short run.[24] But the OECD estimates that the losses sustained by Greece in higher, middle, and lower formally trained personnel through emigration will decline from 112,060 in the period 1961–1974 to 29,230 in 1974–1979, largely as a result of returning students and returning workers from Germany.[25]

It is not only skills that the returning migrants bring back. Changed attitudes toward consumption, work, and the possibilities of change can count. "Their tempo of life quickened." [26]

The Stimulus from Labor Shortage

Under perfectly competitive conditions in comparative statics with a given state of the arts, savings lead to more capital formation, to substitution of capital for labor, and to higher wages. If there is technological progress so that new capital is more productive than the old, labor productivity improves on two scores: the increase in the capital/labor ratio and the improvement in the quality of the capital. There may also be an improvement in the quality of the labor, with education and investment in human capital, and this may constitute a third source of improvement in labor productivity.

But in the conditions of stagnation which exist in many underdeveloped countries, with disguised unemployment or at least underemployment, capital investment is handicapped. The marginal productivity of labor is below the going wage, which means that landlords and entrepreneurs pay family workers out of their share of income. This cuts down the source of savings. In addition, labor becomes an overhead or sunk cost, with a shadow price below the going wage. This discourages capital investment. If there is disguised unemployment and the marginal product and shadow price of labor are zero, it does not pay to invest capital in farming or business enterprise where labor can physically be substituted at all, since the cost of capital at any positive interest rate exceeds the cost of labor. Investment will,

24. Privately communicated by J. Walbroeck.
25. OECD, *Greece*, pp. 135 ff., esp. Table 10, pp. 136–137.
26. Saloutas, *They Remember America*, p. 130.

of course, take place where substitution of labor for capital is impossible, where modern enterprises rely exclusively on wage labor, or where family enterprises expand beyond the limits of the family overhead labor. But there will be a large number of inefficient operators, who barely make ends meet, and technology will change but little.

In an economy which has excess supplies of labor and where investment is stagnant and technology frozen, any shock to the system may push the economy off dead center and speed growth. One such jolt would be a drastic increase in demand, which would take up the labor into effective employment and raise the return to capital. Another is the removal of labor, and still another would be an arbitrary increase in wages. The Black Death in the fourteenth century is said to have given such a shock to the medieval economy of Europe and stimulated capital investment and technological change. A more modern example is the unionization of the garment trades in New York City, which by raising wages made the sweatshop unprofitable and led to the reorganization of the industry with greater capital investment on the part of a smaller number of entrepreneurs, lower costs and prices, and, because of the elasticity of demand for the product, higher output and substantially the same level of employment. A still more modern example is the response of the coal industry in the United States to the raising of wages by the United Mine Workers. This led to a substantial change in technology and capital investment and lower prices, but because of the elasticity of demand and competitive sources of energy somewhat lower output and much lower employment resulted.

This is a dynamic model. It operates only in the presence of capacity for innovation, or unexploited technological opportunities. An additional supply of capital may be endogenous in the model, as already discussed in relation to remittances and the decline in consumption of the labor that leaves, but these were not important in the garment industry, in coal, in French agriculture, and perhaps are not in Mediterranean growth. What counts is that the price system in factor markets begins to produce incentives for change after a period when entrepreneurs and landlords either neglected such opportunities or were unable to respond to them.

Emigration may operate directly on the labor supply of agriculture and stimulate productivity there. This is clearly the pattern in southern Italy and Portugal.[27] In Spain, Greece, and Turkey, however, rural exodus has brought some of the unemployed and underemployed to the city, which provided a large part of emigration. In Spain emigration picked up after the rules permitting the dismissal of industrial workers were relaxed in 1962. Prior to that time, it was possible to dismiss employees for disciplinary reasons but not for economic, except after a long and involved process. The International Bank mission very delicately recommended both the loosening up of this requirement and greater flexibility of wages, pointing out that employers hesitated to take on new ventures when labor was an overhead cost instead of a marginal one.[28] The position of the disguised unemployed and underemployed in Greek towns and cities prior to the large rise in emigration has been effectively described, as well as the impact of the loss of excess labor in improving agricultural productivity in one village, Lofiscos.[29] The position can be suggested by reference to Epirus — a region under planned development from the central government in Athens. This project is said to be "extremely disappointing."[30] Income rose by only 5 percent over a series of years, despite the investment of $4 million for 18,000 people and the employment of 50 technical advisers. Farmers ate the cows provided by the government. In a neighboring region which lacked this attention and lost population through emigration, gross production rose 21 percent over the same period, and the local farmers bought cows without prompting.[31]

Often emigrants pass from the countryside to the city and on to

27. V. Xavier Pintado, *Structure and Growth of the Portuguese Economy* (n.p.: European Free Trade Area, 1964), pp. 73, 79, 95.

28. International Bank for Reconstruction and Development (IBRD), *The Economic Development of Spain* (Baltimore: Johns Hopkins Press, 1963), pp. 343–344.

29. William H. McNeill, *Greece: American Aid in Action, 1947–56* (New York: Twentieth Century Fund, 1957), pp. 21, 55, 95, 147–157.

30. Benjamin Ward, *Greek Regional Development*, Research Monograph No. 4 (Athens: Center of Planning and Economic Research, n.d. [1962?]), pp. 136 ff. and esp. p. 141

31. Interview, OECD Center for Economic Growth, Paris, September 1964.

foreign parts. The Turkish government has been trying to convert the *bidonvilles* of Istanbul and Ankara into established communities, but these settlements serve partly as through stations for emigration to Germany, a country of which many of the Anatolian peasants hear for the first time when they come to the city.[32] In Greece no less than in Spain, internal and external migration are intimately bound up, so that numbers taken from industry or agriculture may result in a final subtraction from the one sector or the other.[33]

Bloodletting need not be stimulating. Exodus can lead to collapse and ghost communities. Manlio Rossi-Doria complains of southern Italian communities without men and compares them to concentration camps.[34] Provided it does not go too far, however, the loss of excess supplies of labor can speed up the growth process through removing the impediments to the effective operation of the price system in factor markets. It is believed, though it would be very difficult to prove the point, that it is this force which above all others — rising exports and tourist receipts, closer association with the rest of Europe, capital investment and foreign aid — has been responsible for the rapid growth of all Mediterranean countries save Turkey. In Turkey, the dent in the underemployment problem — the estimates range up to 9,000,000 underemployed out of work force of 12,500,000 — has been limited.[35]

In the Fei and Ranis model, the turning point for the economy comes when the wage in the agricultural sector reaches the level of that in industry (or some conventional proportion of it which

32. Statistics which show that 65 percent of Turkish emigrants to Germany come from Istanbul and Ankara are virtually worthless since those cities may be the proximate origin only, a residence for only afew months. See Nermin Adadan, *Batĭ Almanyadaki Türk İşçileri vs Sorunlarĭ* ("Turkish Emigration to Germany") (Ankara: Başkanlĭk Maatbaasĭ, 1964), p. 26 (called to my attention by R. Robinson).

33. B. Kayser, *Géographie Humaine de la Grèce* (Paris: Presses Universitaire de Paris, 1964), chaps. 4–5; S. Elvasco, "Quelques considerations sur l'émigration espagnole," *Revue Syndicale Suisse,* LIII (October 1961), 308–310.

34. Manilo Rossi-Doria, "Agriculture and Europe," in Stephen R. Graubard (ed.), *A New Europe?* (Boston: Houghton Mifflin, 1964), p. 408.

35. Nuri Eren, *Turkey Today — and Tomorrow* (New York: Praeger, 1963), p. 144.

balances the labor force in the two sectors) and leaves each sector growing in response to technical progress and the relative allocation of capital between them. In present circumstances, the movement from, say, Greek agriculture to the Greek city is of this sort, but it is difficult to calculate what Greek-European sectoral relationship would be sufficient to cut off the flow from the city abroad or initiate the return of emigrants. It is likely that governmental action will be taken well before this point is reached.

CHAPTER VI

Demand Factors: Exports and Investment

Export-Led Growth

Just a few years ago, experts were explaining the "law of declining foreign trade," conceived in the last century by Werner Sombart, under which there was a tendency for foreign trade to decline as a share in national income.[1] In the economic growth of Europe in the 1950's, on the other hand, it is widely recognized that exports played a prominent part in producing prosperity or at least were closely associated with it. The world market has long been recognized as an engine of growth for countries in the early stages of development. The post-World War II experience has been surprising, however, in that exports led growth in all the fast-growing countries of Europe. Figure VI-1 compares exports of goods and services and gross national product in real terms for 10 European countries and shows that in all cases the rate of growth of exports led that of gross national product. Figures for the trend in the two series are given for the period 1949 to 1959 in Table VI-1 in the same groupings as shown in Table II-1. The gap in the rates is particularly striking in Germany, Italy, the Netherlands, Austria, Denmark, and Belgium.

Some part of the expansion is of no great importance, because it represents intermediate goods being traded back and forth with little value added. The theory of international trade, which might lead us to think otherwise, was developed almost entirely on the basis of trade in final product—that is, goods wholly produced in one country and consumed in another. As the world division of labor becomes more finely articulated, however, the relationship between exports and imports, on the one hand, and

1. K. W. Deutsch and A. Eckstein, "National Industrialization and the Declining Share of the International Economic Sector, 1890–1959," *World Politics,* XIII (January 1961), 267–299.

TABLE VI-1

Volume growth in gross national product and exports and imports of goods and services, 1949–1959
(average annual compound rates)

	Gross national product	Exports	Imports
Germany	7.4	16.7	17.0
Italy	5.9	12.6	9.5
Switzerland	5.2	7.9	7.4
Netherlands	4.8	10.4	8.5
Austria	6.0	16.1	11.2
France	4.5	6.6	6.6
Norway	3.4	6.4	5.4
Sweden	3.4	6.0	7.0
Denmark	3.2	8.0	7.2
Belgium	3.0	7.2	6.5
United Kingdom	2.4	2.7	3.3
Greece	5.9	10.1	9.4
Turkey	5.9	0.9	0.2
Spain	5.2	3.0	8.7
Portugal	4.1	5.2	4.6

Source: ECE worksheets, dated April 4, 1962.

gross national product and especially national income, on the other, becomes less interesting. It is asserted that in a recent year Belgian exports rose by 26 percent and Belgian imports by 27 percent, the greatest part of the rise consisting of shipments of semifinished materials between the Ford plants at Limburg in Belgium and Cologne in Germany, on which value added in the exporting country was small in relation to the value of the product. If foreign trade is already large in relation to GNP, incremental gains in trade of this sort, with small value added, have limited significance for economic growth. Some part — but an unknown proportion — of the gain in foreign trade in Table VI-1 may have been of this character.

Moreover, European foreign trade was unduly low at the end of the 1940's. Depression, war, and painful recovery in which

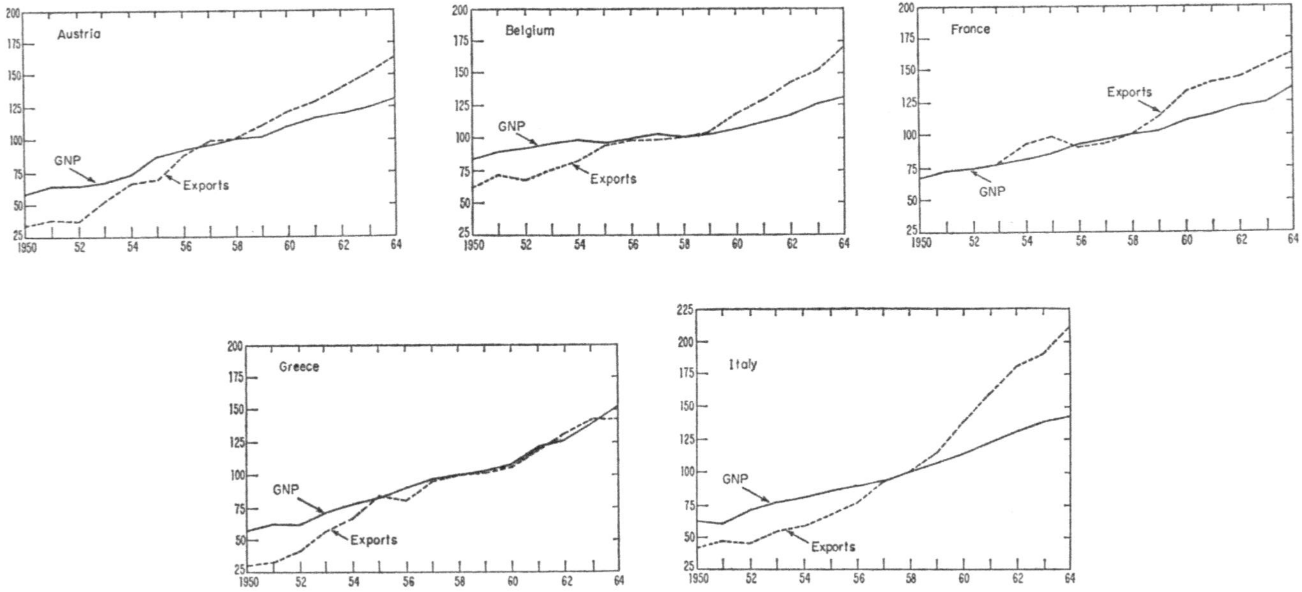
Austria
GNP
Exports
Belgium
GNP
Exports
France
Exports
GNP
Greece
GNP
Exports
Italy
GNP
Exports

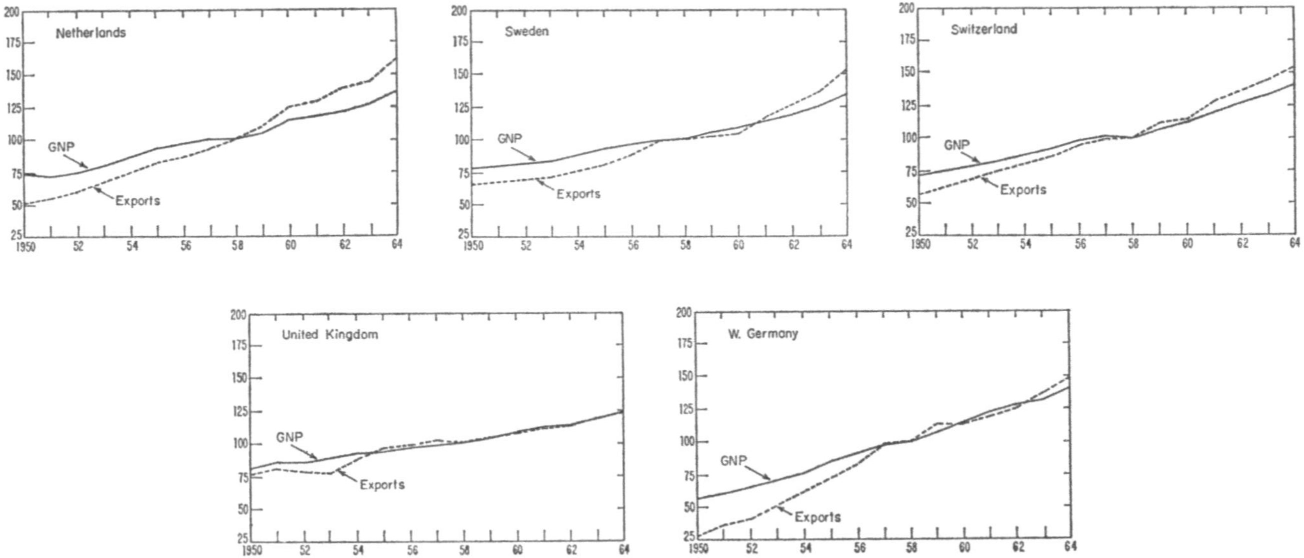

Figure VI-1. Exports and gross national product, in real terms, 1950–1964, for 10 European countries *1958 = 100*

Source: United Nations, *Yearbook of National Account Statistics*, various issues foreign trade had been slow in getting on its feet left the ratios of foreign trade to national output low by long-run standards. Positive steps were taken to bring it back, in the establishment of the European Payments Union (EPU), the removal of quantitative restrictions, the reduction of tariffs, and the establishment of the European Economic Community (EEC) and the European Free Trade Association (EFTA). In addition, the prices of materials rose in general more than the cost of transport in Europe, reducing the natural protection provided by distance. On all these scores, some increase of European trade relative to output was inevitable. To the extent that the rise in exports of final product was faster than that of GNP, however — which cannot be told from Figure VI-1 but which is likely to have been considerable — European postwar growth can be said to have been export-led.

European growth also had a strong element of import substitution in it. The models of export-led growth and import-substitution growth are often regarded as contrasts. This need not be the case. When domestic expenditure grows faster than exports and foreign trade declines as a proportion of total output, they are indeed opposites. But such an outcome is not inevitable. Import substitution involves a shift in the import schedule which may be more than offset by movement along it. If the income elasticity of demand for imports is greater than a factor of one, import substitution can leave the ratio of imports to output higher than before. A shift of the schedule cannot be detected from inspection of the import ratio. There is clear evidence that European growth came in considerable part from a block of countries learning to make for itself a variety of durable consumer goods and producer goods which used to be bought from the United States: automobiles, first of all, perhaps, but also radios, television sets, office equipment, trucks, tractors, airplanes, and so on. In this way, and despite the fact that imports grew faster than output, Europe followed the normal pattern of growth which calls for import substitution.[2] As is claimed by economists who

2. See Hollis B. Chenery, "Patterns of Industrial Growth," *American Economic Review*, L (September 1960), 624–654; Jacques Drèze, "Quelques réflexions sereines sur l'adaption de l'industrie Belge au Marché Commun," *Comptes Rendus de la Société d'Economie Politique de Belgique*, No. 275 (1960), p. 21.

recommend this path to the less developed countries, total imports are larger after import substitution, and in this instance a larger proportion of total income. But the composition is changed.

The import-substitution model has the same balance-of-payments effects as the export-led model, in the first round of spending. The ultimate impact, however, depends upon what happens to expenditure in subsequent rounds. If profits in exports are higher than those in import-competing lines, and the propensity to save out of profits is higher than those from other income shares, export-led growth may result in balance-of-payments surplus when import substitution will not. There is no presumption either way, however, even though export-led growth is likely to raise the ratio of exports to domestic output, and import substitution, because of the offsetting shift along the schedule, is unlikely to reduce the ratio of imports to income. In what follows I focus on the export-led model because that is more readily identified. It is useful, nonetheless, to bear in mind that import-substitution has the same initial effects on growth and the balance of payments, even though the later impacts of the two forces may diverge.

Autonomous or Built-In?

The crucial question is whether expansion of exports among the growing countries of Europe has been an autonomous factor or a result of economic growth. Did the exports produce the growth, the growth the exports, or did the two interact in a virtuous circle? The question arose first in connection with the Common Market. In an important article, Lamfalussy stated that he started out to prove that the establishment of the Common Market had led to the rapid growth of exports, which in turn produced rapid economic growth in the European Economic Community, and found to his surprise that the exports and growth had been surging ahead long before the Common Market came into effect.[3] The counter to this view is the argument that the exports picked up in advance of the actual entry into opera-

3. Alexander Lamfalussy, "Europe's Progress: Due to Common Market?" *Lloyds Bank Review*, No. 62 (October 1961), pp. 1–16.

tion of the Common Market because of anticipation.[4] Businessmen were unwilling to wait the deliberate and limited steps by which the Common Market was to come into being but undertook investment and marketing interpenetration in advance of actual reductions in tariffs. Or perhaps the establishment of the Common Market led to exports and growth by a somewhat different mechanism than mere response to tariff changes, actual or prospective. Prior to the agreement for the Common Market, national markets tended to include a few large firms competing with a host of small ones, with the large firms making a wide variety of differentiated products — the so-called "full line." When the Common Market was formed, these large firms entered into rationalization agreements or cartels with their counterparts in the Common Market, tending to specialize on fewer styles and models. This produced economies of scale, market interpenetration, lower prices, and strenuous competition for the smaller firms, and in this way exports as an autonomous factor resulting from the Common Market can be said to have stimulated growth in advance of actual tariff reductions.

These are not the only autonomous factors. For particular countries, the course of income abroad and the income elasticity of demand for the country's products may determine the level of exports and support the growth process. This has clearly happened for some countries much of the time — the demand for labor which led to the emigrant remittances discussed in the last chapter, for example, or the highly income-elastic demand for tourist expenditures which benefited Spain, Italy, and Greece in the Mediterranean area, and Austria. In 1962 and 1963, even German exports expanded rapidly because of the inflationary process at work in France, Italy, and the Netherlands. But while elements of the structure of various countries' trade — the course of income for its trading partners and the nature of the goods and services sold to them — were important for particular countries all the time and for others some of the time, the structural argument does not stand up overall. It requires that demand

4. Richard Mayne, "Economic Integration in the New Europe: A Statistical Approach," in Stephen R. Graubard (ed.), *A New Europe?* (Boston: Houghton Mifflin, 1964), p. 186.

for European goods and services outside the system grow faster than European aggregate output, which has not been the case, and it would have to explain why this demand was for European (and Japanese) products, not British and American. Trade structure counts for only a limited part of export growth and cannot be used to explain an autonomous export demand.

If the demand for exports does not play an autonomous role, what of supply? The contrast is often drawn between German merchants, eager to export, and those of other countries, especially the British and before 1958 the French, who had a take-it-or-leave-it attitude toward exports and whose products were deficient in "design, quality, delivery dates and salesmanship." [5] Italian-styled clothing sold all over the world as part of the rise of Rome as a center for high fashion, a movement associated with a revival of world interest in various aspects of Italian culture.[6] A remote possibility is that United Kingdom and United States exports were restricted by the rise of British and American overseas investment — in other words, that foreign operations substituted for exports and stimulated growth abroad rather than at home.[7] This is unlikely to have been a significant factor. British market shares declined drastically in some lines where direct investment is limited or nonexistent (textiles) and less in others where it is substantial (soap, machinery). In addition, there is a strongly held view in the United States that direct investment stimulates exports rather than depresses them, through purchases of machinery, equipment, components, and materials, on the one hand, and by means of marketing ancillary lines of goods, on the other. There is no agreed view on the issue. It is more significant that the shares of foreign import markets taken over by Britain

5. On the subject of the German merchants, see W. N. Parker, "Entrepreneurial Opportunities and Response in the German Economy," *Explorations in Entrepreneurial History,* VII (October 1954), 16; H. C. Wallich, *Mainsprings of German Revival* (New Haven: Yale University Press, 1955), pp. 244 ff. For France, see the list compiled in my *Foreign Trade and the National Economy* (New Haven: Yale University Press, 1962), p. 230; and regarding England, see National Economic Development Council, *Export Trends* (London: H.M.S.O., 1963), pp. 15 ff.

6. S. J. Wells, *British Export Performance: A Comparative Study* (Cambridge: Cambridge University Press, 1964), pp. 186–187.

7. *Ibid.,* chap. 3.

and the United States during the period of German, Italian, and Japanese defeat were not strongly held and could be fairly readily rewon when the latter countries made their comeback.

Perhaps the main basis for holding that exports have been an autonomous factor in European growth is export policy, on the part of both government and business. To promote exports, governments have adopted a variety of means ranging from devaluation, remission of excise and income taxes, and subsidies to special depreciation allowances, insurance, easy credit, assistance in purchasing materials, special discounting facilities, permission to raise prices, and so on. Import restrictions have been removed slowly in some instances, and there are widespread claims that nontariff and nonquota means of restricting imports continued after the obvious techniques for holding back imports had been removed by internationally coordinated action. Some export promotion has been competitively offsetting: all the countries of the Common Market remit excise taxes on exports and apply them to imports as part of the harmonization of fiscal charges, an action which is equivalent to a moderate devaluation against the outside world although not against each other. The provision of medium-term export credit by government is undertaken in every country on roughly the same terms. But despite the suspicions of the competition, governmental export promotion does not seem to have been a major factor. Wells concludes that "no substantial part of the German export effort can be explained in terms of specific Government fiscal aid." [8] A study of French export assistance concludes that it was required before 1958 primarily because of the disequilibrium exchange rate and that the real development of French exports occurred after the devaluation when the bulk of the assistance apparatus was abandoned.[9]

Nor can exchange-rate policy be saddled with much of the responsibility, apart from the corrective devaluation of the French franc in 1958 and perhaps the undervaluation of the Austrian schilling in 1952. The 1949 devaluation of all European

8. *Ibid.*, p. 81.
9. René P. André, "Government Action and French Exports" (Master's thesis, Massachusetts Institute of Technology, 1964).

currencies may have left the dollar overvalued.[10] Nevertheless, Britain, with slow export growth, devalued more than the rest of Europe at the time, too much in the view of Harrod and possibly too soon.[11] The German and Dutch upward revaluations of 1961 failed to halt the expansion of exports of the two countries, although there was some evidence that the German export orders fell off even though deliveries continued their upward trend. Over a decade, however, as was the case in the 1950's, the domestic cost and price levels can be expected to adjust to the exchange rate, leaving little if any independent room for exchange policy.

Government policy cannot then be held responsible for the autonomous growth of exports by these positive acts. Overall government policies to promote growth and to maintain stable prices may have prevented exports from being cut off. German exports are said to have been supported by policies of maintaining competition in goods and factor markets or through general measures to maintain "competitiveness or defenses against inflation." [12] This leads us from government policies to business policies, apart from the vague "eagerness to promote exports," and general business performance in achieving higher productivity, lower costs, and lower prices. Specifically, it leads to the question of whether European business went in for highly flexible pricing in export markets, otherwise called price discrimination, or dumping.

The question arises because unit values in exports — that is, relatives of export values divided by indexes of volume — behave differently than domestic prices. It is not surprising that whole-

10. Richard N. Cooper, "Dollar Deficits and Postwar Economic Growth," *Review of Economics and Statistics*, XLVI (May 1964), 155–159.

11. Roy Harrod, *Policy Against Inflation* (New York: St. Martin's Press, 1958); M. June Flanders, "The Effects of Devaluation on Exports: A Case Study, United Kingdom, 1949–1954," *Bulletin of the Oxford University Institute of Statistics*, XXV (August 1963), 197.

12. See Egon Sohmen, "Competition and Growth: The Lessons of West Germany," *American Economic Review*, XLIX (December 1959), 986–1003; Sohmen, "The Dollar and the Mark," in S. E. Harris (ed.), *The Dollar in Crisis* (New York: Harcourt, Brace & World, 1961), pp. 185–200; Angus Maddison, *Economic Growth in the West* (New York: Twentieth Century Fund, 1964), pp. 102, 180.

sale prices should move differently from the cost of living. As Balassa has conclusively shown, domestic prices of services will rise rapidly in countries where productivity is increasing at a rapid rate, since goods and services with low rates of productivity increase feel the pinch of rising wages spreading from the industries of rapid productivity gain.[13] But export prices of manufactures (actually unit values) rose less between 1953 and 1963 than unit wage costs in manufacturing in the United Kingdom and Germany and actually fell when unit wage costs were rising in France and Italy. In contrast, as shown in Figure VI-2, export prices of manufactures rose more than consumer prices or unit wage costs in the United States. United States and United Kingdom export prices rose far more than those of the other countries portrayed, which helps explain their losses in export shares.

A number of hypotheses may be advanced to explain this disparate price behavior at home and in exports. It may be a purely statistical phenomenon, based upon differences in the composition and method of weighting the separate indexes. This is unlikely. It may reflect the particular situation in steel, where United States prices rose substantially in the home market, and held firmly at the high level when production fell, whereas European prices fell sharply with every setback in production.[14] This supports Sohmen's thesis about competition between Europe as a whole and the United States but does not discriminate among the European countries. Or there may have been very different productivities in export sectors and in the economy as a whole, just as existed between manufactures and most services, although why this should apply on the Continent and not in the United States and Britain is difficult to explain. Or, finally, there may have been dumping. Various studies are under way to pin down the factors for this disparate behavior, and pending their results we cannot be certain what the causes were. The issue of whether the development of exports has been an autonomous factor responsible for growth or a part of the growth process

13. Bela Balassa, "The Purchasing Power Parity Doctrine," *Journal of Political Economy,* LXXII (December 1964), 584–596.

14. Egon Sohmen, *International Monetary Problems and the Foreign Exchanges,* Princeton University Special Papers in International Economics, No. 4 (1963), p. 15.

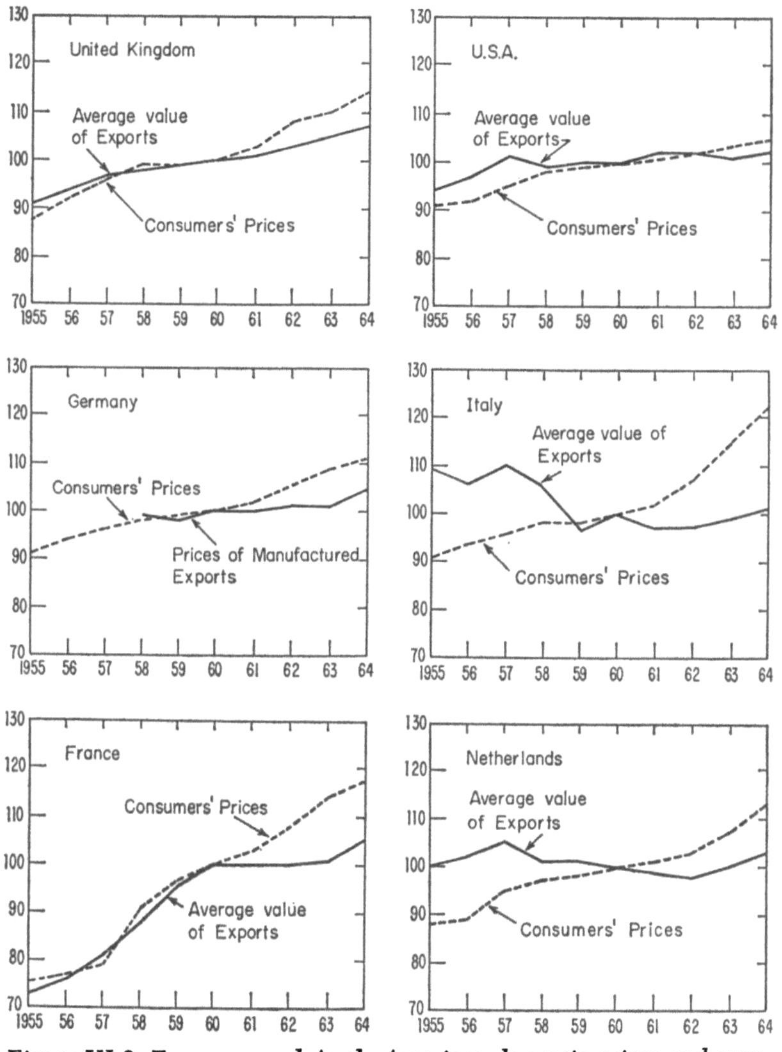

Figure VI-2. European and Anglo-American domestic prices and average export values, 1955–1964 1960 = 100

Source: Organisation for Economic Cooperation and Development, *Main Economic Indicators, Historical Statistics, 1955–64,* Paris, 1966 turns in part, however, on whether exports have grown from dumping or from the differential sectoral productivities.

Unquestionably there has been dumping. Trade in automobiles, for example, is conducted with prices for the domestic and foreign market set independently, as a first approximation, even though import competition may hold down domestic prices in the long run. In April 1962 Volkswagen raised its domestic price $60 to $97 per automobile, citing the rising costs of steel, transport, and labor, but effected no change in export prices.[15] All European automobile companies are said to maintain higher prices at home than in export markets in order to meet foreign charges, duties, marketing costs, and so on. The *Monthly Report* of the Deutsche Bundesbank mentions price concessions on exports, and the U.K. National Economic Development Council observes that British firms pursue a "less flexible pricing policy."[16]

But apart from known cases of price discrimination, most opinion seems to favor the explanation that prices of exports diverge from domestic prices because productivity increases faster in these goods.[17] If this be the case, export growth is an endogenous factor which comes from economic growth itself, and not an independent force. Somehow the system has to get started; but once it is under way, economic growth leads to exports, which lead to profits, to investment, to increased productivity, and back again to more exports — so long as wages do not rise sufficiently to cut off rise in profits. This is the Lamfalussy thesis in *The United Kingdom and the Six* — without the caveat on wages — that exports and economic growth have been barreling along in a virtuous circle in Germany, Italy, the Netherlands, and since

15. *New York Times*, May 31, 1962. The German government took action against Volkswagen and the other producers who followed suit by reducing the import duty on automobiles by 30 percent. Its interest was price stability, however, rather than nondiscrimination.

16. *Monthly Report* of the Deutsche Bundesbank, XVI (January 1964), 31; Development Council, *Export Trends*, p. 15.

17. See Wells, *British Export Performance, passim;* Bela Balassa, "Recent Developments in the Competitiveness of American Industry and Prospects for the Future," in U.S. Congress Joint Economic Committee, *Factors Affecting the United States Balance of Payments* (Washington, D.C.: Government Printing Office, 1962), pp. 29–54; Richard N. Cooper, "The Competitive Position of the United States," in Harris (ed.), *The Dollar in Crisis*, pp. 137–164.

1958 France, while Belgium and the United Kingdom were locked in the vicious circle of low exports and low growth, explained in the early 1950's by inadequate labor supply.

The Virtuous Circle

It is one thing to hypothesize about the virtuous circle; it is more difficult to demonstrate the phenomenon in action. There is no difficulty in proving that rising exports are associated with rising growth, as shown in Figure VI-1 and Table VI-1. Moreover, a number of statistical studies have shown that rising exports are the result of what is called "the competitive effect" — that is, they cannot be explained away entirely by structural aspects of a country's trade, either the commodity structure or the country distribution.[18] As already indicated, the competitive effect may result from price reduction, shown in Figure VI-2, or from greater selling effort, which is nonprice competition.

Table VI-2 shows the percentage change in exports of the developed countries of Europe, plus the United States, broken down for the periods 1953 to 1959 and 1959 to 1963 by commodity effect, market effect, and residual (which embraces the competitive effect). The gap represents the difference in rate of growth per year between total exports of a country and that of the group as a whole. The commodity effect shows what the growth would have been, above or below the average growth for all countries, if each country had retained the same share of each commodity market that it started with in the base period. The market effect both shows the difference between overall growth and that growth which would have been achieved if the country had its base-period share of given commodities in given national markets and indicates whether the country is selling to fast- or slow-growing countries. What commodity and market effects do not account for in the gap is the residual, which serves as a proxy for its competitive ability. This table shows that the com-

18. See H. Tyszynski, "World Trade in Manufactured Commodities, 1899–1950," *The Manchester School,* XIX (September 1951), 272–304; Alexander Lamfalussy, *The United Kingdom and the Six* (Homewood, Ill.: Richard D. Irwin, 1963), chap. 5; Robert M. Stern, "Developments in the Commodity Composition, Market Distribution and Competitiveness of Italy's Foreign Trade, 1955–1963," Banca Nazionale del Lavoro *Quarterly Review,* No. 72 (March 1965), pp. 3–21.

TABLE VI-2

Commodity, market, and competitive effects among European exporting countries, 1953–1959 and 1959–1963 (percent per year)

Country and Period [a]	Growth rate of exports	Overall gap vis-à-vis country gap	Commodity effect	Market effect	Residual (competitive effect)	Increase in unit value
Germany						
1953–1959	13.3	10.0	1.0	1.1	8.0	0.4
1959–1963	10.4	2.5	–0.1	1.8	0.7	1.7
Italy						
1953–1959	12.0	8.1	–0.9	1.6	9.3	–3.1
1959–1963	15.0	9.0	—	0.9	8.1	0.1
Netherlands						
1953–1959	8.5	2.8	–0.9	1.7	2.1	0.6
1959–1963	8.2	–0.4	–0.1	3.5	–3.8	1.0
Austria						
1953–1959	9.6	4.4	—	2.4	–2.0	0.4
1959–1963	8.1	–0.5	–1.0	4.7	–4.2	—
France						
1953–1959	6.0	–0.5	–0.1	–0.8	0.5	–0.1
1959–1963	9.5	1.2	–0.4	–1.8	3.4	0.1
Norway						
1953–1959	6.8	0.5	–0.5	2.6	–1.6	0.1
1959–1963	7.2	–1.6	–1.5	1.3	–1.5	–0.1
Sweden						
1953–1959	6.8	0.5	–1.0	1.1	0.4	0.2
1959–1963	9.7	1.5	–0.6	2.2	–0.1	0.1
Denmark						
1953–1959	7.7	1.6	0.3	1.5	–0.2	0.2
1959–1963	7.9	–0.9	0.6	2.1	–3.6	0.2
Belgium						
1953–1959	7.4	1.3	0.1	2.3	–1.1	0.2
1959–1963	10.1	2.1	–2.3	2.9	–1.5	0.5
United Kingdom						
1953–1959	4.4	–2.4	0.2	–0.9	–1.8	1.8
1959–1963	5.9	–3.3	0.2	–0.9	–2.6	1.2
United States						
1953–1959	3.0	–4.1	–0.7	–0.9	–3.1	1.4
1959–1963	7.1	–1.8	0.7	–2.2	–0.3	0.5

Source: Prepared by Robert J. Gordon, M.I.T., from United Nations trade data.

[a] Total growth rates of exports for countries listed are, for 1953–1959, 6.4, and for 1959–1963, 8.6.

petitive effect was of great importance for Germany and Italy and to a lesser degree the Netherlands in the first period but declined strikingly for Germany, the Netherlands, and Austria in the second. If the data had carried through until 1964, the Italian competitive gain would have been sharply reduced and possibly even reversed. At the same time, the market effect was substantial for Austria, the Netherlands, and Belgium and to a lesser degree the Scandinavian countries (except for Norway) and improved from the first period to the second. French experience does not conform to that of the other principal European countries, because of devaluation in 1958, which gave it a strong competitive benefit in the second period. The British lose a little from their market ties outside the Continent, but their real failure to keep up is attributable to competitive capacity rather than to market or commodity structure.

The breakdown of the table into the two periods broadly confirms the hypothesis of the export-led model with elastic labor supplies up to 1959, and thereafter increasing bottlenecks and stringency, where one European country benefits from inflation in the other. The Netherlands residual loss was, to be sure, concentrated in agricultural commodities and shared widely in many markets, but by and large, the picture, if modified by knowledge of the Italian crisis of 1963–64, supports the hypothesis.

The German Council of Experts has provided a useful demonstration of the mechanism of export-led growth. The increase in output is divided among exports, investment, and consumption, in percent, and a clear pattern emerges in which in successive years first exports, then investment, and then consumption dominate the increase in income.[19] But the generality of the lead of exports is hard to prove more widely. The ECE staff finds a close association between the growth of exports and the growth of gross domestic product, based on the correlation of increases and decreases in exports and increases and decreases of output, but the covariation becomes weaker for most countries if output is lagged a year behind exports.[20] If in a virtuous circle exports

19. Sachverständigenrat zur Begutachtung der gesamtwirtschaftlichen Entwicklung, *Stabiles Geld, Stetiges Wachstum: Jahresgutachten 1964/65* (Stuttgart and Mainz: Kohlhammer, 1965), Table 9, p. 12.

20. ECE internal memorandum, dated April 19, 1962.

lead to increases in output and increases in output lead to greater exports, it is hard to predict whether exports should lead output statistically or output exports. It is curious, however, to find them growing together year by year when the model calls for lags.

Further differences of view turn on the mechanism in relation to price, on the one hand, and profits, on the other. Most of the extant analysis assumes that exports lead to investment which increases productivity and lowers prices and that the new export increase is the result of high price elasticities. But a number of writers are not persuaded that the elasticities are high or that European exports sell much on price. Patrick Boarman ascribes German export successes to technological excellence.[21] E. Rosselle and J. Waelbroeck conclude on the basis of an analysis of covariance that increases in demand lead to increases in profits, which in turn provide the financial support needed further to invest in market expansion. Thus they see no necessity for price reduction, on the one hand, or high elasticities, which they are unable to find, on the other.[22] The residuals in the analysis of Table VI-2 may reflect declines and high elasticities; but they need not. In truth all they imply is that exports have expanded for certain countries over certain periods in ways which differ from those postulated in explanations based on given markets and given commodities. All these models relate higher profits to higher exports, if by a different mechanism. But of course it is possible that lower profits will lead to greater efforts at exporting. J. W. Angell sets out the case on *a priori* grounds: a fall in the rate of profit because of rising costs can lead to intensified efforts to expand sales abroad.[23] And this sequence did emerge in Germany in 1962. The slight recession at home led a number of industries, including especially the electrical, to ask their export

21. Patrick M. Boarman, *Germany's Economic Dilemma, Inflation and the Balance of Payments* (New Haven: Yale University Press, 1964), chap. 7.

22. E. Rosselle and J. Waelbroeck, "La Demande à l'Exportation pour les Pays du Marché Commun, une application de l'analyse de la covariance" (paper presented to the Econometric Society, Zurich, 1964); J. Waelbroeck, "On the Structure of International Trade Interdependence" (unpublished paper, Massachusetts Institute of Technology, 1965).

23. J. W. Angell, "United States International Payment Deficits," *Political Science Quarterly*, LXXIX (March 1964), 5.

departments why they had gone to sleep. The resultant export push was remarkable.[24]

There is, then, no simple, straightforward agreed model of export-led, virtuous-circle growth which can be used to demonstrate that exports led to growth and growth to exports. There is no model so universally accepted that policymakers can feel confident that if they start with exports — achieved perhaps through devaluation as in France in 1958 — they will get growth, or if they start with growth they will achieve exports — in the way the British have contemplated pushing through the import barrier to higher productivity and exports. The thesis of this book is that it makes an enormous difference whether the labor supply and consequently the supply of goods are elastic.

The Balance of Payments

The fact that exports initially grow faster than output does not necessarily mean that the balance of payments will stay favorable. With a domestic accelerator, the increase in exports can lead to higher percentage increases in investment which spill over into imports via the marginal propensity to import and lead to import surpluses. A recent attempt has been made to build a theory of capital movements on this sort of positive-feedback model.[25] But in Europe, especially Germany, rapid growth has been associated with export surpluses — although the fact is not self-evident in Table VI-1 because of the idiosyncracies of the base year in a number of countries. Investment rises, but savings rise more, so that the export surplus is matched by net domestic savings.

This export surplus is connected with the labor supply and income distribution, as discussed for separate countries in Chapters II-V. When the country runs at full employment, or if it had little idle labor to begin with, increases in exports quickly lead to rising wages and immediately increased consumption, without the delay evident in the German example mentioned on p. 34,

24. Interview, IFO-Institut für Wirtschaftsforschung, Munich, 1964.

25. See G. E. Borts, "A Theory of Long-Run International Capital Movements," *Journal of Political Economy*, LXXII (August 1964), 341–359.

and imports rise to offset or reverse the rise in exports. When there is excess labor, however, the rise in profits leads to increased savings, and consumption and imports rise less in percentage terms than exports to keep the balance of payments active.

But there is one important variation within the European countries which until the summer of 1965, at least, spoiled the simplicity of the model. In Germany, and to a lesser extent in the Netherlands, which is another country sharing the Teutonic temperament, a shift from profits to wages had a smaller effect than in Britain or the Latin countries, because households had a high marginal propensity to save.

In the early days immediately after the Korean War and the establishment of the EPU when Germany ran a large import surplus, owing to inventory stocking on credit by businesses, the German government ran a large and disguised budget surplus. Finance Minister Schaefer effected this surplus by means of levying taxes to meet military expenditures which proved to be slow in coming and by putting the tax receipts into special reserve funds for future military disbursement. This high rate of government saving proved to be the counterpart of the balance-of-payments surplus, and was called the "Juliusturm," or Julius Tower, after the place in Spandau where the Bismarck government secreted part of the gold from the Franco-Prussian indemnity of 1871 as a war chest against future need. When the "Juliusturm" was discovered and abandoned about 1954, some economists, including me, thought that the German balance of payments would turn adverse, for the surplus had been produced by the act of saving and seemingly would disappear when the saving ceased. In the next phase, however, the counterpart of the export surplus which remained turned up in the saving of enterprise, largely retained profits which rose faster than investment. Instead of the balance-of-payments surplus or deficit adjusting to the net between savings and investment, as the "absorption" theory of Alexander and especially Johnson called for, net savings adjusted to the balance of payments. The *ex ante* long-run equilibrium of the balance of payments and net savings may not have been realized, but net savings adjusted *ex post* to the balance of payments.[26] It was not until the summer of 1965 when government deficits, combined with business investment, outran the savings of households that the balance of payments turned adverse.

The same mechanism seems to have been at work early in Italy, where the balance-of-payments surplus had its counterpart in industrial profits so long as wages were held down. But an important difference existed. When Italy ran out of labor, the balance of payments turned adverse right away. In Germany and to a lesser extent in the Netherlands with rising wages, household savings replaced corporate savings to maintain net savings and the balance-of-payments surplus. But I conclude from the experience of the rest of Europe that these are the exception. The rule is that exports lead to growth and a balance-of-payments surplus so long as the labor supply is plentiful and goods supply is elastic. When the labor supply runs out, exports lead to investment, inflation, imports, and balance-of-payments equilibrium or possibly even deficit, except in the rare case where households have as high an income elasticity of demand for savings *ex ante* as does business *ex post* — a curious phenomenon perhaps, but one whose existence must be recognized.

A penultimate word on France: in my view, the devaluation of 1958 was necessary but not sufficient to get recovery, just as the monetary reform of 1948 in Germany was necessary but not sufficient to produce the *Wirtschaftswunder*. In the earlier case, production had been growing, and inventories were being built up prior to reform: when reform took place, large stocks of goods moved out of black-market channels and hoards into the shop windows. In the Rueff revaluation, adroit policy gets some credit for the redressing of the balance of payments, but the basis for recovery in the balance of payments was the growth which had gone on from 1949 to 1957. The same tactics applied in 1946 or 1948 would have produced no more in the way of recovery than the devaluations of those years did.

26. See my "Germany's Persistent Balance-of-Payments Disequilibrium," in R. E. Caves, H. G. Johnson, and P. B. Kenen (eds.), *Trade, Money and Growth: Essays in Honor of Gottfried Haberler* (Chicago: Rand McNally, 1965), pp. 230–248.

To conclude, then: European postwar growth was export-led, but the exports were a supply phenomenon as well as a creature of demand. Rising incomes in the other countries of Europe and relatively high price elasticities took care of the individual countries. They took poor care of the slower growers. And for growing Europe as a whole, exports were as much a result as a cause.

Investment

Belief in the importance of demand in economic growth relies heavily on government policy in stimulating investment. In terms of Keynesian analysis, investment raises effective demand through a multiplier and possibly an accelerator; this stimulates employment, and the productivity of the investment enlarges capacity for growth through the Domar supply aspect of the Harrod-Domar model. Policies for stimulating and shaping investment are those central to economic growth.

There is one difficulty which we have already pointed out about discussing this issue in the same chapter with exports. It is true that both exports and investment are the autonomous variables in the Keynesian macroeconomic system. But the policies which help one may hurt the other. The more that demand is stimulated by raising investment, the more domestic prices will rise and cut off exports. Thus Maddison seems to get into trouble when he claims that German policy, for example, kept demand high through fiscal policy affecting investment, consumption, and domestic government expenditure and kept export industries competitive by restraining demand.

But the thesis set out here is that not all investment is important to demand, though some is, and that most investment policies pursued by governments relate to the type of investment which is either neutral with respect to growth or even slows it down.

The ECE evidence of a close association between economic growth and the expansion of the labor force and of low correlations between growth and capital inputs has already been cited (above, p. 26). A more recent and detailed study claims that investment is closely associated with growth for 5 countries — France, Germany, Italy, the United Kingdom, and the United

States — in which after 10.5 percent of gross national product is invested to stand still, an extra 1.72 percent of GNP invested will raise the growth rate by 1 percent per annum. But this correlation breaks down when the attempt is made to add more countries and put them on a per capita basis, to include employment as an explanatory variable in multiple regression, or to disaggregate. T. P. Hill suggests that the addition of southern and northern countries disturbs his regressions because these respectively have mild and severe climates and are densely and sparsely populated, with divergent requirements for social overhead capital. He goes on to note that growth is correlated closely with investment in machinery and equipment and not with residential and other construction. Some construction, like roads, experiences a direct capital/output ratio of infinity because its services are not included in national product.[27]

I suggest that investment policies are either neutral or negative for growth, since most of them are designed to stimulate investment in lines where it will not take place of its own accord, that is, in lines where the productivity of the investment is not self-evident. It is easy to fall into the trap of *post hoc ergo propter hoc* and to attribute high rates of German investment to high rates of investment stimulation. But high activity in investment stimulation produced low rates of investment in France, though investment of high productivity; and wide measures of investment stimulation in England produced equally low rates of investment of low productivity. In Italy, high rates of investment are associated with relatively low rates of stimulation, and stimulation is attempted for the most part not through general investment and depreciation allowances but by special measures to achieve social objective (especially in the south), to assist lagging industries (shipbuilding, coal, and sulphur), and to build infrastructure ("land reclamation, housing, roads, airports").[28] In Germany, moreover, much of the governmental intervention in the investment process was of this same sort, and of dubious assistance to

27. T. P. Hill, "Growth and Investment in International Comparisons," *Economic Journal*, LXXIV (June 1964), 287–304.

28. E. Tosco, "Economic Policy in Italy," in *Economic Policy in Our Time*, vol. III: *Country Studies* (Chicago: Rand McNally, 1964), pp. 146, 149, 150, 156.

growth, notably in shipbuilding, coal, small business, farming, and especially housing.[29]

It is unnecessary to cite again in detail the Norwegian experience with high rates of government and private investment and a low rate of growth. Here is investment policy and little growth. On the Mediterranean edge of the Continent there were high rates of growth, except for Turkey, and only limited investment or investment policy. The explanation that infrastructure requirements were lower there because of mild climate and dense population is hardly convincing. Rosenstein-Rodan maintains, on the contrary, that countries at the earlier stages of growth need intensified rates of investment in infrastructure — especially roads, schools, and hospitals — before they can achieve lower capital/output ratios by investing in directly productive plant and equipment. Such programs of investment as have been undertaken in southern Italy and in Greece, to attract foreign investment and to stimulate the Epirus region, have not been notably successful.

One useful point has been made that the Continent, aside from Belgium, benefited from the destruction caused by the war, which was less severe in Britain and Scandinavia. The benefit was in sweeping away obsolete equipment and in enabling war-torn countries to start with investment in complete units rather than marginal additions to obsolete plants that failed to take full advantage of the technological advances since 1939.[30] Not only were the complete plants more productive per dollar of investment, but standard depreciation rates applied to new equipment produced gross savings not available with older average capital stock where physical wear keeps pace with accounting depreciation. A similar point can be made for countries of rapid population growth through either natural increase or immigration: a widening of the capital stock to maintain the average ratio of capital to population permits a country to take advantage of improvements in technology and continuously to reduce the average age of its capital relative to countries with a stagnant

29. Frederick G. Reuss, *Fiscal Policy for Growth without Inflation: The German Experiment* (Baltimore: Johns Hopkins Press, 1963), pp. 104 ff., pp. 188 ff.
30. See Lamfalussy, *The United Kingdom and the Six*, pp. 106–108.

population. But these effects operate on the productivity of capital — a supply point — and are unrelated to the question of demand.

The conclusion is not that investment is unrelated to growth. To pick up Hill's remark about investment in plant and equipment, the conclusion is that growth-producing investment occurs in industries which are making profits and expanding to make more. Government control has little to do with it. In nationalized French industry or in French industry following out the expansion of the Plan, it may be government capital which is being invested, rather than profits. The same may be the case with IRI (Instituto per la Ricostruzione Industriale) and ENI (Ente Nazionale Idrocarburi) in Italy. In these cases the pull is probably stronger than the push. Investment in response to profit opportunities, though not investment as such, is the engine of growth.

Much of the investment of this sort comes from profits. But it need not. The French example of channeling private savings through governmental institutions back into private hands demonstrates this. But profits help, both in demonstrating the opportunity and in providing the resources. When profits dry up, investment may go forward in cost-reducing opportunities, a procedure which calls for reliance on the capital market, using domestic savings provided by households or government. Or if the rise in wages has stimulated consumption at the expense of total savings, investment may proceed with funds borrowed from abroad. But these issues will occupy us considerably later, in Chapter XII.

CHAPTER VII

Supply Elements: Technological Change and Economic Efficiency

"The Residual"

We have rejected the claim that demand and therefore policies to keep it high and stable are prime determinants of differences in postwar European rates of growth. We turn now to supply. But before pursuing the investigation of the role of labor supply and its critical importance, we may usefully evaluate the claim that two other factors on the supply side constitute independent causes: technological progress and, related to it, the efficiency of the economy. Technological progress embraces, of course, both imitation of the technical advances of other economies and independent invention and innovation. By efficiency of the economy is meant the effectiveness of entrepreneurs in producing the right goods in the right way, given the range of technical alternatives. It depends on a number of factors, and in particular on whether the price system gives the right signals and whether industry and government respond to those signals in the most economical way. It covers, that is, questions of competition, the vigor of entrepreneurship, and the efficiency of nationalized industry.

Technological change and economic efficiency are not the only possible causal factors which could be investigated. Growth has been faster in many countries than can be explained by the weighted inputs of factors of production. The difference was first called "technical progress" since this was the first factor thought of. Later a more eclectic attitude was adopted, and the difference is referred to merely as "the residual." If capital and labor inputs combined on a fixed-weight index grow at one rate and output grows faster, the difference may be explained by a variety of factors, including differences in the level of utilization of capacity, economies of scale, increasing education (which should be counted as investment in human capital but is regarded as consumption), improved economic organization, or perhaps merely technical progress.[1] Differences in utilization of capacity are ignored here, since these are of little consequence in the postwar period in Europe apart from the surplus of manpower. Economies of scale are touched on below in connection with economic efficiency, as is the elusive concept of economic organization, which can be graded as fair, good, excellent. Before we tackle technical progress and economic efficiency, however, it may be appropriate to say a word about the possibility that investment in human capital accounts for the very different rates of growth in Europe.

It is hard to deny that differences in education have some impact on economic growth and that a way to faster growth is to train more students in science and engineering. But it is difficult to establish a close relationship in the short run. Growth through education is roundabout. In the short run, the correlation between expenditure on education and rates of growth is a poor one, and that between numbers of engineers and rates of growth of output and of employment in manufacturing is high only because of the inclusion of eastern European countries with the three western European countries for which data have been mustered.[2] Slow-growing Sweden, Denmark, and Britain spend a larger proportion of national income on education than faster-growing Germany and Italy. While the absolute amounts spent on education rise in every country for which data are available, and in percentage of national income in most, the countries of highest rises in percent of national income spent on education between 1950 and 1955 include slow growers and fast (Sweden and the Netherlands), and so does the smaller class of countries where the proportion of income has declined (Norway and Italy).[3]

1. See E. D. Domar, "On the Measurement of Technological Change," *Economic Journal*, LXXI (December 1961), 709–729; Domar *et al.*, "Economic Growth and Productivity in the United States, Canada, United Kingdom, Germany and Japan in the Postwar Period," *Review of Economics and Statistics*, XLVI (February 1964), 33–40.

2. ECE, *Some Factors in Economic Growth in Europe during the 1950's* (Geneva: United Nations, 1965), chap. 5, Charts 3–4, pp. 15–16.

3. *Ibid.*, p. 8.

There have been increases in education in virtually every country in Europe — lifting the school-leaving age and increasing the proportions of young people enrolled in school at every age group up to that for higher education, 20–24. But it is difficult to see theoretically why it should be the change in numbers of educated people which would affect differential growth rates rather than the proportions. And there may be some significance to the fact that the three countries with the highest proportion of young people receiving higher education — the United States, Sweden, and Norway — are all slow growers, while Austria, France, Greece, Italy, Portugal, Spain, Switzerland (and Turkey and the United Kingdom) are at the bottom of the list with only 3 or 4 percent of the 20–24 age group enrolled in educational institutions (Turkey 1 percent).[4]

Education, like technological progress, is difficult to quantify. More significant than numbers enrolled in school may be the fact that the French Grandes Écoles, which used to prepare their students for military life, including the calculation of artillery trajectories, now anticipate the entrance of graduates into business or the economic side of government. On the other hand, economic growth in Austria has been great despite the decline in prestige of her once-great universities, a decline most marked perhaps in medicine but ramifying beyond that field.

The difficulty in identifying the residuals in Europe with education or investment in human capital may be the result of too short a time horizon, and it may still be true that Britain needs more colleges of engineering and business administration to stimulate growth, whereas German education could adopt a less utilitarian bias. But it is awkward on the scanty evidence to make the case that education is the strategic factor, differences in which account for differences in European rates of growth in our period.

Technological Progress

Technological progress is another elusive concept that is difficult to measure statistically. It is possible to count engineers, expenditure on research and development, and even inventions without having a clear idea of the rapidity of technical advance.

4. *Ibid.*, p. 21.

But it is ridiculous to adopt the view that because you cannot measure it, it does not exist. Countries evidently do proceed at different paces in technology, both in imitating the technology available in the rest of the world and in devising their own. And these differences seem to have an impact on relative rates of growth.

The assertion has been made that since the technical possibilities open to European countries are substantially similar, technical progress cannot be given an independent role in explaining economic growth in 1950's.[5] This assumes first that technical progress proceeds only through imitation — except perhaps for one outside country like the United States — and that imitation is automatic and advances at a pace of its own which is necessarily uniform between countries. Neither assumption is valid. While it is true that much of European rapid growth vis-à-vis the United States has consisted in imitation, entrepreneurs have been readier to imitate in some countries than in others, and there have been invention and innovation as well.

European imitation has been important. It has been regarded as a cause of the European balance-of-payments surplus and the United States deficit, especially from 1958 to 1961 when there was doubt about the competitiveness of United States exports. According to this reasoning, equilibrium had been achieved with levels of costs and prices which took account of faster technical progress in the United States than in Europe before and immediately after the war. When European imitation picked up and narrowed the technical gap, the pre-existing set of costs and prices left post-1949 exchange rates undervalued.[6]

European narrowing of the technological gap has also been important for faster growth in Europe than in the United States. The spread of modern technology to Europe was retarded by difficulties in recovering after the two world wars; but once these

5. Angus Maddison, *Economic Growth in the West* (New York: Twentieth Century Fund, 1964), p. 81.

6. See my "The Cause and Cure of the United States Balance of Payments Disequilibrium" (written in 1960), in *Europe and the Dollar* (Cambridge, Mass.: M.I.T. Press, 1966); P. A. Samuelson, *Stability and Growth in the American Economy* (Stockholm: Almqvist & Wiksell, 1963), pp. 46–47; H. G. Johnson, *Economic Growth and Public Policy* (McLean Lecture at Ontario Agricultural College, 1963), pp. 4–5.

difficulties had been overcome, using the large backlog that had been built up worked productivity miracles. The process was aided under the Marshall Plan by productivity teams—Europeans visiting the United States and United States experts touring Europe. It was also assisted by United States direct investment in Europe and by licensing of American technology to European business.

It is not clear why imitation should be thought to proceed equally in all countries. The opportunities for imitation are surely different when one country, with destruction, imitates with complete plants and another can only piece out existing equipment with particular items (see above, p. 130). Or technological progress may be slow in certain industries producing standardized materials in an unchanging way, as the Belgians claim is true of their specialties (see p. 74). The will to imitate may differ, too. It is probably impossible to demonstrate that the British drive to imitate is lower than that of France, Italy, or Germany, but casual empiricism supports the view. Finally, the blocks to imitation may vary from country to country, as trade unions here resist changes in productive techniques and others there do not. It is hardly a random event that the book on persuading trade unions to accept productivity improvements should be written about the experience of an American company in Britain (see p. 81n.). The same company either felt no need to change its output and wage practices in other countries in Europe, had less difficulty in getting changes accepted, or, least likely, lacked an equal historian. Resistance to technical change is partly a function of national labor attitudes, which may depend upon the labor supply. But technical progress based on imitation can surely differ from country to country.

A variant of the view that the same technology is available to the world suggests that industries everywhere are divided into two classes as Mrs. Lutz divides them in Italy: Class I, or modern industry, where the same techniques are used ubiquitously regardless of factor proportions and factor prices, and Class II, which embraces artisan and handicraft enterprises and where productivities differ widely. Rapid productivity growth consists of shifting a country's industrial weight from Class II to Class I, as Mrs. Lutz maintains has been true in Italy and as Norman

Macrae claims would have taken place in Britain had it not been for interruptions in demand. But ECE studies do not bear out this contention. Labor productivity, which is the only available measure of technical progress, and which as an index suffers from failure to eliminate the impact of capital, differs more widely for given sectors and for given branches within manufacturing than it does for sectors and branches within a given country.[7] Labor productivity in all countries moves faster, on the average, for chemicals than for textiles, and for metal-making and -using industry than for food, drink, and tobacco. Nonetheless, labor productivity in chemicals grew at 1.3 percent per year in Austria and 1.8 percent in Denmark, as opposed to 11.2 percent in Italy and 7.6 percent in Germany, and the rate of increase in productivity in food, drink, and tobacco in Italy at 7.2 percent was higher than the highest metal-making and -using figure, 6.6 percent, again in Italy.[8]

Moreover, the pattern by which inventions occurred virtually at random but innovations got under way in the United States and spread by imitation to Europe lost much of its force after the war. French technical virtuosity in aircraft, automobiles, computers, desulphurization, glass-making, electricity transmission, machine tools, and railroad locomotion has been discussed elsewhere and referred to above (p. 60).[9] One could also mention optical jigs, earth-moving equipment, nuclear fission, and electrogenerating equipment. France's percentage of GNP devoted to research and development in 1960 is so low as to evoke surprise, especially in view of relatively high French expenditures for defense, which may use up as much as 40 percent of research and development funds. The percentage at 1.1 compared to 2.5 for Britain may be understated, but the innovations of commercial utility are undeniable.[10]

Other innovative activity in Europe is more questionable. The

7. ECE, *Some Factors in Economic Growth in Europe,* chap. 3, Tables A-8, 11.
8. *Ibid.,* pp. 57, 15.
9. See my essay, "The Postwar Resurgence of the French Economy," in Stanley Hoffmann *et al., In Search of France* (Cambridge, Mass.: Harvard University Press, 1963), pp. 148 ff.
10. ECE, *Some Factors in Economic Growth in Europe,* Table V-1, p. V-5.

Austrian contributions in oxygen process for steel and in sintering metallurgy have been mentioned in Chapter III. The first was widely applied in Germany. Switzerland and Sweden have reputations for turning out high-quality products of technical ingenuity. German continuous rolling equipment installed during the war was the envy of Britain, along with the large presses in the Volkswagen plant at Wolfsburg. But these were mere extensions of American techniques. The major innovation, partly negative, was the Volkswagen itself and the refusal to embody annual design changes, making a virtue out of the original necessity to amortize jigs over a large number of stampings. The Volkswagen Microbus, the NSU Wankel gas-turbine engine, the vacuum process in metal coating, and continuous improvement of chemical products, synthetic fibers, and electrogeneration equipment qualify Germany as an innovative country despite its lag, partly imposed by the Allies, in computers, nuclear science, and aircraft. Italy scored in design rather than in new products, though the scooter opened up a new market at home and abroad.

It is worth noting that preliminary IFO studies on German productivity, largely labor productivity, show very fast progress in Germany in petrochemicals and in electrogeneration but relatively slow progress in the fastest-growing export branch, machinery.[11]

The opposite side of the coin is the difficulty in finding substantial British innovations during the period. The Calder Hall design for a nuclear-energy power facility was an early one quickly rendered obsolete. A number of failures have been recorded in the aircraft and missile field, failures of design and effective production. An outstanding success to put in the scales is the Pilkington process for producing flat glass by flotation, a process which rendered a brand-new French plant in the United States obsolete.

There is thus something to be said for the possibility that technical progress played an independent role, including both imitation and innovation. This would hardly be true of the Mediterranean countries, where imitation took place, to be sure, but the gap between average technology in these countries and best practice in the United States probably widened rather than

11. Interview, IFO-Institut für Wirtschaftforschung, 1964.

narrowed. And it is difficult to embrace Scandinavia, the Netherlands, or Switzerland in a theory which ascribes much weight to technology. There may be something to Belgium's being held back by its preponderant weight in industries with slow technical progress; to British entrepreneurs' and labor's resistance to change; and to French, German, and Italian entrepreneurs' (including in the French and Italian cases, at least, governmental entrepreneurs) effectiveness in both narrowing the technical gap with the rest of the world and branching off on their own.

For lack of data, it is hard to evaluate the importance of these differences in technical advance. It is probably positive, but not substantial.

Economies of Scale

As already mentioned, the IFO-Institut für Wirtschaftforschung in Munich has estimated a model of economic growth for Germany that indicates the presence of important economies of scale, alongside a modest rate of technical progress. More than a hundred regressions were run before arriving at an equation

$$Q = \text{constant}\, f\, (K^{0.34}\, L^{0.75}\, M^{0.23}\, e^{0.02t})$$

where Q is real output, K is capital, L is labor employed, M is imports, and e is a technical progress factor (trend) of 2 percent a year. Since the coefficients of K, L, and M add to more than 1.0, the model shows increasing returns to scale. The model was estimated for the 22 years ending in 1957 (apart from the war gap) but is said to show a good fit for the period from 1957 to 1961. As a supply model, it is based upon the assumption that everything produced is demanded. Changes in income distribution make little difference to either consumption or investment. Investment is a simple linear function of output, without lags. The function ignores not only the gap from 1938 to 1950 but also the changes in the geographic area of Germany.[12]

The methods used by the IFO-Institut have not gone unchallenged, and the principal criticism has been leveled against the use of pre- and postwar data for different areas in fitting a single

12. See K. C. Kühlo, "Bases for an Analysis of Growth," *German Economic Review*, II (4th Quarter 1964), 289–297. My observations are also based on an interview at the IFO-Institut, 1964.

production function.[13] There seems to be little doubt that the "residual," that is, the positive difference between the rate of growth of output and that of weighted inputs of labor and capital, was small prior to the war and substantial afterwards.[14] But the question of economies of scale must be left for further resolution by the statisticians insofar as Germany is concerned, and economies of scale in other countries remain to be demonstrated.

One hypothesis for this subsequent testing would be that economies of scale prevail in certain sectors of the economy, though not in others, and that the Class I industries of Mrs. Lutz or the durable consumer goods cited by Macrae have increasing returns while others do not. The presumption, however, is that nothing of any generality can be demonstrated. Chemicals and metal-using industries tend on the whole to have faster growth rates in Europe than food, drink, and tobacco, or textiles, clothing, and footwear, or timber and furniture, or leather and rubber. But shares in output of chemicals and metal-using industries are not widely different between Germany and Britain or in the slower-growing categories named, and rates of growth in Germany have been as high as or higher than British rates in the soft goods, as shown in Table VII-1.

Competition

Reference has also been made to Sohmen's theory that economic growth is a function of the degree of competition.[15] Supposedly competition spurs growth through improved efficiency in resource allocation. Where prices are set competitively and enterprise responds vigorously to the dictates of the price system, one gets an approximation not only of static optimum but also of dynamic. Sohmen has mainly asserted his view in com-

13. E. Helmstaedter, "Steigende Skalenerträge der deutschen Wirtschaft," *Jahrbücher für Nationalökonomie und Statistik,* CLXXV (December 1963), 473–500. The article criticized was C. Gehrig and K. C. Kühlo, "Okonometrische Analyse des Produktionsprozesses," *IFO-Studien,* No. 7 (1961), pp. 175–237. Cited by D. Willey, "Changes in British and German Manufacturing Productivity, 1951–62" (preliminary and summary draft of a dissertation submitted to the International Economics Workshop, Columbia University, 1965) p. 76.

14. Willey, "Changes in British and German Manufacturing," p. 48.

15. Egon Sohmen, "Competition and Growth: The Lesson of West Germany," *American Economic Review,* XLIX (December 1959), 986–1003.

TABLE VII-1

German and British rates of growth and shares in manufacturing, 1949–1959, for selected branches

	Median rate of growth in Europe, Canada, and United States (percent per annum)	Share in manufacturing (percent of total)		Rate of growth (percent per annum)		Ratio of German rate of growth to British
		German	British	German	British	
Chemicals	9.3	12.1	9.0	12.8	6.8	2.1
Metal-using industry	6.7	32.7	40.6	13.5	4.2	3.2
Leather and rubber	4.3	2.6	1.5	9.1	4.0	2.3
Food, drink, and tobacco	3.6	11.3	11.0	9.7	2.2	4.2
Timber and furniture	3.1	3.6	2.7	5.9	2.4	2.5
Textiles, clothing, and footwear	2.7	15.0	14.1	7.2	0.2	36.0

Source: ECE, *Some Factors in Economic Growth in Europe during the 1950's* (United Nations: Geneva, 1964), chap. 3, Tables 7–8, pp. III-12 and III-13.

paring Germany and the United States and has not attempted to apply it in detail to the separate countries of Europe except for some references to Britain. But even the narrower statement of the doctrine has been sharply attacked on a variety of grounds: that the German government interfered with the functioning of the price system in many areas such as rent, savings, and bottleneck sectors; that the capital market does not function competitively; that his argument proceeds by eliminating successive reasons until only one is left; that he fails to deal with Henry Wallich's conclusion that trust-busting was not a success; that he neglects the growth of the labor supply; and that he fails to take into account the low proportion of consumption and high proportion of net investment in national income (the comparison of gross investment being misleading because of low levels of replacement in Germany).[16]

Sohmen's contention also suffers from its inapplicability outside

16. On the capital market, see K. W. Roskamp, "Comment," *American Economic Review*, L (December 1960), 1015–1018; on labor supply, A. I. MacBean and W. G. Shepherd, "Comment," *ibid.*, pp. 1018–1022; on net investment, R. G. Opie, "Comment," *ibid.*, pp. 1022–1025. See also Egon Sohmen, "Reply," *ibid.*, pp. 1025–1031.

the Germany-United States context and perhaps the Germany-United Kingdom one. Fast-growing Austria has little in the way of perfect competition, and much of Italian and French growth took place in industries and plants owned, operated, or controlled by government. Slow-growing Belgium is not notoriously monopoly ridden. And so on. Moreover, his 1959 forecast (probably written in 1958) that German growth would slow down because of reconcentration and a massive merger movement was premature, to say the least, and runs contrary to the French position where mergers have been part of the growth mechanism. The functional relations between monopoly and growth are not fully worked out, although it is clearly right that competition can energize stagnant industries riddled with restrictive business practices. Sohmen may be correct that differential monopoly contributed to differential rates of growth in Europe, especially in the Germany-United Kingdom comparison, but it is necessary to render the Scots verdict of "not proven."

Entrepreneurship

In Schumpeter's analysis, the entrepreneurial function was innovation. On this basis it has already been discussed. But another entrepreneurial function of great importance is business organization. The point can be made that the supply of keen business enterprisers who are concerned to produce efficiently, with minimum cost and maximum profit, differs from country to country. Some evidence on the differences between France and Britain has been presented elsewhere, and it is known that the postwar change of heart of French entrepreneurs made them turn away from mere preservation of family enterprises to more dynamic effort in expansion and greater readiness to accept change.[17]

Here again, the leading countries of Europe have been studied, but not the smaller ones. German entrepreneurship was distinguished for the enormous effort it put out during the first half of the 1950's, though this tapered off as the decade neared its end.[18] The urge to reconstruct, to restore economic and social

17. See my *Economic Growth in France and Britain, 1851–1950* (Cambridge, Mass.: Harvard University Press, 1964), chap. 6, and my "Postwar Resurgence of the French Economy," pp. 148 ff.

18. Henry C. Wallich, *Mainsprings of the German Revival* (New Haven: Yale University Press, 1955), chap. 12.

position, to reaccumulate capital, is a well-known one. Jesse Pitts, the sociologist, remarks that the French aristocracy is uninterested in economic matters except when it has lost a fortune through some misadventure, at which time it buckles down with energy and determination.[19] This is the obverse, perhaps, of the Duesenberry effect, under which a family that suffers a loss in income has difficulty in adjusting its consumption downward and is left with greater consumption and less savings than a family which approached the same level of income from below.

Outside of Germany, France, and Britain modern entrepreneurship has been studied but little.[20] In Italy, the names of Professor Valetta of FIAT and the late Sr. Mattei of ENI, the nationalized oil enterprise, stand out as prominent islands in a sea of ignorance. But there is little of a solid basis to enable one to judge whether Belgium and Scandinavia had a different and inferior quality of entrepreneurship compared to Austria, Italy, Spain, and Greece.

One interesting contrast has been adverted to in the country sketches: the success of Austria and more recently Germany and Switzerland in adopting capital-intensive techniques in investment as compared with Britain's failure in the same connection. Part of the British failure may be owing to the country's investment in small marginal increments rather than large quantum jumps called for by destruction. But only part. British entrepreneurship had the incentive of sharply rising labor costs to move in capital-deepening rather than capital-widening ways, and it seems to have failed to do so. Evidence exists in all countries that capital-widening — more of the same — is an easier type of investment to undertake than new and different methods. There is evidence that Germany, and belatedly Switzerland, have responded to rising wage rates by adopting labor-saving innovations. It has been suggested to me, for example, that Swiss inter-

19. Jesse R. Pitts, "French Values and Their Implementation by Social Classes before World War II" (seminar paper, Center for International Affairs, Harvard University, 1957); Pitts, "The Bourgeois Family and French Economic Retardation" (Ph.D. thesis, Harvard University, 1957).

20. David Granick, *The European Executive* (New York: Doubleday, 1962), deals largely with Britain, France, and Germany. The earlier study of F. H. Harbison and E. W. Burgess, "Modern Management in Western Europe," *Journal of Sociology*, LX (July 1954), 15–23, compares French, Belgian, and Italian entrepreneurs with American.

est in labor-saving machinery has been increasing, though it is still not very large, and that the United States exposition of automation in Zurich in 1963 made a big impression on Swiss businessmen.[21]

In Austria, however, capital-deepening was adopted without the stimulus of high labor costs. Investment was deepening rather than widening not because of effective entrepreneurial adaptation to relative factor prices but as an independent phenomenon associated with German project designs, Russian removals, and the United States aid.[22] Austrian entrepreneurship followed the path of least resistance into projects of steel sheet and artificial fiber which had been laid out by the Germans for their own operation with their own needs and resources in mind.

Again, therefore, differences in the quality of entrepreneurship may explain a lot, but there are large gaps in the information needed to establish the case. The Austrian counterexample suggests the danger in leaning too heavily on a one-dimensional explanation.

Government Intervention

At an early stage of the discussion in Britain, I. M. D. Little brought out a book entitled *The Price of Fuel* (Oxford: Clarendon Press, 1953) which made the effective point that nationalized industry in Britain was wasting resources by setting the overall price of coal too low and failing to establish the appropriate differentials among different grades. In addition, the Central Electricity Authority has been accused of encouraging the misuse of electricity by holding down prices to domestic users and holding up the price for industrial consumption, with the result that productive use of power was discouraged and its expensive use of space-heating encouraged. Sir Robert Shone and H. R. Fisher in fact have held the different practices in the pricing of publicly owned industry in Britain and the Continent to be one of the factors responsible for the slow growth of pro-

21. Interview, Zurich, 1964. It is said that Swiss peasants have motorized their little plots and rigged plastic pipelines to carry milk from summer pastures in the Alps to the village. Labor and horses are gone, but the capital/labor ratio is less than optimal, and in many instances there has been mechanization without cost reduction.

22. Interview, Austrian Institute of Economic Research, Vienna, 1964.

ductivity in the United Kingdom.[23] The point goes well beyond national ownership: French nationalized industry, especially in aircraft, automobiles, electricity, gas, and railroads, and possibly in coal, is acknowledged to be efficient and has in fact developed sophisticated techniques for evaluating investment projects.[24] In Britain, on the other hand, it has been stated that governmental techniques for checking investment proposals by the nationalized industries are rudimentary and that nothing like adequate cost-benefit analysis is undertaken.[25] On both scores, then, the pricing of output and the calculation of inputs, there are differences in governmental efficiency.

While the record of Britain was admittedly weak up to the second half of the 1950's, that of the Continent was not perfect. The most flagrant violation of price efficiency — violation in the sense of ignoring marginal costs — has been in coal. Coal prices have been held low for the benefit of consumers, and efficient mines have been taxed to subsidize the inefficient, virtually since the creation of the European Coal and Steel Community in 1950.[26] The record of the Community in steel is not bad, but that in coal has been appalling, with support of the Belgian coal mines of the Borinage long after the 5-year period of grace to which they were entitled, failure to carry out the mandate to permit competition within the Community, and return of the problem to the nations, which moved away from the efficient, international solution by keeping out cheap American coal and by taxing cheap imports of fuel oil. Waste in agriculture exists in every country. And just as the British government supported the fish industry, which according to Macrae should have been allowed to expire because of its inefficiency, so the German and

23. Sir Robert Shone and H. R. Fisher, "Industrial Production and Steel Consumption," *Journal of the Royal Statistical Society*, Series A, CXXI, Pt. 3 (1958), 293. Cited by PEP, *Growth in the British Economy: A Study of Economic Problems and Policies in Contemporary Britain* (London: George Allen & Unwin, 1960).

24. Pierre Masse, *Le choix des investissements: Critères et méthodes* (2d ed.; Paris: Dunod, 1964).

25. See P. D. Henderson, "The Use of Economists in British Administration," *Oxford Economic Papers*, XIII (February 1961), 5-26.

26. Richard L. Gordon, "Coal Pricing and the Energy Problem in the European Community" (Ph.D. thesis, Massachusetts Institute of Technology, 1960).

French governments subsidized shipbuilding, housing, handicrafts, agriculture, and, in the case of the German government, West Berlin.[27] Karl Roskamp claims that on balance the German government contributed to the efficiency of capital formation by its intervention — a claim which could not be made for British governmental direction — but much of the intervention was designedly wasteful, involving subsidies to various interests, even though it probably reduced rather than fostered equity in the system.[28] And despite the rationalizations of *Sozialmarktwirtschaft* after the fact, it seems correct that German intervention like French was empirical rather than based on doctrine. When British, French, and German governments all intervene on an *ad hoc* basis, and French and German intervention by and large helped whereas British did not, it is possible to blame the nature and skill of the intervention. A more likely interpretation, however, would ascribe the differences in outcome to deeper-seated forces which intervention did not affect seriously in any of the three countries.

One debating point can be made against the view that the differential rates of growth in Europe are ascribable to differences in efficiency emanating from competition, entrepreneurship, or the character of governmental enterprise and intervention in private enterprise. It is this: on no *a priori* basis can the character of enterprise or the skill of governmental intervention be judged higher in Portugal, Spain, and Greece than in Belgium, Britain, or Scandinavia, and yet the growth rates are an order of magnitude higher. (Admittedly a comparison of rates of growth at very different levels of income has only limited significance.) For skill of government it is difficult to set a higher standard than the Scandinavian countries unless one takes the view that they are disposed to overintervene on socialist doctrinal grounds — and the capital/output ratio in Norway gives grounds for disquiet at the least. But surely their entrepreneurs are more responsive to economic stimuli, and their experience with intervention in government has brought them to a very advanced point in this

27. See Frederick G. Reuss, *Fiscal Policy for Growth without Inflation: The German Experiment* (Baltimore: Johns Hopkins Press, 1963), chap. 15.
28. K. W. Roskamp, *Capital Formation in West Germany* (Detroit: Wayne State University Press, 1965), p. 208.

area, especially taking into account the homogeneity of viewpoint and political and economic discipline of these countries (less in Belgium perhaps than elsewhere) in the early postwar years.

Economic efficiency is an elusive subject. There may be something to the case that the free-market economies have been more efficient than the Socialist — though the Netherlands and France "plan," and Germany, Italy, and Austria are not that "free." The subject is full of interesting topics of investigation, but one has the feeling that many of them lead in circles like the trails of a cottontail rabbit. The possibility that differential rates of growth in Europe have been the result of differences in technical progress or in the "overall efficiency" of the economy, apart from redistribution of labor among sectors of the economy, cannot be ruled out as an explanation, but it is not highly persuasive. Let us leave it in suspense and proceed to discuss the labor market.

CHAPTER VIII

National Labor Markets

The domestic and foreign aspects of the labor supply in a country cannot properly be separated. As we have seen, international migration can alter the mobility of the domestic labor supply, either through upgrading native workers, as in Switzerland, or through returning former emigrants to different regions and occupations from those from which they set out, as in Italy and Greece. But while the distinction is analytically overdrawn, it is convenient in exposition and is used to separate this chapter from the next.

The Domestic Elasticity of the Labor Supply

Elasticity of the labor supply can be regarded either overall or in particular expanding or contracting sectors of the economy. Overall, the major domestic factors touched upon have been unemployment for Germany and Italy, underemployment in Portugal, Spain, and Greece, and a high rate of natural increase in the Netherlands and the Mediterranean countries. For given sectors, the major force in all countries has been the movement of labor out of agriculture and small independent operations into larger-scale manufacturing and services. It is perhaps time to deal with elasticity more systematically, however, and to break down the domestic factors into: (1) the natural rate of increase, which determines, with a lag, the population of working age, 15–64; (2) participation rates, which determine the percentage of the population of working age that constitutes the labor force; and (3) within the total, the rate of unemployment, with the complex subsidiary questions of open unemployment, disguised unemployment, and underemployment. These factors operate on the total elasticity. With regard to the elasticity affecting particular sectors, there is additionally the question of mobility — itself capable of division into mobility of those already employed (which can be from firm to firm, occupational, and geographical), and the higher mobility of entrants into the labor market. All these factors affect the numbers at work. The total labor input, moreover, is finally affected by the hours worked, which raises questions of the work week, overtime, and vacations.[1]

These matters cannot be dealt with fully in a short chapter. It is useful, however, to remind the reader of the OECD studies on manpower, which seek to order the statistics from country to country to make them comparable.[2] A table prepared by the ECE covers the sources of manpower from 1953 to 1962 in Belgium, Germany, the Netherlands, Norway, and the United Kingdom — a limited assortment of countries for which complete data can be assembled. Unhappily neither exception to the Lewis model among the developed countries (Austria or France) nor any of the less developed countries is included. The table (used here as VIII-1) shows the complexity of the sources of labor overall, including immigrants. Even so, it fails to make the distinction between independent workers and employees that went into Table II-3, above, on Germany.

The natural rate of increase has been substantial and steady in the Netherlands, substantial but declining in Italy and the other Mediterranean countries, rising in France (which experienced a demographic revival after World War II), and positive but low elsewhere in Europe. Germany and to a lesser degree France have gaps in their population tree, especially in males in the 40–50 age group. The mid-1960's bring a limited pickup in new entrants into the labor force, as the postwar increase in birth rate, after the wartime decline, begins to have its effect. Large rates of natural increase in the future, however, are excluded for all but the Netherlands and France.

Participation rates follow different patterns from country to country, especially for young people, depending on schooling, and women, depending on a variety of factors. Table VIII-2

1. For a review of some literature on the work week and vacations, largely on France, see Guy Berger, "De Quelques Travaux Recents sur La Reduction de la Durée de Travail," in *Bulletin Sedeis* (Société d'Études et de Documentation Economiques, Industrielles et Sociales), No. 924 (July 1965), Supplément (Bibliographie).

2. OECD, *Manpower Statistics, 1950–1962* (Paris, 1963).

TABLE VIII-1

Sources of manpower in selected western European countries, 1953–1962

(thousands)

Country and year	Change in civilian employment	Source of supply of civilian employment: Decrease in unemployment	Source of supply of civilian employment: Decrease in the armed forces	Source of supply of civilian employment: Increase in the active population	Determinants of the increase in the active population: Demographic factors and migration	Determinants of the increase in the active population: Changes in activity rates
Belgium						
1953	−25	−9	−10	−6	6	−12
1954	21	11	−1	11	3	8
1955	44	42	5	−3	1	−4
1956	40	38	10	−8	−4	−4
1957	34	18	10	6	−3	9
1958	−30	−37	6	1	1	—
1959	−29	−22	1	−8	−1	−7
1960	21	22	3	−4	1	−5
1961	46	25	4	17	5	12
1962	34	40	4	−10	7	−17
Western Germany						
1953	515	120	—	395	325	70
1954	565	40	−5	530	387	143
1955	830	290	−5	545	378	167
1956	585	170	−20	435	371	64
1957	450	100	−85	435	135	300
1958	165	−20	−45	230	250	−20
1959	230	205	−55	80	182	−102
1960	400	240	−65	225	120	105
1961	355	80	−50	325	159	166
1962	280	20	−30	290	180	110

Netherlands						
1953	59	36	–20	43	25	18
1954	99	28	–14	85	33	52
1955	85	21	2	62	40	22
1956	81	13	2	66	41	25
1957	46	– 12	2	56	40	16
1958	– 29	– 46	3	14	52	– 38
1959	55	21	1	33	55	– 22
1960	75	28	– 2	49	46	3
1961	72	14	– 1	59	70	– 11
1962	68	5	—	63	96	– 33
Norway						
1953	– 3	– 2	– 1	—	5	– 5
1954	6	1	– 1	6	7	– 1
1955	9	1	– 3	11	9	2
1956	—	– 2	2	—	7	– 7
1957	7	– 1	– 3	11	9	2
1958	– 10	– 9	– 2	1	10	– 9
1959	6	1	1	4	12	– 8
1960	15	6	—	9	8	1
1961	18	4	1	13	5	8
1962	14	– 2	—	16	7	9
United Kingdom						
1953	121	34	7	80	8	72
1954	378	55	26	297	9	288
1955	329	46	36	247	14	233
1956	220	– 17	42	195	– 10	205
1957	92	– 47	59	80	16	64
1958	–182	–144	88	–126	58	–184
1959	122	– 6	49	79	117	– 38
1960	438	95	47	296	134	162
1961	291	36	44	211	144	67
1962	170	–122	32	260	343	– 83

Source: ECE, *Economic Survey of Europe in 1962*, Pt. I: *The European Economy in 1962* (Geneva: United Nations, 1963), chap. 2, p. 22.

TABLE VIII-2

European school enrollment ratios by age groups, ca. 1958

	Percent of age group enrolled	
	15–19	20–24
Norway	36	10
Sweden	32	11
Belgium	32	6
Netherlands	33	5
France	31	4
Switzerland	23	3
Denmark	19	6
Germany	18	5
United Kingdom	18	4
Greece	17	3
Italy	16	4
Austria	13	4
Spain	13	3
Portugal	9	3
Turkey	3	1

Source: ECE, *Some Factors in Economic Growth in Europe during the 1950's* (Geneva: United Nations, 1964), chap. 5, Table 11, p. 11.

shows the variety of European experience with respect to schooling in 1958 or thereabouts. Increasing private and public attention to education has raised the compulsory school-leaving age and increased voluntary interest in secondary and university study to reduce the percentage of youths in the labor force. The proportion of youth in school is clearly related to the level of income reached but much less certainly to the rate of change in income.

Table VIII-3 shows the changing participation percentage of women in the labor force from 1950 (in some cases only 1954 or 1955) to 1961. The very high percentage for Turkey is misleading, since most of the Turkish labor force is engaged in agriculture, where female participation is taken to be complete. In other countries, the range is still wide, from 57 percent in Austria to 20 percent in Portugal. The strong social disapproval of women working in the Netherlands has been mentioned earlier.

TABLE VIII-3

Percentage of women participating in the labor force, 1950 and 1961

	1950	1961
Turkey	—	70.7
Austria	51.8	57.2
Sweden	n.a.	53.2[a]
Denmark	50.3 (1955)	51.9
Germany	48.5 (1955)	49.3
United Kingdom	42.9	48.8
France	47.2 (1954)	45.6
Switzerland	39.1	42.0 (1960)
Greece	—	38.9
Belgium	33.4	37.1
Norway	36.3	35.5
Italy	24.7 (1954)	32.4
Netherlands	28.8 (1954)	30.0 (1957)
Spain	17.4	20.9
Portugal	25.9	20.6 (1960)

Source: OECD, *Manpower Statistics, 1950–1962* (Paris, 1963).
[a] OECD, Manpower and Social Affairs Division, *Labour Market Policy in Sweden* (Paris, 1963), p. 23, states that participation rates for women rose from 30 percent to 40 percent in the 1950's and are likely to rise to 50 percent in the 1960's.

Participation of women in the labor force in Italy is low but increasing. What is perhaps most striking is the failure of any clear-cut pattern to emerge, related either to levels of development, as in Table VIII-2, or to region. In Scandinavia, Sweden and Denmark have high rates of participation; the Danish is rising, while the Norwegian is much lower and falling. Spanish and Portuguese rates are low as befits a Latin culture but, if the figures can be believed, are moving in different directions. The major gains in female participation were in Austria, a fast grower, and Britain, a slow one. Some part of the increases may have taken place in part-time work, especially in Italy.

The ECE maintains that activity rates act as a safety valve, changing to bring the active proportion into line with demographic realities. In the United Kingdom, with frequent changes as shown in the last column of Table VIII-1, the elasticity is in men at the ages of entering and leaving the labor force, 15–19 and 60–69, married women from 15 to 24, and single women at all ages except 20–29, when participation rates are already high. This may be true in the United Kingdom, where youthful employment and affluence have been a feature of the postwar period. For most of the Continent, however, higher rates of school enrollment and a rising trend limit elasticity of males at the youthful end of the market; more education and lower marriage ages reduce it for young women; work for older women in much of the Continent, especially the Netherlands and the Latin countries, is subject to social disapproval. Everywhere there is a lack of part-time jobs, which have been a feature of the postwar employment market for women in the United States.

It is difficult, therefore, to find a very high degree of labor elasticity based on domestic factors, apart from various forms of unemployment, except in the countries of rapid population increase — the Netherlands, the Mediterranean countries, and prospectively France — and in those countries where there has been a substantial rise in women at work, Austria and Britain. But in the last case, with males actually declining, and women and immigrants from the Commonwealth representing the entire gain, the quality of the labor force has fallen.

The major elasticity factor of the prewar period — unemployment — existed abundantly in Germany after the influx of expellees and refugees and in Italy despite debate over the exact numbers.[3] The underemployment of the Mediterranean countries, including Italy, has also been discussed, along with the measurement controversy it evokes. Some considerable unemployment existed in Belgium from 1950 to 1954, averaging 180,000 out of a labor force of 3,500,000, or more than 5 percent. This held down wages during the period, but demand was lacking. Once the demand picked up, growth followed, and beginning in 1955 unemployment declined sharply.

Unemployment was excluded in Britain, the Netherlands, and Scandinavia by a political consensus that was resolved to fend

3. See the 5-part, 15-volume proceedings of the Italian Commissione Parlamentare di Inchiesta sulla Disoccupazione (Rome: Atti, 1953); summarized and analyzed in "*Quaderni*" *della Rassegna di Statistiche del Lavoro*, Quaderno VIII (March 1954).

off the experience of the 1930's. For the Netherlands this made little difference for the labor supply, given the safety valve of high natural increase *cum* emigration, which was gradually allowed to languish. For Britain and Scandinavia, however, limited unemployment maintained by high internal demand meant that the labor supply had low overall elasticity. It is wrong to conclude, as Paish comes close to doing, that British growth could be stimulated by cutting back and producing unemployment. Repressing demand obviously reduces the rate of growth. What is called for to achieve the supergrowth enjoyed by the Continent is more demand, preferably provided from abroad or obtained abroad (through income-elastic or price-elastic exports and rising output plus falling costs in exports), plus some unemployed or other source of elastic labor supply, already in existence or created out of thin air.

Unemployment is frequently taken to be the single most important variable in determining the course of wages. A. W. Phillips' pioneering study of the relations between the level of unemployment and the percentage increase in the price level is the best-known formulation of the point.[4] As shown in Table VIII-4, an international Phillips curve developed for 5 countries in Europe (and 3 outside, which we discard) reveals an excellent correlation between rate of increase in wages and unemployment across the 5 countries. However, the statistical basis of the unemployment figures is weak, and the wages fail to reflect uncertain amounts of wage drift. Moreover, it is difficult analytically to see why the Phillips relationship should be expected to hold exactly for different countries with different degrees of labor mobility and readiness to import migrant labor. Rather, different countries would be expected *a priori* to have the curvature or kink in the nonlinear function occur at different stretches. It will be remembered, for example, that Paish believed that the price level would not rise at all above 2.25 percent unemployment. Table II-6 above shows the Italian unemployment rate on the ISTAT basis reaching 3 percent in 1962 (6 percent on the Ministry of Labor calculations) when the wage rate began its 42 percent rise in 2 years.

4. A. W. Phillips, "The Relation between Unemployment and the Rate of Change of Money Wages in the United Kingdom," *Economica*, XXV (November 1958), 283–299.

TABLE VIII-4

The Phillips relationship in Europe, 1960[a]

	Wages (percentage increase)	Unemployment (percent of labor force)
Germany	10.0	1.0
France	7.1	1.9
Sweden	6.9	1.7
United Kingdom	6.0	2.4
Italy	4.2	4.3

Source: Joseph W. Gabarino, "Income Policy and Income Behavior," in Arthur M. Ross (ed.), *Employment Policy and the Labor Market* (Berkeley and Los Angeles: University of California Press, 1965), p. 66.

[a] The figures for unemployment are for 1960; the increase in wages is the 1961 index less the 1959 index divided by twice the relative for 1960.

If we shift from the total economy to a disaggregated basis, domestic elasticity of the labor supply is great for some industries and low for others. It is important to distinguish between expansion and contraction. In unskilled occupations — domestic service, menial service in hotels, restaurants, or municipal sanitation, agriculture, mining, construction, and some dirty or unpleasant jobs in metal-making and metal-using — elasticity may be high for relative demand decreases and low for increases. In less disfavored industries, on the other hand, elasticity of the labor supply turns on the mobility of domestic labor: mobility which can be distinguished in a number of ways, by business unit, occupation, and region.

Loyalty to the business unit, generally the family enterprise, makes for reduced labor mobility. In countries at early stages of development, loyalty to the family is translated into following in the father's occupation and unwillingness to leave the family farm or business. At a later stage, there may be loyalty of the "faithful retainer" to the family enterprise at a much larger and more efficient scale of operation, with equally negative effects on mobility. It is difficult to prove a weakening of these loyalties, apart from the decline in the French family firm, but it is virtually self-evident.[5] The European data for testing firm mobility

5. See, for example, Alessandro Pizzorno, "The Individualistic Mobilization of Europe," and Alain Touraine, "Management and the Working Class

are limited. In Britain, turnover in manufacturing industries involves between 30 and 40 percent of the labor force, and in France the movement is about 20 percent.[6] While new government research on labor mobility is under way in France and Britain, OECD studies have adduced little on these countries and nothing on the rest of the Continent that would compare, for example, with the data for the United States. A 30 percent turnover a year, however, should provide room for shifting the labor force and suggests that loyalty to the firm is not an inhibiting factor.[7]

Occupational mobility has improved with the spread of mass production and the breakdown of craft skills. The apprentice system continues in Europe, but semiskilled labor is increasingly flexible as a consequence of greater familiarity with machinery on the farm and in daily consumption. Here again there may be some asymmetry, with older workers much less mobile because of rapid obsolescence of skills and because perquisites such as extra holidays must be given up if seniority is lost. Occupational mobility is very much in the minds of national and international labor officials, and training and retraining schemes are expanding rapidly. Statistical demonstration of what occupational mobility is and how it has changed is difficult if not impossible. Spatial mobility within countries for domestic workers differs from country to country and is linked to regional loyalty or the lack of it, to channels of mobility, availability of housing, and a host of other factors. There are many studies of the phenomenon, historical and current.[8] While much remains to be learned about

---

in Western Europe," in Stephen R. Graubard (ed.), *The New Europe?* (Boston: Houghton Mifflin, 1964), pp. 265–290 and 370–400, respectively. On the demise of the French family firm, see David S. Landes, "New-Model Entrepreneurship in France and Problems of Historical Explanation," *Explorations in Entrepreneurial History*, I (Fall 1963), 56–75.

6. Guy Routh, "Geographical Mobility of Manpower," in OECD Joint International Seminar on Geographical and Occupational Mobility of Manpower (Castelfusano), *Supplement to the Final Report* (Paris, 1965), Report No. 2, pp. 7–8.

7. A 1965 report by a group of experts for the OECD, however, states that gross mobility rates have been from 10 to 40 times changes in net employment *and* that movements of labor have been preponderantly wage-insensitive (OECD, *Wages and Labour Mobility*, Paris, 1965, p. 17).

8. See, for example, Arthur Redford, *Labor Migration in England, 1800–1850* (Manchester: Manchester University Press, 1926); Peter Schran, *Re-*

the subject, it is recognized that in France, Britain, and Greece, for example, workers move from the farm into industry, first to the neighboring village, next to a nearby town, and then to the metropolis. Lateral movement from one place on the periphery to another in, say, France is unusual and difficult. The story is frequently repeated of the miners of the Midi who replied to a question whether they would move to Lorraine by asking, "Who would bring the cemetery?" The immobility of the Bretons is notorious. But geographic mobility in France is greater than generally believed.[9] And there is evidence that the intermediate steps between farm and Paris may be in the process of being short-circuited, for Paris has gained almost a million people from the provinces in the 10 years ended in 1964, people who moved to improve their position despite the possession of a job at home and the necessity for 40 percent of them to accept inadequate housing. Some 10 percent were willing to consider a return, and 50 percent wanted to stay under any circumstances. The remaining 40 percent would be willing to return to the provinces provided they could have better jobs, incomes, and chances of advancement.[10]

In the Netherlands, a relatively compact country, a marked increase in spatial mobility has taken place by means of com-

---

search Report on Migration and Urbanization in Germany, 1840–1910 (Berkeley: University of California, Institute of Industrial Relations, n.d. [late 1950's?]); Alain Girard and Pierre Meutey, *Développement économique et mobilité des travailleurs: L'Individu, la profession, la région* (Paris: Éditions de l'Institut d'Études Demographiques, 1956); B. Kayser, *Géographie humaine de la Grèce* (Paris: Presses Universitaires de France, 1964). See also the many publications of the Manpower and Social Affairs Directorate of the Social Affairs Division of the Organisation for Economic Cooperation and Development, especially H. Krier, *Rural Manpower and Industrial Development* (Paris, 1961); Guy Barbichon, *Adaptation and Training of Rural Workers for Industrial Work* (Paris, n.d. [1963?]); and the final reports and supplements to the final reports of the Castelfusano and Wiesbaden International Joint Seminars.

9. Laurence Wylie, *Village in the Vaucluse* (Cambridge, Mass.: Harvard University Press, 1957); Girard and Meutey, *Développement économique et mobilité des travailleurs;* Claude Vimont, "Occupational Mobility of Manpower," in OECD Joint International Seminar (Castelfusano), Report No. 1, p. 18.

10. "Paris' Provincial Immigrants: One Million since 1954," *France Actuelle,* XIII (October 1, 1964), 6–7.

muting in buses without disturbing the strong attachment of Dutch workers to their place of residence. Frontier workers also move in buses; Belgians, for example, go to work in the DAF automobile plant, and Dutch go to jobs in the Ruhr. Only Friesland is so remote that plants have been brought to the workers rather than the reverse.

Germany has had a tradition of long-distance transfer, however, and Italy has lately combined movements from the south to Rome with those from south to north, as well as from farm to town within the province. The tradition of long-distance migration of German workers from the farms of Pomerania, Mecklenburg, and East Prussia to the steel mills of the Ruhr was powerfully assisted after 1945 by the destruction and uprooting caused by the war and its aftermath. The housing shortage made it difficult to move, perhaps, but attachment to a particular corner of the soil had been destroyed by previous transplanting of much of the German population. One reason for the lack of adaptation problems in the German labor supply has been the "extreme mobility that the Germans went through during and after the war." [11]

In the 1880's southern Italian labor migrated overseas to the Americas rather than internally. Once a start was made and relatives or friends had settled overseas, these channels kept flowing, despite the distance and expense. Moving to northern Italy involved a different dialect and an unfriendly reception. In the 1920's, the movement overseas was cut by United States restrictions and domestic migration was substituted, as a growing population in southern Italy found few employment opportunities. In 1929 internal migration was forbidden to prevent the crowding of unemployed into the cities where housing was lacking. The restrictions were renewed in 1939 and again after the war in 1946. Gradually, however, when demand for labor in the north picked up, they eroded until they were finally removed in 1961. The southern Italian laborer moved north without regret despite the slum character of the housing which faced him in Turin and

11. See M. Erixson, summary of interviews in Germany, in "Adjustment of Rural Manpower to Industry: Practical Policies and Programs" (mimeographed material for OECD Working Party, 1964), p. 22.

Milan, turning his back finally on his birthplace. The driving force was not only income but a desire to rise socially.[12] Where industry moved south, its first recruits were from a group who had already moved off the farm into casual employment largely in construction in the town. These men had expectations which rose faster than their salaries, retained their old fatalism and nepotism, and resented the discipline of the factory.[13] But the old way of life was ruptured.

Housing shortages have presented a formidable barrier to geographic mobility in Europe. Even when there has been adequate housing in regions of expanding employment, ownership of a house has deterred potential leavers. And as already noted for Britain, possession of a rental contract for a house or apartment below the full market value is equivalent to ownership of property equal to the capitalized value of the difference between the actual and economic rent.

Bringing Employment to the Workers

One means of overcoming immobility of the worker is to have the plant move to him. Two variants may be distinguished: one where declining industry leaves a trained work force available with its housing for new occupations; another where industry moves to the countryside or to commercial towns with no industrial experience with the idea of training an industrial work force from existing unskilled labor. The first variant is encountered in a number of countries of Europe: Britain, where Ford built an

12. Guido Baglioni, "The Italian Workers Moving from the South to the North of Italy," in OECD Joint International Seminar (Castelfusano), Case Study No. 7; see also Magda Talamo, "Techniques for Adapting Rural Workers to Industry," in OECD Joint International Seminar on Adaptation of Rural and Foreign Workers to Industry (Wiesbaden), *Supplement to the Final Report* (Paris, 1965), Report No. 2, pp. 158–161. By contrast, 90 percent of Greek men and 82 percent of Greek women who were asked in 1959 why they were leaving the country restricted their answers to "work opportunities" or "income" (National Statistical Service of Greece, *Report of the Exploratory Survey into Motivations and Circumstances of Rural Migration,* Athens, 1962, p. 22).

13. Paolo Vigorelli, "Sincat Company of Catania" in OECD Joint International Seminar (Wiesbaden), Case Study No. 1; Paolo Sylos Labini, "The Problem of Precarious Employment: The Case of Sicily" (paper presented to the International Labour Office Conference on the Problems of Employment in Economic Development, Geneva, 1963).

entirely new plant in the depressed area of Lancashire; Germany, with its new Opel plant at Bochum (which took advantage of the miners leaving voluntarily or being forced out of coal) and its Volkswagen plant for export at Bremen; France, where the Dunkirk steel mill combined access to imported iron ore with availability of labor, though the necessity to construct additional housing existed. Moving plants to new industrial locations has been practiced elsewhere in France, without great success, and is widely endorsed by trade unions and government in Germany.

Getting industry to start in depressed areas is relatively easy for so-called scavenger industries, which rely on cheap labor and take advantage of the low rates of pay that women will accept, for example, while their husbands remain unemployed. Getting modern and efficient industry to move to or start in these areas is more difficult. Sometimes it is undertaken spontaneously, as in the case of the Opel plant at Bochum; often with powerful financial inducements from the state, as in Britain and France. It is stated that the Robert Bosch Company, which moved away from the heart of Stuttgart, gets its labor supply by buying up unprofitable textile firms for the sake of closing down textile production and converting the female labor to work on magnetos, generators, and so on.[14] The labor may not be of the right sort, nor capable of adjusting through training. Few of the unemployed textile workers of New England, for example, ended up working in the Boston area's Route 128 electronic plants. But the infrastructure exists and can readily be made to function efficiently. Bringing work to depressed areas is difficult perhaps, but not so difficult as bringing it to rural areas.

There is a voluminous historical literature and growing current documentation on the attempt to head off the rural flow to the cities by bringing the plants to the countryside.[15] Social argu-

14. Interview, European Coal and Steel Community, Luxembourg, 1964.

15. For historical background, see "Urbanization and Regional Balance" in my *Economic Growth in France and Britain, 1851–1950* (Cambridge, Mass.: Harvard University Press, 1964), chap. 11; Étienne Juillard, *La Vie rurale dans la plaine de Basse-Alsace* (Strasbourg and Paris: Le Roux, 1953); H. J. Habakkuk, "Family Structure and Economic Change in Nineteenth-Century Europe," *Journal of Economic History*, XV (March 1955), 1–12.

For more recent examples, see OECD Joint International Seminar (Wiesbaden), especially the case studies by Paolo Vigorelli, "Sincat ments strongly favor the attempt: the preservation of family and community, the prevention of depopulation of the countryside. One strong argument supports it on the economic side: economy in construction of new housing. But economic experience more generally is not reassuring. Too often the peasant worker tries to keep the farm going at the same time that he undertakes factory life, is efficient in neither capacity, and exhausts himself. Holidays at the plant are used for farming. In Eure-et-Loire, the union writer accuses a number of plants of the speed-up, offering 70 or 80 hours of work a week and letting employees choose to work through all 4 weeks of paid vacation. Accident rates are high. At Rennes, on the other hand, Citroën management seeks to create not a worker-peasant but a worker living in a household of peasants, with the schedule arranged so that he can stay home two or three days a week. Initially, labor costs were high. More recently, the capacity of the workers satisfies the bosses, and output occasionally passes that of the Paris factories. In the Netherlands there was no social difficulty between the locals who spoke Friesland and the invaders who spoke Dutch; in Haute Savoie on the other hand, despite the same language, there is little inclination to mingle, and the wives of workers from Paris feel isolated.

There are further economic problems: the isolation of management and the difficulty of conducting business in those lines — finance, design, law, and advertising — that call for rapid interchange with specialists, possible only through face-to-face communication; the unavailability of materials and components in emergency and the consequent greater cost of inventories. Most dangerous, it seems, is that there is a finite ceiling on the ultimate labor supply of native workers. When Lorraine ran out of young people who could be drawn from the countryside, it had to turn (in 1953) to the North Africans who had been brought in to

Company of Catania"; Roelof Terpstra, "N. V. Philips Gloeilampenfabrieken, Drachten, Netherlands"; Pierre Servoz, "The Gambin Company in Haute-Savoie, France"; and Roger Louet, "The French Department of Eure-et-Loire." See the case study of the Citroën Company in Rennes, discussed both by Eliane Mossé, "Problèmes de localisation dans l'industrie automobile (mimeographed, École Pratique des Hautes Études Centre d'Études Économique [Paris], 1956), p. 83; and in E. Dimitrias, paper on France, in OECD, "Adjustment of Rural Manpower to Industry," pp. 20–21.

build new plants.[16] The isolated automobile complex at Sochaux in the France-Comté and the Michelin tire plant at Clermont-Ferrand have come up against the limits of the local labor supply, and in the latter instance, having failed to recruit sufficient numbers of Bretons and Basques, the company is constructing new plants elsewhere.[17]

Unions, Companies, and the Domestic Labor Supply

The rest of this chapter is devoted to a brief discussion of the attitude toward new recruits, mobility, technical change, and other elements of labor elasticity on the part of major European economic institutions — trade unions, companies, and government. The discussion here is necessarily limited. Foreign workers and incomes policies, in relation to this topic, are treated in Chapters X and XI, respectively. Moreover, as an economist specializing in international trade and economic growth, I lack the qualifications to deal with such specialized topics and am likely to fall into error. It is nonetheless inappropriate to neglect the topic altogether.

The basic question for trade unions is whether they are interested in their worker-clients broadly or parochially; whether, that is, they put the national interest and long-run concern for growth ahead of the local, specific, regional, or craft interest in the short run. The point has been put positively by a Swedish union representative who said that the Swedish labor movement is for the elimination of all occupational and geographic monopolies in the labor market and for the provision of more opportunities for mobility, in the interest of the union members.[18]

16. Girard and Meutey, *Développement économique et mobilité des travailleurs,* p. 127.

17. On Peugeot, see André Blanc *et al., Les Régions de l'Est* (Paris: Presses Universitaires de France, 1960), p. 109; on Michelin, Pierre Estienne and Robert Joly, *La Région du Centre* (Paris: Presses Universitaires de France, 1961), pp. 70, 98.

18. Per Holmberg, "Sweden," in OECD International Trade Union Seminar on Active Manpower Policy (Vienna), *Supplement to the Final Report* (Paris, 1964), p. 172. This view does not go undisputed. The contrary opinion is that Swedish unionism is a slot machine into which the worker puts his substantial dues and expects periodic wage increases. See Walter Galenson, *Trade Union Democracy in Western Europe* (Berkeley and Los Angeles: University of California Press, 1961), p. 72. Galenson observes, p. 83, that the Swedish labor movement has debated the desirability of

Whether wages rose owing to monopolistic organization of the labor market in Italy has already been discussed. We decided that the Italian unions were too weak to be effective monopolies. The same is largely true of France and of trade unionism in Portugal, Spain, Greece, and Turkey.

In Germany, wide division exists between those who believe that the union movement is weak and those who regard it as farsighted and concerned with long-run rather than short-run objectives. On the side of the weakness interpretation is the fact that Hitler and the Nazi Labor Front destroyed the indigenous movement; restored only with difficulty by the Occupation forces, it then had to meet the substantial competition of unemployed expellees, refugees, and ultimately foreign workers. Sohmen argues that the unions' early achievement of the right of codetermination (*Mitbestimmungsrecht*), or the right to union representation on company management boards, is an indication of strength, but this can be taken as a pursuit of the shadow of prestige because of incapacity to obtain the substance of larger wage increases.[19] Some writers take the position that Boechler, Rosenberg, Brenner, and other German labor leaders, however aggressive in manner, were convinced at heart that the way to raise real wages was to keep growth high and prices stable, which led them to restrain wage demands. Whatever the truth about weakness or farsightedness, the outcome is plain: during the 1950's, wage rates grew less rapidly than productivity, labor conflict was minimal, and yet real wages doubled in the decade.

Specifically on the subject of mobility, German trade unions, like the British, come out strongly for bringing the jobs to the workers rather than the workers to the jobs.[20] The basis for this atti-

---

increasing labor mobility geographically, occupationally, and by industries to give the workers wide freedom of choice. It may be mentioned that the national bargain deals only with the minimum wage, and the need to negotiate actual wages locally encourages wage drift.

19. See Egon Sohmen, "Competition and Growth: The Lesson of West Germany," *American Economic Review*, XLIX (December 1960), p. 991; this position is somewhat modified in his "Comments on Competition and Growth: A Reply," *American Economic Review*, L (December 1960), 1029–1030.

20. See H. Beermann, "The Trade Union Attitude towards an Active Manpower Policy," in OECD International Trade Union Seminar on Active Manpower Policy (Vienna), *Final Report* (Paris, 1964), pp. 147–148.

tude may be social rather than economic, resting on a concern for the maintenance of family, community, and housing. It nonetheless fosters local monopoly. Evidence on the other side is that German trade unions, and in fact all Continental unions, embraced the inward movement of workers off the farm, seeking to add the inflow as union members and to ensure that the newcomers conformed to union standards rather than cut wages.[21]

Given the ease of busing, Dutch trade unions can hardly affect mobility much. In other questions of national policy, they have been both powerful and cooperative. Belgian unions spent the early days of unemployment after 1950 agitating on regional questions that were partly concerned with pockets of unemployment but were not unrelated to the political division between Flemish and Walloon regions.

It is in Britain that the question arises in its most critical form as to whether the trade-union movement helped or hurt mobility. Probably, by and large, it hurt. Craft organization limits occupational mobility and piles up jurisdictional disputes. Usurpation of power from the national bodies by local shop stewards encourages militancy at the national level and labor hoarding by business. There is possibly little that British trade unions can do to stimulate labor mobility, given the lack of housing and the availability of some housing at rentals below the market. But the unions have played into the hands of immobility.

There is little current literature on European union attitudes toward technical change. During the Marshall Plan days, most non-Communist unions favored it. British unions are traditionally opposed. The German paper submitted to the Vienna union seminar on manpower policy fulminated against automation. The success of the French railways in reducing their staff from 492,000 in 1946, swollen by reconstruction, to 370,000 in 1955 after electrification is perhaps more a testimony to the skill of management than to the cooperation of unions, which may have been opposed and weak.[22] Perhaps it is legitimate to charge Brit-

21. Solomon Barkin, "Trade Union Policies and Programmes for National Internal Migrants and Foreign Workers" (unpublished paper, representing the personal views of Mr. Barkin, circulated by OECD, 1965).

22. Girard and Meutey, *Développement économique et mobilité des travailleurs*, pp. 43–57. Staffs were redistributed geographically, with housing arranged. Retirement was speeded up and recruiting cut off, but there

ish craft unions with obstructionism toward technical change and to withhold judgment on others for lack of evidence.

Trade unions are in an awkward position today. It is hard to maintain ancient ideologies of revolution and protest with national income per capita rising rapidly. It is equally difficult intellectually to focus on strictly business unionism, maximizing the short-run wage and the local monopoly, without regard to effects on the national economy, when the economic interrelationships are evident to all. But the union leaders are paid to serve the workers, not the national interest. The result is that only unions which are convinced of their weakness can be aggressive in putting forward the claims of their following. Strong union leadership is in a cleft stick: it can go through the motions of vigorous attack on industry but settle on a moderate basis, as seems to have been the German pattern; or it can modify its demands from the beginning and risk losing authority, as in Britain. The big advantage of moving from "black" wages to rapidly rising official rates, as in the Netherlands in 1963, is that it restores the capacity of the trade unions to lead.

Management's attitude toward mobility does not require much discussion. It is for it in labor. In France native firms have learned not to discharge redundant workers precipitously as did G. M. Frigidaire and Remington Rand, both under the pressure of Common Market competition and with such a brisk demand for labor that the workers were quickly placed. Under certain circumstances, when all other things are equal, plants will move to locations where labor is more abundant, as in the automobile-industry instances cited earlier. With things unequal, no. And when labor is tight and the firm expects to stay in business, the labor mobility that might come from discharges gives way to hoarding so that the firm is in position to meet requirements in the next expansion. Companies undertake a certain amount of training even with the knowledge that they will lose some trained labor to their competitors. They will scour the countryside for workers and in some cases build housing with their own funds.

---

were no discharges. The contrast is with the British railroads (see above, p. 85). The analogue is John L. Lewis' policy in the American coal industry, a monopolistic solution, and Fawley (see above, p. 81).

Their interest in such cases is evident. One can mark management down in favor of mobility.

Government's Role

Government's role in labor elasticity is many-sided and is still discussed here without reference to foreign workers or incomes policy. This leaves a long list of issues: regional policies of development to bring work to the labor; national employment services, training, housing, transfer assistance, etc., to bring workers to the jobs; and legislation on redundancy provisions, unemployment relief, etc., which bear on employers' readiness to discharge workers and workers' tolerance of unemployment.

On the whole, government measures to stimulate the movement of plants to workers have not been successful. The regional development plans of Italy and Norway have undistinguished records. Strong tax advantages in France have produced investments outside of Paris, Lyon, and Marseilles, but the process seems not to be self-perpetuating. British efforts through town-and-country planning to divert investment from the south and east of England to northern Ireland, Scotland, and the Liverpool-Manchester area are no triumph of economic engineering. Unemployment rates remain higher in the north and west than the south and east, and workers still drift southeast. Belgian firms move away from rather than to the Borinage. The Greek program to attract foreign capital has had some success in the Athens area, where large numbers of the underemployed from the countryside have moved. Despite some spontaneous business movement to workers, already cited, however, the regional attack on more effective use of the labor supply through redistributing investment has achieved only modest results. The reason would seem to be that conventional subsidies offered to business to undertake regional investments are inadequate in relation to the high rates of return required by business on risky investments.

European governments have tackled the task of moving workers to the job with increasing assiduity since the end of the 1950's and have been moderately successful except in housing. Employment services have been perfected in most countries, although only a third or so of hiring takes place through them. The French organization was founded in 1945 and has recently been expanded with training and counseling services. The impressive German Bundesanstalt für Arbeitvermittlung und Arbeitlosenversicherung (BAA), started in 1952, operates a wide variety of services. Belgian legislation in the area was enacted along modern lines from 1959 to 1961 in connection with Belgian planning, stimulated by declining unemployment. The most substantial extension of governmental responsibility in questions of mobility has been in Sweden, which has undertaken to subsidize the costs of transfer from one community to another and has been successful. While housing shortages handicap mobility, only one third of the workers helped return to their original residence.[23] A particularly interesting example of a national employment service in action under pressure is afforded by the French response to the return of the Pieds Noirs from Algeria in 1962. Instead of 500,000 returnees in 3 years, there were 800,000 in a single year, of whom 250,000 were in the "active" category. A wide divergence existed between the manpower needs of France and the skills of the repatriates, many of whom, additionally, were disinclined to work. But under boom conditions placement was effected readily.[24]

Many government policies directed to other objectives affect the elasticity of the labor supply, notably military call-ups and releases and the extension of education. In taxation, moreover, effects on work incentives may not be obvious, and once a tax system has been adopted, it may be difficult to adjust to eliminate disincentives. In a narrow field, the Dutch have reduced taxes for married working women to offset the penalty of the progressive income tax on incremental income. Similar steps are contemplated in Sweden. More important may be the Swedish deliberate step in switching from income to excise taxes. The Continental turnover or value-added taxes, instead of highly progressive personal income taxes and in some countries company profits taxes, have a definite effect on mobility. Taxing

23. See Gunnar Lindström, "Sweden," in OECD International Management Seminar on Active Manpower Policy (Brussels), *Supplement to the Final Report* (Paris, 1965), pp. 8–9.

24. Bernard Vrillon, "Active Manpower Policy in France," *ibid.*, p. 9, and Appendix, pp. 34–38. The figure 250,000 is an estimate and differs from the estimate cited on p. 65.

labor, which is part of value added, and exempting investment creates an incentive to substitute capital for labor. British Chancellor of the Exchequer Thorneycroft contemplated a tax on labor in 1961, and the measure was advocated by Sargent specifically for the purpose of discouraging labor hoarding.[25] On the whole, too little thought has been given to the impact of the general structure of taxation on the elasticity of the labor supply, but the possibility exists that it has favored the Continentals and operated against the Scandinavians, Dutch, and British.

In some areas, government has manpower policies but is unable to prevent labor and employers from going their separate ways. The French Plans contemplated maintaining at a high level the number of hours of work, but once Renault gave in to the unions and added a fourth week of vacation, the concession spread.

The most complex area in which government has to operate to affect labor mobility is in the field of severance pay and unemployment compensation. To maintain them at high levels is to encourage labor in accepting mobility. Workers will care less if they are dismissed, and the pressure for full employment at all costs will be reduced. It is on this account that Sargent and many others recommend increasing these rates in Britain. At the same time, high rates of severance pay have complex effects on business. They encourage the substitution of machinery for labor, which is useful in a full-employment economy but has contributed to structural unemployment in Italy. And they encourage overtime rather than new hirings and hoarding rather than dismissals. Here again is a neglected field of inquiry, where labor economists have regarded the questions as belonging to public finance, and public finance experts have ignored the labor market. Swedish discussion of active manpower policies includes reference to the investment reserves, an incentive scheme for transferring investment from prosperous times to periods of slack by remission of profits tax.[26] Apart from the questions of stability, and of relief of disincentive taxation for women, the impact of the European tax system on labor mobility is virtually not discussed.

25. J. R. Sargent, *Out of Stagnation: A Policy for Growth,* Fabian Tract No. 343 (London: Fabian Society, 1963), pp. 25–26.

26. See Lindström, "Sweden," in OECD Management Seminar (Brussels), p. 10; OECD, *Labour Market Policy in Sweden* (Paris, 1963), pp. 31 ff.

Problems of overfull employment are, of course, new. It takes time to adjust from finding any job for the worker to finding the right job, by which is meant the job that will contribute the optimum to output and welfare. In a period of overfull employment, the French employment service still requires firms to justify dismissals.[27] Much of the burgeoning literature and part of the spurt of interest in active manpower policies are the proximate consequence of the presence of activist personalities in the Manpower and Social Affairs Division of the OECD, which is somewhat in the lead of the Social Affairs Division of the EEC and far ahead of the International Labour Office (ILO) in its involvement with full-employment manpower policies. But the *force des choses* is important too. Full employment ineluctably brings concern for manpower policy, and in particular for attempts to increase the elasticity of the labor supply, with management support for a certain distance and with labor-union collaboration, indifference, or active resistance in the various countries. The Belgian story is perhaps symbolic: there was little interest in the question of manpower policy so long as unemployment was substantial, but beginning in 1959, with waning labor reserves, measures were enacted to use labor more effectively.

In the domestic field, the economic view of the labor market is confused with a variety of social considerations. The Manpower and Social Division of the OECD is in the Social Directorate. The elasticity of the labor supply is mixed in with the social problems of the elderly, handicapped, youthful, and badly housed. While this confusion is large in the domestic field, it is dominant for foreign labor. Economic and social policies less frequently converge here and more frequently diverge. It is time then to turn to the integrated international markets for labor in Europe.

27. Vrillon, "Active Manpower Policy in France," in OECD Management Seminar (Brussels), p. 11.

CHAPTER IX

Integration of Labor Markets in Europe

The Decline of Overseas Emigration

European economic policy immediately after World War II contemplated large-scale emigration overseas. The countries whose emigration overseas had been cut off — the Netherlands, Spain, Greece, and to a lesser extent Italy — naturally considered resumption. A series of international bodies, from the United Nations Relief and Rehabilitation Administration (UNRRA) to the International Refugee Organization (IRO) established in 1946 and the Intergovernmental Committee for European Migration (ICEM), created in 1951, hoped to tidy up Europe by spreading European displaced persons throughout the world but mainly in underpopulated areas.[1] German expellees from the eastern territories and refugees from the Eastern Zone initially thought they would stay in West Germany only in transit to other continents. The suggestion as early as 1951 that emigration could not cope with these numbers and that West Germany had to provide a solution came as a shock.[2]

In the first years after the war, there was considerable intra-European movement. Italian emigration within Europe reached a peak of 89,000 in 1948 and declined thereafter to 22,500 in 1954 as the overseas movement built up.[3] Britain turned to Polish ex-servicemen, refugees, and Italians to meet her needs for nurses, domestic servants, miners, and foundry workers in a scheme

1. ILO, *International Migration, 1945–1957* (Geneva, 1959), chap. 2.
2. See Preface by Edgar Salin to Friederich Edding, *The Refugees as a Burden, a Stimulus and a Challenge to the West German Economy*, Research Group for European Migration, Study No. IV (The Hague: Nijhoff, 1951), p. viii.
3. See G. Parenti, "Italy," in Brinley Thomas (ed.), *Economics of International Migration: Proceedings of a Conference Held by the International Economic Association* (London: Macmillan, 1958), p. 86.

which began with a bang in April 1947 and came to a whimpering end in 1950.[4]

Gross emigration overseas from Europe reached a peak in the period 1949–1951, declined slowly to the end of the decade and quickly after that.[5] Greek, Spanish, Italian, and Portuguese workers emigrated less and less overseas and in more rapidly increasing numbers to Germany, Switzerland, France, and Belgium. Dutch assisted emigration overseas was allowed to dwindle, though the measures were not removed from the books. Only British emigration overseas continued at the same level, occasionally spurting in a period of balance-of-payments crisis and recession as Gallup polls recorded discouragement.[6]

The Special Relations

The "special relation" in quotation marks in Britain typically refers to the political ties with the United States. In the present context, however, what is meant is large population movements into the Netherlands, Britain, France, and West Germany from outside western Europe, each of which involved a special relationship with an external source. The Dutch brought 300,000 immigrants to their crowded country after the independence of the Netherlands East Indies, one tenth "pure-blooded" Dutchmen and most of the others with some degree of Dutch blood.[7] For the Germans it was East Germany and the former German territories now under Russian and Polish administration. For

4. J. A. Tannahill, *European Volunteer Workers in Britain* (Manchester: Manchester University Press, 1958), p. 26.

5. ILO, *International Migration, 1945–1957*, p. 165, gives figures up to 1957. There is no handy comparable collection of data for the period since that time, though on intra-European migration see OECD Joint International Seminar on Adaptation of Rural and Foreign Workers to Industry (Wiesbaden) *Final Report* (Paris, 1965), Report No. 1, pp. 1–35. The rise in intra-European migration is self-evident; for the decline in extra-European, see International Bank for Reconstruction and Development (IBRB), *The Economic Development of Spain* (Baltimore: Johns Hopkins Press, 1963), p. 85; Instituto Centrale di Statistica, *Annuario di Statistiche del Lavoro et dell'Emigrazione*, vol. IV (1962), Table 13, p. 28, *et passim.*

6. Julius Isaac points out that responses to the question "If you were free to do so, would you like to go and settle in another country?" have doubtful validity, since the question is entirely academic (*British Post-war Migration*, Cambridge: Cambridge University Press, 1954, pp. 249, 293).

7. How to Handle Immigrants," *Economist*, CCXIV (March 6, 1965), 1008.

France it was Algeria with its European residents, largely French, and the native North Africans. For Britain it was the Commonwealth and in particular the subjects of the West Indies, Malta, Pakistan, and India. It is an interesting commentary on the homogeneity of western Europe that it was found necessary to halt the inward movement into both France and Britain in 1962, despite strong political ties to the areas providing the immigrants. The movement from East Germany was stopped at the same time by outside forces through the construction of the Wall in August 1961. The Asian movement to the Netherlands was naturally limited in size and duration.

The quality of these infusions differed substantially. The German expellees in 1950 were much more heavily weighted toward wage earners and the service industries than were the West Germans proper (Table IX-1). The incomers possessed "a real drive

TABLE IX-1

Social and economic distribution of expellees compared to that of domestic West German work force, 1950
(percentages)

Social structure	Expel-lees	Rest of labor force	Economic structure	Expel-lees	Rest of labor force
Self-employed	5.2	16.5	Agriculture	13.5	24.9
Unpaid family workers	1.8	16.7	Industry and mining	48.6	41.2
Government officials	3.7	4.0	Commerce and transport	12.0	16.2
Employees	14.1	16.3	Service industries	25.9	17.7
Total	100.0	100.0	Total	100.0	100.0

Source: Hilde Wander, "Migration and the German Economy," in Brinley Thomas (ed.), *Economics of International Migration* (London: Macmillan, 1958), p. 207.

for achievement which proved a real stimulant to the economy . . . , introduced new industries and production methods . . . , and above all promoted a spirit of competition which had a beneficial effect on productivity."[8] The French Pieds Noirs came in greater numbers from government and administration than the French labor force, as mentioned in the previous chapter, were not initially eager to build back their economic position, and felt no loss of social standing.[9] The Algerians in France and the colored subjects from the Commonwealth had only limited skills. The emigrants from Jamaica were possibly skilled by West Indies standards, but the standard was so low that it was said of their migration that it lowered the average level of skill in both countries.[10]

Jamaican work habits were not the main drawback, however. As bus conductors, hospital attendants, and busboys and waiters in cafes, they perform a useful function in London, being "exceptionally good in jobs which require a personal touch."[11] They got on well at work but not at home. Jamaican family life was chaotic by European standards; the immigrants had access only to the worst housing and took care of it in sluttish fashion. Relations with their neighbors were bad, as the Notting Hill riots in 1958 attested. It was this difficulty of assimilation that led to Conservative action to restrict Commonwealth immigration in 1962, reaffirmed by the Labour government in 1964.

French limitations on Algerians and colored members of the Communauté had the same sort of social origin but were based on much less bad feeling. Freedom of access to Metropolitan France had been promised to both, in the Evian Agreement with Algeria and in the treaties giving the African colonies south of

8. Hilde Wander, "Migration and the German Economy," in Thomas (ed.), *Economics of International Migration*, p. 207.

9. *Le Monde*, June 21–22, 1964, p. 12, carried an article on the integration of 35,000 Pieds Noirs in the Toulon region, discussing how effectively they farm abandoned land. The issue of July 22, 1964, however, had an article, the first of a series on the Pieds Noirs, entitled "Un Millions de Pieds Noirs Parmi Nous," with a subtitle which translates as "Economic Reclassification and Social Declassification." The second article in the series, dated July 23, 1964, mentions that some returnees preferred not to stay in France but to move on to Argentina or Peru where they could practice the kind of farming they developed in Algeria.

10. W. F. Maunder, "The New Jamaican Migration," *Social and Economic Studies*, IV (March 1955); cited by Gene Tidrick, "A Cost-Benefit Analysis of Jamaican Emigration to the United Kingdom, 1953–1962" (unpublished paper, Harvard University).

11. Pearl Jephcott, *A Troubled Area: Notes on Notting Hill* (London: Faber & Faber, 1964), pp. 101, 83.

the Sahara independence within the Communauté. But chaos in Algeria in 1964 repelled the masses of Algerians who had returned to their country after Evian. Some 53,000 Algerians came to France in the first three months of 1964, the same number as in all of 1963. On April 10, 1964, the governments of France and Algeria agreed not to suspend migration but to organize it quarter by quarter, the French indicating how many they wanted to receive, Algeria how many it wanted to let go.[12] Provision was made for medical checkups, since 70 to 80 percent of the tuberculosis patients occupying hospital beds in France are foreign workers, largely Arabs and Africans.[13]

The movement of Africans to France is controlled primarily by the African countries themselves. It is estimated that 97 percent of the African workers, who live together in cellars, hangars, and dormitory hotels in utmost squalor, are from the Sarahole tribe, which is divided among Senegal, Mali, and Mauretania and is nomadic at home as well as abroad. These people, maintaining a tribal organization while living in Paris, keep good relations with the French but have high rates of unemployment and illness.[14]

Regional European Integration in Labor

Besides the ambitious effort of the Rome Treaty, there have been two other systematic attempts to integrate labor markets: the Belgium-Netherlands-Luxembourg economic union, or Benelux, and the Common Market for Labor in Scandinavia. The second has some importance, the former none.

The Benelux agreement concluded between governments in exile in London during the war provided for free movement of goods, capital, and labor. The movement of industrial goods was freed with difficulty. That of agricultural products was delayed until the problem was merged with the wider task of establishing a single regime for agriculture in the EEC. But when the free movement of labor was put into operation and the barriers to migration were lifted in 1956, nothing happened. The Dutch as before migrated to Australia and Canada, and the Belgians con-

12. *Le Monde,* April 10, 1964.
13. *Le Figaro,* December 23, 1963.
14. Michel Legris, "40,000 Voluntary Slaves: The Black Worker in France," *Le Monde,* February 21, 22, 23, 1963.

tinued to stay home or in a few cases to commute over the border, but to France as much as or more than to the Netherlands.

The common Nordic labor market, which went into operation in July 1954, has been more effective than the Benelux provisions regarding labor movement. The major movement is a temporary one from the other members of the market to Sweden, which had already exempted Danish, Finnish, and Norwegian citizens from the regulations regarding labor permits as early as 1943. From 1955 to 1957 the movement of labor from all three of the other countries to Sweden apparently increased.[15] Danish and Norwegian numbers in Sweden then remained fairly stable at 19,000 and 10,000, respectively, from 1959 to 1962, but the number of Finns rose from 37,000 to 51,000 over the same period.[16] All non-Scandinavians need work permits, and some can obtain them after their arrival in Sweden, but Italians, Greeks, Turks, and people of a few other countries must have the permit before they arrive. Immediately upon arrival, foreign workers are required to present a request for admission to the Swedish trade unions. No collective transfer can take place without agreement of the trade unions.[17]

The European Economic Community

Large-scale international movements of European nationals are not new. Prior to 1918 all labor movements were unrestricted by governments. Between 1860 and 1914, for example, the number of foreigners in Switzerland quintupled, reaching 600,000 or 15 percent of the population. These foreigners were spread more evenly over Switzerland than the present foreign workers; they traveled as individuals and were accompanied by their families, so that 54 percent were employed, compared with 72 percent today.[18] Foreigners in Germany amounted to 950,000 in 1907, or

15. ILO, *International Migration, 1945–1957,* Table 44, p. 138.

16. OECD Joint International Seminar on Adaptation of Rural and Foreign Workers to Industry (Wiesbaden), Table 32, p. 32.

17. J. Svennilson, "Liberalization de la politique suédoise d'immigration dans l'après-guerre," in Maurice Byé *et al., Demain l'Europe sans frontières* (Paris: Plon, 1958), pp. 147–148. Dr. Svennilson italicizes the information about trade unions.

18. Richard Zollinger, "Zur Bevoelkerungs- und Gesellschaftsstruktur," *Schweizerische Zeitschrift für Volkswirtschaft und Statistik,* 100th Year, Nos. 1–2 (March-June 1964), pp. 29–31.

the same order of magnitude as that reached in 1964, 3.4 percent of all employees, as contrasted with 4.4 percent later; but the 1907 group came generally from Austria-Hungary (43 percent) and Russia and Poland (25 percent collectively) instead of from the Mediterranean countries.[19] France had 1,160,000 foreigners in 1911, 1,500,000 in 1921, and 2,700,000 in 1931, immigration having been sought to make up the manpower losses of World War I.[20]

Following World War I, population movements became so large that it was necessary for governments to subject them to control. Three classes of labor were distinguished: the repatriate, the refugee, and contract labor, a form which was held in low esteem as suitable mainly for Chinese and Hindu coolies and prohibited in the United States by the Foran Act of 1885. Especially prominent were Italian stonemasons, Polish miners, anti-Fascist Italians working as common laborers, and, after 1937, Spanish political refugees. Employers sought contract labor; labor unions resisted it. The French needed workers for postwar reconstruction and led the way in developing a system of organized, selected, and controlled immigration.[21] Foreign workers were the last in, first out. During the 1930's, the French *police des étrangers* rounded up foreign workers, took away their visas, loaded them on trains, and expelled them to Poland and Italy.[22]

Immediately after World War II, there were problems of meeting particular needs for workers and finding jobs for people unwilling to be repatriated. In 1953, the Organization for European Economic Cooperation (OEEC) adopted its first rule to restore wider freedom of movement. It established that native workers had to be given priority over foreigners for 4 weeks (8

19. See chart, "Foreign Workers in the Federal Republic," *German Tribune,* No. 170 (July 3, 1965), p. 11.

20. "Les Travailleurs étrangers en France," *Notes et Études Documentaires,* No. 3057 (January 23, 1964), p. 3.

21. Eugene Kulisher, *Europe on the Move: War and Population Changes, 1917–47* (New York: Columbia University Press, 1948), pp. 250–251.

22. Haut Comité Consultatif de la Population et de la Famille, *L'Accueil des étrangers en France* (Paris: La Documentation Française, 1963), p. 22; Georges Mauco, "Alien Workers in France," *International Labour Review, XXXIII* (February 1936), 190: "In practice, the administrative authorities try to encourage voluntary departures by creating reduced fares for the return journey, and they have even organized collective departures by special trains."

weeks in France) in the event of an opening. At the end of that time, the foreign worker was placed on the same footing as the native.

The Rome Treaty provided for the creation of a common market not only in goods but in capital and labor. The first two regulations affecting the movement of labor, Nos. 3 and 4, were issued immediately after the treaty took effect, and they established the interchangeability of social-security systems. It was recognized that foreign workers had a right to housing of a normal sort, but since housing everywhere was in short supply and few workers could be accompanied by their families, it was provided that allowances to families left behind in the country of emigration would be paid immediately instead of after the normal waiting time of 6 years. Two subsequent regulations regarding labor have been issued, No. 15 of 1959 and No. 38 of 1964. The first reduced the OEEC priority period from 4 weeks to 3 but both exempted from the waiting requirement jobs where a specific foreign person was named and declared certain areas out of bounds for foreign immigration. Under Regulation 15, foreign workers were given the right to vote in works-council elections but not to hold office. Under Regulation 38 they could hold office after serving for 3 years. The main thrust of Regulation 38 was to give the foreign worker who was a citizen of a member of the Common Market full national treatment with domestic workers except where a member state declares that a profession (for example, croupiers in Belgium) or a region (Brittany) constitutes a problem requiring an exception and justifies the declaration. Under the regulation there is no need for a foreign worker from one EEC country in the market of another to indicate whether he has a wife and whether he intends to bring her. National treatment nonetheless prevents wives from moving to a community unless the family is provided with adequate housing; and if the Italian worker in Belgium, France, or Germany cannot find housing which the authorities deem adequate, he cannot bring his wife.

The Rome Treaty and the regulations under it do not make an enormous difference between the treatment accorded to members and nonmembers. Italy has some preference but recognizes it as unimportant. Greece and Turkey are associate members and thereby entitled to privileges of members without themselves, yet, undertaking the reciprocal obligation to allow recruitment freely in their territory. But membership and associate membership are not that important in a competitive market. Spain and Portugal, which have not negotiated associate status with Brussels, have separate treaties with the members that give them virtually the same treatment. Switzerland, which is not in the Common Market, also has treaties with the various countries of emigration which, until recently, left her able to attract such foreign labor as she needed and was willing to take. And the Netherlands, which is really not interested in the immigration of workers from the Mediterranean area, can avoid a large-scale inflow merely by remaining passive.

The Character of Competition for Foreign Labor

National treatment will be of great importance in the event of a recession. The 1934–35 action of the French in pushing close to 1 million foreign workers out of the country and making them bear the brunt of the unemployment is not likely to be repeated. Some German observers in fact claim that the foreign workers with a year's contract have an advantage over the native who can be discharged on 14 days' notice. Under conditions of full employment, however, institutional regulations are perhaps less important than the economic aspects of the bargain — such as pay and housing, the recruiting mechanism, accessibility to the home country — and these are qualified by certain noneconomic factors: the availability of compatriots, including people from the same family, village, or region; the readiness of the community to welcome strangers, which also bears on the ease of assimilation in the event that the temporary worker decides to stay permanently and which is a function of the strangeness of language, diet, and culture.

Propinquity favors Spanish and Portuguese immigration to France, Greek and Turkish to Germany, and Italian to Switzerland, southern France, and southern Germany.[23] Propinquity counts, especially with respect to the cost and difficulty of return-

23. For a map of the routes of foreign workers to Germany, see BAA, *Ausländischer Arbeitsnehmer: Erfahrungsbericht 1964* (Nürnberg, 1965), p. 23.

ing home for holidays or in some few cases to vote, to help with the harvest, or for family occasions. But there are other factors. For Iberians and Italians, the similarity of the Latin cultures and language favors France, Walloon Belgium, and French- and Italian-speaking Switzerland over Flemish Belgium, the Netherlands, Scandinavia, Germany, and German-speaking Switzerland. Languages of different kind present more problems than those of like character, in terms of inflection, link words, and word order, so that an Italian will feel more at home with the music of French than with the sound of German, without knowing a word of either.[24] The Greeks have particular skill at spoken languages; the Turks very little. This obviously tends to favor Greek settlement abroad and to limit Turkish migration to short stays.

Private migration tends to flow in channels, guided after the initial settlement by family, friends, villagers, and regional compatriots. In a group of 17 Italians in a small textile plant in Switzerland — 12 women and 5 men — 5 were related by blood, and 6 had been connected by friendship or acquaintance back in Italy.[25] These private connections are not totally disrupted when recruiting takes place through official agencies such as the BAA, since this agency offers a worker who passes the general intelligence and medical tests a series of alternative positions, often as many as five, and the choice may be affected by noneconomic factors.

There is a trade-off between income and the ease of social adjustment, one which differs from person to person. It is a banal truism that the worker wants to return — if he could get the same wage at home as he does abroad.[26] He cannot do so, however, and the question, therefore, is what combination of money wages and benefits is sufficient to make him leave his family and go abroad or take his family abroad; or if he is already

24. Stanley Rundle, *Language as a Social and Political Factor in Europe* (London: Faber & Faber, 1946), pp. 38–39.

25. Emil J. Walter, "Empirische Beitraege zum Problem der Italienischen Fremdarbeiter in der Schweiz," *Schweizerische Zeitschrift für Volkswirtschaft und Statistik*, 98th Year, No. 1 (March 1962), p. 76.

26. See, e.g., "'European' Wages Luring Spaniards," *New York Times*, May 26, 1963.

abroad, what changes would induce him to move to another country or to return home.

This competition is very much at work currently. The August 4, 1964, Swiss agreement with Italy on immigration (though ultimately not ratified) was designed to improve Swiss benefits for Italians because Italian workers were returning to Italy and moving on to Germany.[27] Foreign workers in Belgium and France are being bid away by German mines and plants.[28] Italian employers have been advertising for trained Italian labor in newspapers in Switzerland and southern Germany. Having already cut his roots to his native land, the foreign worker is peculiarly mobile. Unrestrained by ownership of property or burdened by possessions, he can readily effect geographic changes. Investment in a single foreign language may tend to keep him in a country or countries, but many of the workers, like the Turkish miners who moved from the Borinage to the Ruhr, know none, and even the 12,000 Moroccans who left French coal mines for transfer to Belgium, the Netherlands, and Germany found the language transition less significant than the pay packet.[29]

One significant counter in the competitive scale is housing. Farbenwerke Höchst furnishes housing to its foreign workers, 2 or at most 3 to a room instead of the standard 4, deliberately as a measure of competition. The company recruits partly by informal word-of-mouth channels and attracts workers through their friends and relations. The attractiveness of accommodations plays a part in this program.[30] The BAA sponsors a series of community centers for foreign workers — primarily to occupy them when they are not at the plant or sleeping and to keep them away from the Bahnhof — and is conscious of the competitive advantage this gives Germany over Switzerland and France.

The competition is not entirely at the atomistic level. When

27. "Die Wanderarbeiter in Europa," *Neue Zürcher Zeitung*, June 24, 1964.

28. See *Le Figaro*, June 12, 1964, which discusses a "decided flight" of Italian workers from France to Germany. "Les Travailleurs étrangers en France," *Bulletin d'Information du Bureau Économique et Sociale* (February 1963), p. 18, notes that the younger Italians are being bid away, leaving France with the older.

29. *Le Monde*, April 10, 1964.

30. Interview, Höchst, 1964.

Belgium signed an agreement with Turkey over immigration, it hoped to be able to avoid providing social-security benefits at the same level as to Belgian citizens. Turkey had been able to obtain the local level from other countries, however — there are unsubstantiated stories of family allowances being paid to Turkish workers with 4 wives and 33 children — and Belgium had to fall in line.[31]

In pre-World War I migration to the United States, immigrants were used as strikebreakers. This is not true in Europe today. Foreign workers go out on strike immediately with their native colleagues. The trade unions that are agreeable to the employment of foreign workers — the German, Swiss, Belgian, and, after persuasion, the French — insist on equal pay for foreign workers.[32] The slogan "equal pay for foreigners" is a fallacy, of course, if it is thought that this means that immigrants do not reduce wages. Increased supplies of labor reduce wages, relatively, if not absolutely, even if foreigners are paid the same wages as natives.

The slogan of equal pay does not inhibit wage drift, upgrading, and the development of a dual market in labor — at least in the short run. "It is notorious that foreigners get the hard work, the difficult work, the night shift." [33] The movement of Swiss workers out of hotel-keeping and textiles and into the civil service and the chemical industry has been touched on earlier, along with the fact that the metal-transforming industries lose more of their Swiss workers to other occupations than they gain from agriculture, hotel-keeping, and construction (see above, p. 44). An EEC official suggested casually that while all agreements in Belgium call for equal pay for foreigners and citizens, and foreigners get the wages specified in collective agreements, they get the minimum and the Belgians get 50 to 60 percent more. But

31. "Per Moneta," *Der Spiegel*, No. 41/64 (October 7, 1964), p. 51. Other articles describing the problems of foreign workers as a whole are "Les Soutiers de l'Europe," *Le Monde*, June 23, 24, 25, 26, 1964; Edouard Roditi, "The Peaceful Invasion," *Reporter* (October 12, 1964), pp. 13–15; Walter Hallstein, "Fremdarbeiter in Europa," *Die Zukunft*, No. 13/14 (July 1964), pp. 27–30.

32. J. Benard, "Economic Policy in France," in *Economic Policy in Our Time*, vol. III: *Country Studies* (Chicago: Rand McNally, 1964), p. 309.

33. *Le Figaro*, April 10, 1964.

with time and assimilation, noncompeting markets slip into competition.

There is no up-to-date study of housing for foreign workers. The EEC commissioned several papers on the subject early in the history of the problem, 1958.[34] Since that date, the real upsurge in the movement of foreign workers has occurred, on the one hand, and very considerable progress in housing construction has taken place, on the other. It is hard to know how the race has come out, but it is likely that housing for foreign workers has improved substantially in Germany, fallen behind in France, and remains bearable in Switzerland, with substantial construction, and in Belgium, with foreign workers occupying the somewhat substandard housing that had been evacuated in the Borinage. In 1958 when there were only 160,000 foreign workers in Germany, as contrasted with 1 million in 1965, it was stated that one third of the housing was good, one third average, and one third insufficient. The study that offers this estimate suffers, however, from including among the migrant workers some 40,000 Dutch citizens, many of whom were born in Germany and could be fully reabsorbed there. The verdict on French housing was that one fourth was satisfactory, one third acceptable, 23 percent insufficient, and 18 percent very insufficient. In Germany the unemployment insurance fund made DM 200 million available in loans for the construction of worker housing in 1960–61, and an additional DM 191.5 million up to the end of the year 1964. While DM 50 million were designated especially for housing for married workers, the loans for the most part were to construct housing for single workers, since in this way more workers could be accommodated per DM spent. An estimate by the BAA states that only 10 percent of the foreign workers in Germany at the end of 1964 were interested in bringing their families to Ger-

34. EEC Commission, Direction Générale des Affaires Sociales, *Synthèse des Rapports Établis sur les Conditions de Logements des Travailleurs Migrants dans Trois Pays de la CEE* (V/5522/61, Brussels, 1961). The three reports synthesized were: J. Seraphim, "Les Conditions de Logement en Republique Fédérale d'Allemagne des Travailleurs Migrants des États de la CEE" (V/6671, 60-F); L'Institut nationale d'études demographique, "Le Logement des Travailleurs Migrants en France" (V/7/61-F); L'Institut de l'Université de Liege, "Les Conditions de Logement des Travailleurs Migrants" (V/6137, 60-F).

many, which limits the problem. It is recognized, however, that the longer large numbers of foreign workers remain in Germany, the more will want families along.[35] Housing of foreign workers has proceeded by stages in the several countries: first temporary barracks, then modern housing with a limited number of single workers per room and cooking facilities in the building where the native diet can be provided, finally housing for workers spread through the community to prevent the creation of special sections or ghettos of foreign workers.[36] Governments in the countries of emigration interested themselves at an early date in the housing of their citizens abroad. The Spanish government objected to the housing accorded to Spanish miners in the Netherlands in 1963. After a strike, they left the country. It is said that when the Italian Labor Minister visited homes in Germany and complained about Italian workers sleeping in double-decker beds, the Federal Minister of Labor suggested that he was not fully informed of how his compatriots lived in their own country.[37]

In housing, as in the question of whether to group workers in the plant by nationality or to mix them with Germans, the separate firms are on their own.[38] In the Buderus plant in Wetz-

35. BAA, *Ausländischer Arbeitsnehmer: Erfahrungsbericht 1964,* p. 14. In France, where the housing conditions of foreigners are not known in detail but are suspected to be bad, a census was planned after the population census of 1962 (Haut Comité Consultatif de la Population et de la Famille, *L'Accueil des étrangers en France,* p. 80).

36. "Einsatz von ausländische Arbeitskräften bei der Ford-Werke A. G., Stand Ende Dezember 1963," generously made available by the Ford-Werke, Cologne, mimeographed, p. 20. Foreign personnel work at the Ford-Werke is under the direction of Giacomo Maturi, who has written *Arbeitsplatz Deutschland: Wie man südländische Gastarbeiter verstehen lernt* (Mainz: Krausskopf, 1964). This book unfortunately is concerned almost exclusively with interpreting Italian temperament to Germans.

37. "Per Moneta," *Der Spiegel,* p. 50.

38. It was rumored in Germany that the Volkswagenwerk at Wolfsburg separated the Italian from the German workers after disturbances. I am informed by the company, however, that while there was local unrest in 1962 owing to the differences in temperament and difficulties of adjustment, these have long since been forgotten and Italian and German workers, along with those of other nationalities, work side by side (letter dated January 15, 1965). It is of some interest that the construction of the Wolfsburg plant of Volkswagen was originally undertaken in 1938 with a contingent of 3,000 unemployed Italians sent by Mussolini (Walter Henry Nelson, *Small Wonder: The Amazing Story of the Volkswagen,* Boston: Little, Brown, 1965, pp. 81–82).

lar, the foreign workers are combined with Germans in teams of 3 or 4 workers, largely making foundry products. The foreigners soon evince a desire to make up their own teams in order to raise their earnings under piece rates, but this is not encouraged. Individuals, moreover, work at rates that German workers believe would, if continued, damage their health. After 1½ to 2 years, however, the foreign workers ask for easier jobs even if it means a drop in earnings of DM 1 an hour.[39]

If the Mediterranean peoples compete in the northern European market with local labor, they also compete with each other. The most competitive market, perhaps, is the German. The first German recruiting of Italian unemployed in the 1950's took place in 1956 at the suggestion of the Italian government, interested in finding occupations for its unemployed. The sharp rise, moreover, took place in 1960 and 1961 before the Wall went up in Berlin. In 1960 beginnings were made toward recruitment of Spanish and Greeks, which increased as it became more difficult to obtain Italians, and a net return flow to Italy got under way. Figure IX-1 gives numbers for foreign labor recruited through the German commissions abroad, representing the BAA and German employers. Many more workers from Italy and Greece traveled to Germany as tourists and found jobs through local offices of the BAA. The figure also fails to record the fact that the BAA began to recruit Portuguese in substantial numbers after the conclusion of an agreement in March 1964, reaching the figure of 3,400 by the year's end. If the BAA's experience in other countries were repeated, this number might rise to something on the order of 40,000 a year. Figure IX-2 shows the separate movements of Italians, Spanish, and Portuguese into France from 1946 to 1962.

The Mediterranean countries compete elsewhere than in northern Europe. Increasingly, as labor markets tighten, migration will take place among these countries as well. Not only did Swiss agriculture have to turn to Spaniards when Italians proved difficult to get, but Italian employers have hired Spanish and Greek workers for seasonal work, and there is a call for Spanish maids

39. Georg Mai, "The Buderus'che Eisenwerke, Wetzlar," in OECD Joint International Seminar on Adaptation of Rural and Foreign Workers to Industry (Wiesbaden), *Supplement to the Final Report* (Paris, 1965), pp. 65–66.

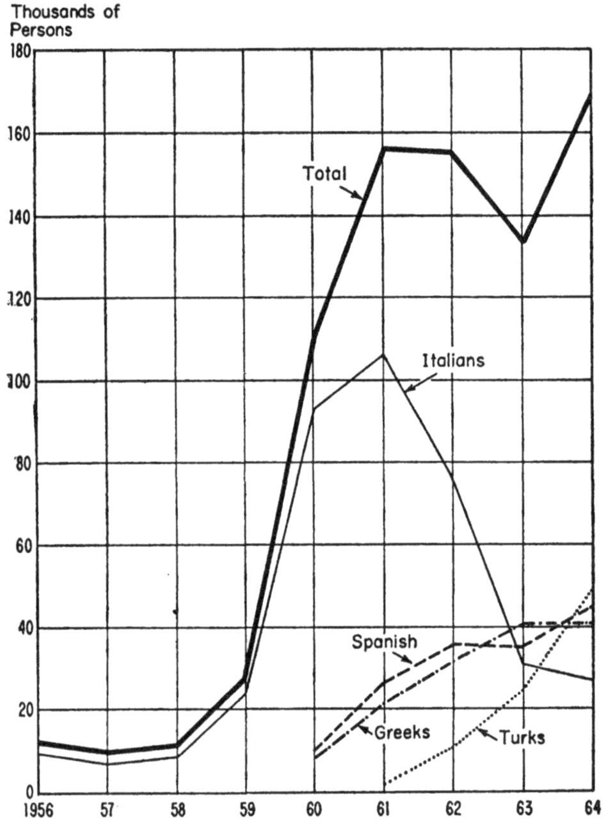

Figure IX-1. Foreign workers recruited abroad annually by German commissions, 1956–1964

Source: Bundesanstalt für Arbeitsvermittlung und Arbeitslösenversicherung, *Ausländischer Arbeitsnehmer, Erfahrungsbericht 1964,* Beilage zu Nr. 2 der ANBA vom 26 Februar 1965

in Rome to piece out the shortage. In Greece, a manufacturer threatens to turn to North Africa for labor if emigration continues to deplete the labor market.[40]

Some firms mix their foreign workers; others try to cling to particular nationalities to achieve economies in the use of lan-

40. See E. Dimitrias, summary of interviews in Greece, in "Adjustment of Rural Manpower to Industry: Practical Policies and Programs" (mimeographed material for OECD Working Party, 1964), p. 12.

guages, provision of local diet, worker housing, and so on. Where a firm specializes, the foreign nationalities may be determined by historical accident, implying largely Italian dominance since they were first in the field; later some other national group may replace the returning Italians. Ford, for example, specializes in Italians and Turks. Other firms indicate a preference for one nationality or antipathy against another, as shown in the following remarks:

Company X had Italians originally. It has now shifted its preference to Spanish who seem more productive. They are sick less, or possibly

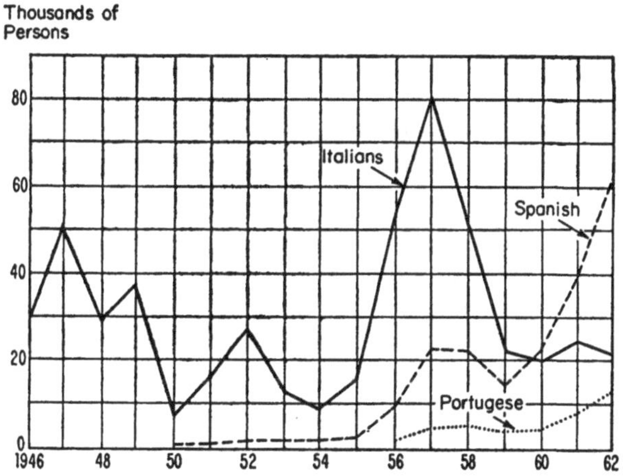

Figure IX-2. Immigration of permanent workers into France, 1946–1962

Source: "Les Travailleurs étrangers en France," *Notes et Etudes Documentaires* (La documentation française), No. 3057, 23 janvier 1964

they, unlike the Italians, do not take full advantage of the sick-leave and sickness-insurance provisions.[41] Their turnover is not so high.

41. The BAA statistics on illness do not bear out the widespread impression that the Italians take advantage of sick leave. There was something to the point with reference to Italian women, but Italian men and Italian workers as a whole as of October 1, 1964, had a lower rate of illness (4.95 percent) than Spanish (5.26), Greek (5.60), or total German and foreign workers combined (5.47). (BAA, *Ausländischer Arbeitsnehmer: Erfahrungsbericht 1964,* Sec. 12, p. 13.) More important is the fact that the foreign sickness rates seem high relative to the totals, given the concentration of foreign workers in the younger age groups.

Ninety percent of the remaining Italians have been with the company for an extended period and are really integrated.

The Spanish workers are also more individualistic than the Italians. They are more difficult to recruit in adequate numbers. The Greeks are easier to recruit, but not such good workers. . . . Foreign women are engaged in packing. They are Spanish and Greeks. They are fully interchangeable with the German women.

There are no Turks.

The first problem with the Greeks before learning to talk German is to teach them to read with the Latin alphabet. . . . This is a special disability of Greeks, who have difficulty reading instructions. It is easier to fit in Italians and Spanish. But the Greeks learn to speak German and to get along in it verbally faster than the Italians and Spanish. . . .

All these workers come from the deep country, but the Greeks are the most backward and have to be shown about electric switches, the functioning of the WC, the use of washing facilities, and the need for them, etc.[42]

A source reports from the Netherlands that Spanish workers seem to have less adaptation difficulties, but when they occur, they are more serious. According to this source, the Spanish also work harder, with a 2 percent rate of absenteeism as opposed to 5 percent for the Italians.[43] Some employers have preferences for nationals who come from a greater distance from the work place, so that they are not continuously going home for leave as the Italians do. But the Bundesbahn offers the Greeks and Turks cheap excursion rates for home leave, and the railroad itself is a preferred employer because workers ride free on the system. Turnover for foreigners on the railroad is particularly high, however, because many work for it for short periods at low salaries to travel home for weekends and soon quit.

The Skills of Mediterranean Labor

The limits to northern European recruitment of Mediterranean workers are probably set by the availability of skilled workers. After a time it is difficult to substitute unskilled for skilled work-

42. Interview notes, German firm, 1964.
43. M. Erixson, interviews in the Netherlands, "Adjustment of Rural Manpower," p. 25.

ers. It is true that the availability of unskilled workers from Europe helped the United States move to mass production and away from dependence on hand work. Much of the Mediterranean labor has gone on the assembly line in Europe. But common labor cannot be used without limit. Technological improvements reduce the need for unskilled hands: in Sweden, for example, it is found that road building is no longer suitable as a form of public works to raise employment, because it is no longer labor-intensive.[44] The disproportion between the 950,000 open jobs in Germany and the request for only 45,000 foreign workers, mentioned in an earlier chapter, suggests that foreign labor cannot meet German needs for skilled help. The point is made explicitly by the EEC.[45] As anyone who has seen the advertisements for professional and skilled labor in the Saturday *Frankfurter Allgemeine Zeitung* will know, the demand for skilled labor in 1964 was insatiable.[46] French official literature on the point states that the professional training of the Italians is satisfactory, especially in building, but that the same cannot be said for Spanish, Portuguese, Greeks, or more recently the Turks.[47]

Grave difficulties present themselves in an international market in equating skills between countries. A German skilled worker has gone through apprenticeship and after that needs a fixed number of years of work experience to qualify as a skilled carpenter, mason, joiner, and so on. When foreign labor is hired abroad, there is considerable difficulty in fixing skill equivalents. A building-construction firm in Frankfurt with 50 percent of its labor made up of foreigners said that it could go no higher in percent of foreign workers because of the skill problem. There are fine skilled workers among the foreigners, but the difficulty is sorting them out from the larger number who claim that they have learned a skill.[48] After some experimentation, the BAA

44. G. Lindström, "Sweden," in OECD International Management Seminar on Active Manpower Policy (Brussels), *Supplement to the Final Report* (Paris, 1965), p. 7 of mimeographed version.

45. EEC, "Les Problèmes de Main-Oeuvre dans la Communauté, en 1964" (mimeographed, 1964), p. 97.

46. I counted 37 pages of "tombstone" advertisements in the issue of July 4, 1964, and 40 pages in that of July 11. Maturi (*Arbeitsplatz Deutschland*, p. 9) refers to the *Inseratkrieg* ("advertisement war").

47. "Les Travailleurs étrangers en France," p. 24.

48. Interview, 1964.

commissions abroad undertook to test so-called skilled workers in practice. The annual reports furnish a small amount of information on "qualified workers," assembled in Table IX-2, from

TABLE IX-2

Qualified labor recruited for Germany, 1962–1964

	1962		1963		1964	
Nationality	Number	Percent of total recruited	Number	Percent of total recruited	Number	Percent of total recruited
Italian	15,060	19.6	4,483	14.1	5,411	20.4
Spanish	4,507	12.4	3,125	8.9	2,456	5.5
Greek	4,741	14.8	4,552	11.2	3,185	7.8
Turkish	5,160	46.8	4,233	18.1	9,268	16.9
Portuguese	—	—	—	—	203	11.3

Source: BAA, *Ausländischer Arbeitsnehmer: Erfahrungsbericht 1962* (Nürnberg, 1963), p. 12, and *Erfahrungsbericht 1964* (Nürnberg, 1965), p. 21.

among those recruited directly abroad. Other skilled labor may arrive in Germany by traveling privately.

Training opportunities are sought in foreign travel by individuals and governments alike. Some non-Europeans in German coal mines, largely Japanese and Koreans, have been sent for training by their respective governments. Under an agreement with the Egyptian government 2,000 so-called *praktikants* from Egypt work for a year in German business after a year in technical business colleges. The Finns have 200 young people studying the hotel business in Germany, learning to cater to German tourists. But these are of course very few compared with the opportunities for acquiring skill made available to the peasants of Anatolia, Epirus, Calabria, Asturias, and Vila Real. The Mediterranean governments frequently seek to provide for training in their agreements with northern European countries. Some training efforts have been undertaken, especially in Italy, by German firms and by the European Social Fund of EEC. But progress is limited.

For one thing, it is hard to teach skills unless the student can read or write the language of the country. Many German firms offer classes in the language, but takers are few and are easily discouraged, and no great success results.

What is impressive, however, is the speed with which raw countrymen become adjusted to factory work. The Buderus company notes that preliminary training varies from 4 weeks to 3 months, depending upon the type of job, and that training for certain jobs, such as casting polisher, mould emptier, caster, machine caster, is given after further experience and may take another 3 months.[49] The Ford-Werke training period lasts 4 to 6 weeks for welders and *Ausbeuler* (workers who knock dents out of metal). No distinction is made in advance between domestic workers and foreigners, if they know the language. Locksmiths and electricians have been trained among the foreign workers at this plant. A few skilled Italians trained in a technical institute run by Italians with Ford help in Cividale have been used as machine-tool makers after 8 months of special training at Cologne.[50]

The speed with which ordinary illiterate labor takes its place in the foundry or on the assembly line raises significant questions about the elaborate program of training the Hungarian refugees after 1956 and the widely expressed view in the United States that in today's world one must finish high school to work in a factory.

Cultural Integration

To the economist, integration means competition in the same market, and the test of complete integration is factor-price equalization, the one price which prevails in a single market.[51] To sociologists, on the other hand, integration has meant assimilation, represented in one significant dimension by easy intermarriage. Cultures become fused in a melting pot, and differences are eliminated.

The notions of a melting pot and assimilation are currently being modified and replaced by that of cultural pluralism, in

49. Mai, "The Buderus'che Eisenwerke, Wetzlar," p. 65.
50. "Einsatz von Ausländischen Arbeitskräften," p. 17.
51. See Gunnar Myrdal, *The International Economy* (New York: Harper, 1955), chap. 1.

which the separate cultures are held to coexist. Cultural integration takes place when the separate cultures interact and affect one another, but there is no necessity for them altogether to merge their identities.[52]

Studies of assimilation in Europe refer to the early spurt of postwar migration and were sponsored by UNESCO. As such, they dealt largely with Poles in Britain, Belgium, and France, with Italians in Belgium and France, and Algerians in France.[53] There is little work in existence or under way on cultural integration of Mediterranean peoples in Switzerland or Germany. While the earlier studies lay out the factors which bear on the decision to stay or return to the country of emigration — length of stay, density of settlement, marriage to a local, sending children to school in the new country, location of foreigners by residence, and so on — these have not been investigated with respect to the new conditions that obtained after the wave of migration beginning in 1959.

The economic importance of cultural integration or assimilation turns partly on whether the immigrant becomes a permanent member of the national labor market or not. So long as he is mobile, able to move from one job to the other, as in Germany

52. See W. D. Borrie *et al.*, *The Cultural Integration of Immigrants* (Paris: UNESCO, 1959), esp. chap. 5. See also Nathan Glazer and Daniel Patrick Moynihan, *Beyond the Melting Pot: The Negroes, Puerto Ricans, Jews, Italians, and Irish of New York City* (Cambridge, Mass.: M.I.T. Press, 1963); *Daedalus* (Spring 1961) — issued as vol. XC, no. 2 of the Proceedings of the American Academy of Arts and Sciences — especially the paper by Milton M. Gordon, "Assimilation in America: Theory and Reality."

53. See René Clémens, Gabrielle Vosse-mal, and Paul Minon, *L'Assimilation Culturelle des Immigrants en Belgique, Italiens et Polonais dans la Région Liégoise,* Travaux du Seminaire de Sociologie de la Faculté de Droit de Liége (Liége: Imprimerie Vaillant-Carmanne, 1953); Alain Girard and Jean Stoetzel, *Français et Immigrées, L'Attitude française, L'Adaptation des Italiens et des Polonais,* Travaux et Documents, Cahier No. 19 de l'Institut National d'Études Demographiques (Paris: Presses Universitaires de France, 1953); Institut National d'Études Demographiques, *Français et Immigrées, Nouveaux Documents sur l'Adaptation, Algériens-Italiens-Polonais, Le Service Sociale d'aide aux Emigrants,* Travaux et Documents, *Cahier* No. 20 (Paris: Presses Universitaires de France, 1954). See also J. Zubrzycki, *Polish Immigrants in Britain: A Study of Adjustment* (The Hague: Nijhoff, 1956). These studies are analyzed with others in J. Zubrzycki, "Across the Frontiers of Europe," in Borrie *et al.*, *The Cultural Integration of Immigrants,* chap. 9, pp. 159–180.

but not France or Switzerland, or able to move from one country to another, he adds greatly to the elasticity of the national labor supply.[54] When he returns permanently, he reduces it substantially. When he settles and puts down roots in the local scene (of the country to which he has emigrated), he reduces it somewhat because, with normal housing and schooling for his family, he is less mobile than earlier.

The risks a country takes by depending on foreign labor, which might move out en masse and leave certain occupations unattended, are discussed in the next chapter. Here it is possible only to collect certain opinions as to whether the Mediterranean workers will return to their own countries or not. It is useful in this connection to note that the general belief in a difference between American and European experience — holding that emigrants to the United States intended to stay, while those within Europe intend to return — may be true *ex ante* but is sharply overdrawn *ex post*. The eastward movement across the Atlantic in 1897–1918 was equal to 47 percent of the westward, and of those 2 million returnees after 1908 who replied to a questionnaire 77 percent had been in the United States less than 5 years, a further 18 percent only from 5 to 9 years.[55]

The French say that the decision whether to stay abroad or not is made only after 4 or 5 years.[56] An Italian official told me that the typical Italian going to Switzerland would take his family if he could, would stay 5 or 6 years, but would then return. Indeed, he always planned to return.[57] An informed view sug-

54. French and Swiss labor permits are given for one job only. In Switzerland, a permanent resident can take any job, but only 80,000 of the 480,000 Italians living in Switzerland have the right of permanent residence. The August 1964 agreement would have reduced the time period of temporary residence necessary to acquire permanence from 10 to 5 years, had it been ratified. A survey of Italian immigrants in Bouches-du-Rhône in France found that the restriction to remain in the same occupation for many years weighed heavily on immigrants (L. Mourgues, "L'Assimilation des Italiens dans les Bouches-du-Rhône," *Information Sociales*, No. 8, September 1954, p. 906; quoted by Borrie *et al.*, *The Cultural Integration of Immigrants*, p. 108).

55. Simon Kuznets and Ernest Rubin, *Immigration and the Foreign Born*, National Bureau of Economic Research, Occasional Paper No. 46 (New York, 1964), pp. 22, 30 n.

56. Haut Comité Consultatif de la Population et de la Famille, *L'Accueil des étrangers en France*, p. 21.

57. Interview, Division of Emigration, Italian Foreign Office, 1964.

gested, however, that if the Italian man did bring his family to Switzerland, his chances of returning were low.

Only a small percentage of Italians working in Germany would remain there, 7 percent according to one source, 5 percent, or half of the 10 percent who were married, according to an expert in the Federal Agency for Labor Recruitment and Unemployment Insurance. Perhaps 20 percent of the Greeks would settle in Germany, but it is too early to tell. The Turkish consul in Frankfurt believes that 10 to 15 percent of the Turkish workers would stay, especially those who marry German women. Buderus' experience is that about 30 percent of all foreign workers have stayed 3 or 4 years and seem to be settling in for a longer stretch, but it may be too early to make reliable estimates.[58]

Italians are believed to remain permanently in Belgium and especially Luxembourg. The latter has an extensive anti-Fascist tradition. The Italian workers formerly were not allowed to stay in Luxembourg, but as work at the iron mines expanded, the regulations were changed, and schools were even established with instruction in Italian. Luxembourg now has the highest proportion of foreigners in Europe, 33,000 out of a working force of 100,000. One official concerned with labor supply believed that 60 percent of the Italians in Belgium would settle permanently. An uninformed opinion was offered to the effect that 100 percent of the Spaniards arriving in Belgium were interested in staying.

A French report states that 45 percent of immigrants repatriated, but the calculations are not convincing. There were 1,750,000 foreigners resident in France at the time of the 1946 census, plus 875,000 immigrants over the years to 1962, for a total of 2,625,000. Some 425,000 foreigners were naturalized over the same period, and 1,800,000 foreign residents were counted in 1962, for a total of 2,225,000. The difference, or 400,000, left France. This is 45 percent of the immigrants.[59] But conditions in 1962, with many recent immigrants, were not comparable to 1946, with the bulk of the foreign residents of long standing. The figures do not reflect the position in the steady state.

French official opinion, however, shares the general view that those foreigners with families stay, whereas the single workers

58. Mai, "The Buderus'che Eisenwerke, Wetzlar," p. 68.
59. "Les Travailleurs en France," p. 14.

are unstable and likely to return. The French social structure with its liberal and even laissez-faire attitude favors assimilation. French requirements for labor eased after November 1963, when military service was reduced, and will decline sharply as the large classes of postwar youth enter the market. Even if new additions to the labor force are not needed, however, it is imperative that France hold on to foreigners currently in the country, a situation that poses a substantial challenge.[60]

60. *Ibid.*, pp. 21–24.

CHAPTER X

The Costs and Benefits of Labor Migration

Is Migration a Good Thing?

The costs and benefits of migration have been discussed in earlier chapters in many of their aspects — for the country of immigration in the case of Switzerland in Chapter II, and for the countries of emigration in Chapter V. The present treatment serves to recapitulate and sketch out an analysis appropriate to a broader and more general attack on the question of whether European migration has been and continues to be a good thing on balance. It is not, I hasten to make clear, a formal econometric calculation of costs and benefits in modern welfare-economic terms. The writer lacks the technical capacity to push the analysis far. In addition, it is not clear that a single answer can be distilled from the aggregate of the various possible approaches.

At the level of the individual employers and migrants, international migration can be said to be a good thing on the basis of revealed preference: employers hire foreign workers, and workers migrate to jobs abroad. Economic and social approaches to the problem may give different answers, however, with no easy way to net out a single result if the outcome should be positive on one score and negative on the other. Moreover, there may be different answers in the short run and in the long. In economic terms, a single outcome could be derived with the help of an appropriate shadow rate of interest: at high rates of interest the short-run calculation dominates; at low, the long. It is far from clear, however, that the shadow rates appropriate to, say, Germany and Switzerland should bear any relation to their market rates of interest, much higher for the former than for the latter. For lack of a numéraire, on the one hand, and of a social rate of interest, on the other, it is not apparent how short-run and long-run social advantages can be compared. Again, some allowance must be made over time for risk. If Switzerland benefits economically in the short and long run without too great social costs, is she warranted in continuing immigration if there is an increasing risk that a sudden exodus of foreign workers would leave the economy high and dry? This calls for an appreciation of the real risks so that they may be compared with present and prospective gains. Finally, of course, there is the difficult question of comparing benefits and costs between countries, in arriving at an overall judgment. If Germany benefits a little and Greece is hurt a lot, should the net be calculated on the basis of countries, relative populations, relative populations adjusted for income per capita, or how? In the light of these imponderables, it is evident that this chapter can do little more than suggest what the issues are.

Private Calculation of Costs and Benefits

For private employers and migrants, the benefits exceed the costs; otherwise the employment of the foreign worker would not take place or, if undertaken in error, would not continue. The fact that benefits exceed costs does not of course guarantee that migration will occur. It may be prevented by ignorance or by outside interference. But where the movement occurs, it is evident that the benefit was in excess of the cost, or at least was thought to be prospectively. The fact that one third of the emigrants break their contracts and return is suggestive of a discrepancy between prospect and actuality and indicates a social cost.

For employers, the added costs of hiring foreign workers over domestic at the same price are many: recruiting, translation and interpretation, accidents, absenteeism, and especially turnover. The turnover rate in Germany for foreign workers is 23 percent a year compared with 11 percent for all workers, foreign and domestic.[1] In some opinion, the domestic German turnover con-

1. BAA, *Ausländischer Arbeitsnehmer: Erfahrungsbericht 1964* (Nürnberg, 1965), p. 12. The Buderus Company reports rates of 12 percent for Germans and 47 percent for foreign workers (OECD Joint International Seminar on Adaptation of Rural and Foreign Workers to Industry [Wiesbaden], *Supplement to Final Report*, Paris, 1965, p. 68). Professor François Sellier of the University of Alençon is studying the rates of turnover in particular German plants and has kindly communicated some individual

tinues inordinately high, not only as a result of high demand but also because substantial proportions of the expellees and refugees have not decided on a permanent residence. The Ford Company has 1 interpreter for every 150 foreign workers.[2] One of the tasks of the interpreters is to explain the dangers of carelessness in the presence of machinery and to seek to bring down the high rate of accidents.

Absenteeism is related to turnover. Sickness rates were discussed in the last chapter. But special provisions for leave have been worked out by a number of companies to enable foreign workers to visit the home country. Buderus, for example, gives full annual holiday with pay and up to 3 weeks' unpaid leave for a man returning to his home, with a contribution of 70 marks toward the price of his ticket.[3] In France, the Algerian worker needs to return to North Africa periodically for periods up to 2 months, and most employers authorize this without breaking the contract. These workers are generally absent 2 months in 18 or 24.[4] These prolonged absences, which have their counterpart at harvest and planting time in less developed countries, are disruptive and expensive, but are preferred by employers as a precaution against workers' failure to return from the home country after the holidays.

Added expenses for housing construction are undertaken by some companies, though not exclusively for foreign workers.

---

plant material. Perhaps the most interesting item is the differences among various foreign groups in their capacity to last in the Hamborner coal mines, where 1,500 of the 13,500 workers employed in 1963 were non-German. The figures show that the Italians, Spanish, and Greeks were able to stand work in the mines less well than Turks, Japanese, and Yugoslavs. A breakdown at the end of 1963 showed that 50 percent of the first group worked less than a year and only 22 percent were still employed, whereas the respective percentages for the others were 17 and 61. The comparison is distorted by the fact that the Turks were numerous among the most recently hired, but even when the Turks hired in 1963 are eliminated, the percentages change only to 19 and 40, respectively ("Belagschatz und Sozialberichts," in the Hamborner & Thyssen Bergbau house organ *Der Förderturm,* 29th Year, No. 5, May 1964).

2. Interview, 1964.

3. OECD Joint International Seminar on Adaptation of Rural and Foreign Workers to Industry (Wiesbaden), pp. 68–69.

4. "La Main d'Oeuvre étrangère en France," based on a lecture by Ferdinand Besse, published by the Confédération Français des Travailleurs Chrétiens, in *La Revue du Militant Formation,* No. 41 (January 1962), p. 7.

Company policy varies widely depending upon the size of the housing need, accessibility to a large labor market, and perhaps social responsibility. Where a company wants to attract and hold large numbers of foreign workers, it is likely to build decent housing for single workers, and may be forced by the competitive situation into the provision of married housing in order to hold staff. It is possible that some investment in housing is defensive, with a low payout on the average but undertaken to prevent losses of workers. At the margin, the investment would be undertaken because it paid off.

The private costs borne by the foreign worker are largely in the level of living and in social displacement. Since migration is voluntary, the costs may be taken to be less than the benefits, except where the worker has been unable to support homesickness and separation, the real cost of migration, and has broken his contract to return home. (Breaking a contract to take a better job in another plant is indicative not of underestimation of the cost but of an opportunity to increase the benefit.) That these social costs are high for the worker and for his family left behind there can be no doubt. But there are other social and economic costs, like the probability of having an accident or working so hard to obtain cash and eating so cheaply that the worker undermines his health. In these cases the doctrine of revealed preference is little reassurance for the outside observer since it is evident that the dangers have been underestimated through ignorance. The Italian and Greek governments have adopted policies of full information about the conditions to be met by the emigrant abroad. Even with such policies, however, it is clear that no government can ensure that its citizens evaluate the prospective costs of emigration accurately.

Short-Run Economic Benefits and Costs

The ECE describes the economic significance of immigration as ability to meet the needs of undermanned sectors of the economy — mining, agriculture, domestic service, and many branches of agriculture; greater mobility; and ability to regulate the inflow to meet national needs. These are all different aspects of increased elasticity in the supply of labor. The benefits for the exporting country are stated to be relief of population pressure, help for the balance of payments, and in frequent cases the acquisition of skills.[5] A young economist attempting an economic calculation of the benefits for the country of emigration aggregated estimates for the return flow of remittances, plus the decline in consumption of the emigrants, less the decline in production ascribable to the loss of labor.[6]

As we have attempted to show earlier, these views are unduly restricted. In the country of immigration, short-run elasticity of the labor supply has a favorable impact on wages (holding them down), on profits (holding them up), on investment and growth, and on price stability. High rates of savings and of remittance abroad of the average emigrant make him contribute more to supply than to demand and thus hold down inflation. (This was less true of the Europeans moving to France from Algeria after 1962, since their Algerian losses had been made good in whole or substantial part by government subsidy, and their need to replace their real property gave a strong push to demand.) In the country of emigration, the removal of excess labor and the movement of the marginal product of labor to the conventional level of wages can stimulate growth there as well. The acquisition of skills is, as the ECE observes, a more problematic result, depending upon whether the emigrating workers learn anything useful abroad and whether they return after learning it. This is a long- not a short-run benefit.

Short-run economic costs for society are the consumption incurred in the country of immigration and the production foregone in that of emigration. The remittances paid by the country of immigration are also a cost, although they are below the increase in output out of which they are accumulated. The gain in elasticity of supply of labor in the country of arrival occurs at some expense of supply elasticity in the country of departure, but since that is already excessive — or is until the labor supply dries up, as in Italy in 1963 — the cost in the country of emigration is usually unimportant. Similarly there is no cost in the

5. ECE, *Economic Survey of Europe in 1962,* Pt. 1: *The European Economy in 1962* (Geneva: United Nations, 1963), chap. 2, p. 24.

6. G. Psacharopoulos, "The Economic Aspect of the Greek Emigration Problem" (term paper in the Graduate Department of Economics, University of Chicago, 1964), kindly communicated by Professor T. W. Schultz with the agreement of Mr. Psacharopoulos.

country of immigration corresponding to the gain from better allocation of resources leading to growth in the country of emigration.

Within the total for the country, immigration benefits noncompeting groups and hurts competing ones. Competition increases with time, so that the early gains of noncompeting groups are later cut. The normally expected economic impact that the addition of more labor will hurt domestic labor may not hold, first because domestic labor differentiates itself from foreign, by occupation and by nominal grade within the same occupation — wage drift affecting the domestic labor much more than the foreign. Second, of course, domestic labor benefits from the growth. There seems to have been no need to hold wages on the imported labor below its marginal product in the early stages (but above the average product in the country of emigration), as Abba Lerner has suggested, in an effort to turn off the opposition of domestic labor to immigration. Even with labor unions insistent on equality of wages, where immigration was encouraged (Germany) and tolerated (Switzerland, Belgium, and France after 1958) by the trade unions, noncompeting groups and wage drift have produced the Lerner result through the market place. The opposition of British, Scandinavian, Dutch, and Austrian unions to immigration seems to have been less an economic decision based on calculation than an instinctual distaste for foreigners (in Scandinavia, non-Scandinavians). Equally, in Germany the trade-union welcome to immigrants seems to have had its origin in uneasy consciences about the Third Reich's treatment of foreigners rather than in close economic calculation. The official view is that the unions are aware of the necessity to stimulate the influx of foreign manpower after the heavy losses of men in the productive years during the war.[7] In actuality, the fact that the Germans as a whole refer to "guest workers" rather than foreign workers and that the churches, charitable organizations, and even trade unions undertake a remarkable program of social work among the foreign workers reveals an effort to blot out the memory of the German treatment of "foreign workers"

7. M. Erixson, summary of interviews in Germany, in "Adjustment of Rural Manpower to Industry: Practical Policies and Programs" (mimeographed material for OECD Working Party, 1964), p. 28.

during World War II. In France weak unions opposed immigration prior to 1958 and then let it be forced on them with good grace, justifying the development in terms of the international traditions of Socialist and Christian unions. The Swiss case is unclear for lack of material, but there seems to be a difference between the position of labor, which was opposed to immigration so long as upgrading took place, and the employers, who favored more labor-market competition.[8] One suggestion for compromising between the economic benefit of cheap foreign labor and the social cost of too many foreigners was advanced as a semi-ironic suggestion by a Swiss economist: limit immigrant permits and then auction them off to employers to collect for the state the difference between what the foreigners were willing to work for and their value to enterprise.[9]

On a short-term basis, therefore, the benefits greatly outweigh the costs. Migration, like mercy, blesses him that gives and him that takes. The difficulties begin only when we move to the levels of longer-run economic costs and benefits and to the social problems.

Long-Run Economic Costs and Benefits

First take the country of immigration. In the early stages of the Lewis model, high profits permit the country to focus on productive capital. Because the foreign workers will accept low levels of accommodation — without their families and the concomitant need for schools, hospitals, and housing — investment in social-overhead capital can be kept relatively low. This is the opposite of the Rosenstein-Rodan model of growth in which a country starts with a heavy investment in social-overhead capital with a high capital/output ratio and only later, when the infrastructure has been built, is able to step up the rate of growth by

8. Note the statement by the Swiss trade-union official at the International Trade Union Seminar on Active Manpower Policy: "In the case of seasonal workers, it would be better if the work permit were issued only in respect of a given job, restricting labor mobility of foreign labor in this respect. This is perfectly justificable [*sic*]" (OECD International Trade Union Seminar on Active Manpower Policy [Paris], *Supplement to Final Report,* Paris, 1964, p. 177).

9. Interview, Zurich, 1964.

diverting investment into directly productive capital.[10] In the present case, men crowd into barracks and slums in the short run, as they did in the Industrial Revolution in Britain and in the period of heavy immigration in the United States. They are not content to do so for long. Moreover, there is a difference in the present competitive situation, with more than one country bidding for foreign labor, as contrasted with the weak municipal governments in Britain in the eighteenth century and the nineteenth up to the last 25 years and with the monopoly position of the United States as the Mecca of European emigrants. One country might get away with slums; no one country among four can do so.

The long-run benefits and costs may be unequally divided, with firms content to have wages held down even when they find it necessary to add equipment to go with the increments of labor, but governments bearing the burden of the social investment. Where housing and schools are provided by industry, as does occur, this asymmetry of cost and benefit is not so sharp. It can be significant, however, and give rise to differences of interest between enterprise and taxpayers.

Many economists suggest that the short-run gain of the Lewis model is bought at the cost of the long-run benefits from growth through increased substitution of capital for labor. In this view, steady wages maintain profits and support capital-widening. In the long run, the secret to growth is capital-deepening, with which steady wages interfere.

This raises a question in which our ignorance is profound. The steady level of wages did not inhibit rapid technological change in Britain in the period from 1815 to 1873, nor did rising wages after the latter date prevent the slowing down of technical progress up to World War I.[11] More currently, as we have seen, Britain has had a relatively slow rate of increase in productivity with a limited labor force and rising wages, whereas Germany has been able to shift smoothly from capital-widening to capital-

10. See P. N. Rosenstein-Rodan, "Notes on the Theory of the Big Push," in H. S. Ellis and H. C. Wallich (eds.), *Economic Development for Latin America* (New York: St. Martin's Press, 1961), pp. 57–73.

11. See my *Economic Growth in France and Britain, 1851–1950* (Cambridge, Mass.: Harvard University Press, 1964), chap. 7.

deepening as called for by the classic mechanism. In France, technical changes seem to have been relatively independent of the labor position. In Switzerland it may be true that the availability of large numbers of foreign workers prior to 1964 slowed down the movement toward automation and more capital-intensive methods, but the evidence is far from complete.

Analogously, the argument that immigration adds to mobility of the labor supply can be turned inside out by noting that obtaining high elasticity with immigrant labor enables a country to escape the necessity of making its domestic labor more mobile — a task with which it should get on. The Renault works recruited a contingent of Italians in Abruzzi in 1962 because it was unable to induce a sufficient number of Bretons to leave Brittany for the Flins plant outside Paris. This is regarded as a case where international migration replaced rather than supplemented internal mobility, just as capital-widening made possible by immigration may forestall capital-deepening that might have occurred otherwise.[12] But that it would have occurred otherwise, of course, cannot be taken for granted.

For the countries of emigration, the balance of long-run pluses and minuses is not so close. There is a chance of benefit to growth from the acquisition of skills, as has been noted. The improvement in land/labor and capital/labor ratios is permanent, and the stimulus to capital formation from more effective factor price tends to perpetuate itself. There may be political unrest — as when Asturias miners in the Ruhr send back contributions to their striking brethren in Spain, or when workers under Iberian dictatorships turn restive after having breathed the more democratic air of northern Europe. (From some points of view these results would be counted good.)

There is a risk, however, feared especially by Greece and in southwest France, that the exodus may go too far. Rather than stop at the optimum population, it may continue through inertia to reduce population to suboptimal levels. This is the cry of the bucolic sage (and agricultural economists), who worry that villages will be reduced to levels where they cannot support a variety of services necessary to civilization — doctors, schools,

12. Guy Barbichon, *Adaptation and Training of Rural Workers for Industrial Work* (Paris: OECD, n.d. [1963?]), pp. 24, 34.

distribution networks, and so on. There may be something to it. Experience in other countries, however, especially the increase in mobility made possible by the automobile, suggests that the fear of the deserted village is exaggerated. Ireland is perhaps a country which pushed emigration so far as to hurt, and the possibility must be recognized that the channels connecting Greek citizens with the outside world are so deep and wide that the country is in danger of being drained of its best citizens on a permanent basis.[13] But the Italian case is reassuring. Emigration helped growth. Growth stopped emigration and gave rise to a return flow. The particular localities left in the exodus did not receive back their complements of labor and householders, and the internal mobility induced by the return of southerners from Switzerland and Germany to northern Italy involves a cost in the need for new investment in the north, and a waste in the abandonment of lodging, some built with remittances from north of the Alps, in the Mezzogiorno. But the growth model based on emigration does contain the ability to reverse the movement. There is no inevitability that emigration will go too far.

We have touched above (pp. 98–100) on the plausible view that adult labor is capital, embodying the cost of its upbringing, and that poor countries should not export it. This view was found analytically unsatisfactory. It is just as valid to regard emigration as capital-saving, the permanent emigrants eliminating the need at home for productive and social capital at the average capital/labor ratio, just as, in the long run, immigration increases the need for capital in the receiving country.

Social Costs and Benefits

In the present section, the word "social" is meant in a broad context to include political, cultural, and sociological matters — everything, indeed, that comes under social science with the exception of the economic. Once "outside" economics, there is a temptation to say that the social aspects of emigration are all negative, with costs outweighing the benefits for the individuals

13. Note that the adult-education provisions of the Greek development plan for Epirus included instruction in the German language (Benjamin Ward, *Greek Regional Development*, Research Monograph Series, No. 4, Athens: Center of Economic Research, n.d. [1962?], p. 143 n).

concerned, for society, and for the polity. There are perhaps political gains for the nation experiencing a faster rate of growth as a result of either immigration or emigration. Added population may also contribute to political weight in the international equation, which leads France to seek to make up war losses through the addition of permanent immigrants. But the more general social and political aspects at first blush look negative. In the country of immigration: increases in crowding, crime, disease, cultural tension. In the country of departure: loss of the vigorous, the healthy, the youthful; breakup of the family; discontent with local conditions after the return. In both countries: the disturbance of political, religious, cultural, and in some cases language balance. This last can be seen both for Switzerland, where the several balances are of great importance, and for Greece, which has worried lest heavy migration from Macedonia disturb the political balance along the border with Albania, Yugoslavia, and Bulgaria.

One rather subtle political drawback is that, without provision for easy acquisition of citizenship, migration gives rise to the existence of a large group of disenfranchised people. They can perhaps vote by absentee ballot in the homeland, though the majority of their concerns are probably where they work and live. Not represented, they have no one to look out politically for their requirements. An important advantage of the German refugees and French Pied Noirs in the homeland after repatriation is that they had political power to enforce attention to their needs. The emigrants to the United States were quickly enfranchised and organized into political machines, with some undesirable features perhaps but responsive to the needs of the group. As yet there is no evidence of a breakdown in the difficult task of changing citizenship in Europe, so that the mass migration tends to create a class of *fliegende Südlander,* like the Wagnerian "Flying Dutchman," who are politically and possibly socially suspended between countries.

The suggestion that the social aspects of migration are all negative must be qualified in several ways. Some of the points made are exaggerated; some of the social distress is voluntary and is accepted in exchange for economic gain when the migrant has a choice; the list neglects some values which are positive.

The notion that the rate of crime among immigrants is higher than for local citizens and that emigration abroad exposes a young man to an iniquitous environment can be said to be exaggerated.[14] Exactly the same accusation was made against immigrants in the United States in 1890, but when the figures were corrected for age and urban/rural proportions, the foreign rates turned out to be the same as for native-born whites.[15] In the same fashion, the German Kriminalamt insists that rates of crime among foreign workers are no higher than among residents of German origin.[16] It is difficult to believe that a population which has a large element of single men separated from wives, fiancées, and women of the same culture should have no higher tendency to criminality than the permanent members of the settled community into which they are introduced. There may be something of a stretching of the facts by the authorities to reassure the local populace and to encourage it in acceptance of the "guests." The explanation for the impression which comes from reading the European press that foreigners have a higher crime rate than native-born peoples is that the crimes of the former are regarded by the press as more interesting and attract greater publicity. This is the exaggeration of social costs.

Voluntary distress occurs where a migrant worker clings to a very low standard of living despite a comfortable income, in order to send home as much as possible for consumption by his remaining family or in order to achieve more quickly the target

14. Consider, for example, the following passage from an article which in English would be titled "Exaggerations?" *Tovima* (Athens), February 12, 1965 (kindly communicated by the American Embassy, Athens):

"Seventy out of a hundred Germans are willing to work one hour a day longer, provided all the foreign 'guests' will return home. . . . But why should the Germans be willing to work longer? The answer is given by a French reporter. Unlawful prostitution, suspicious bars, alcoholism, narcotics, and misunderstanding. Besides these, the girls, even second-class, are very expensive, and so the 'guests' in order to be able to make their monthly remittances to their old parents, fiancées, or even wives are forced to steal and smuggle. It may also be added that besides the 'good' workers, many ex-convicts, smugglers, professional thieves, etc. have arrived in Germany, and they waste no time in finding and creating gangs. Result: violence in the streets, whole neighborhoods terrorized, and daily problems for the German police. . . ." (translation by M. Chacholiades).

15. John R. Commons, *Races and Immigrants in America* (3d ed.; New York: Macmillan, 1924), pp. 168–169.

16. "Per Moneta," *Der Spiegel*, No. 41/64 (October 7, 1964), p. 56.

amount of savings for which he has emigrated. In this case, the social distress can be condoned as it has been traded voluntarily for remittances or savings. Such malnutrition as occurs is likely to be of the voluntary sort. There is food enough in Europe, and, even though the Turk or the Portuguese may not be able to find an abundance of the kind of cooking he likes in the short run, kitchens available for cooking in the foreign style, canteens with foreign dishes, or restaurants catering to the foreign palate quickly respond to effective demand, for entry in these lines of endeavor is easy.

The situation in housing is more complex. Given the shortages remaining from the war and the varying success of European governments and construction industries in meeting it, housing of a decent standard for foreign single men but especially for foreign married couples and families may be impossible to obtain except at profiteering prices. Where companies or governments have not provided sufficient decent housing at moderate prices, slum landlords, frequently of the same nationality as the residents, move in to provide sleeping space of inadequate comfort and sanitation at prices which enable the foreign worker to meet his remittance or savings goal. Even where adequate housing is available, the disposition may still exist to work overtime at the risk of health and to submit to substandard accommodation in order to reach the savings target sooner. However, there may be a difference in attitude and understanding between the foreign workers and domestic landlords which gives rise to real costs. The foreign worker rents decent housing and overcrowds it with his compatriots and colleagues to such an extent that he pushes it into the slum class. This argument is used by landlords everywhere when they discriminate against minority groups, and it must be admitted that there is some truth in it. In this case the substandard living conditions are voluntary on the part of the tenant but involuntary from the landlord's point of view.

Finally, it must be stressed that there are positive social benefits to migration. For the Germans, the arrival of the "guest workers" provides an opportunity for atonement of past sins and for understanding cultural differences rather than condemning them out of hand. This is the theme of Maturi's book, *Arbeits-*

platz Deutschland.[17] The need for unintended political liberalization in Spain has been mentioned and can be regarded as positive. But the largest social benefit, albeit one that does not go uncontested, is the opportunity to reduce narrow nationalism and to build a European entity.

Migration may be regarded as a symptom rather than as a means. The Scandinavian countries have a loose community of identity: labor movements are allowed freely among them. They hold themselves slightly aloof from the rest of Europe. Therefore they limit inward migration. When the national identity is threatened, as is claimed in Switzerland and as has been the case in Greece, the desirability of building the larger entity is questionable.

There may be a question here of what is an optimum-sized social and political unit. The question cannot be answered without specifying the criteria or the variables to be maximized or minimized. The increase in economic, social, political, and cultural contact among Europeans, however, suggests the need for more and more institutions that transcend 1967 national boundaries, and efficient coordination of these institutions may in due course require supranational arrangements on a European scale. The development of a European-wide labor market with movement back and forth over present national boundaries might make a contribution to that long-run objective, so long as the movement stays within limits.

The Economic Risks of Dependence on Foreign Labor

Dependence on foreign labor in the 1930's provided a useful safety valve against domestic unemployment, since the foreign labor could be shipped home. This occurred in France and Switzerland. Today it is no longer possible to use foreign labor as the marginal unit.[18] It might be possible for a country like Switzerland not to rehire seasonal workers, but an attempt to push out

17. Giacomo Maturi, *Arbeitsplatz Deutschland: Wie man südländische Gastarbeiter verstehen lernt* (Mainz: Krausskopf, 1964).

18. In the Netherlands it was stated by Minister Veltrop, sometime before June 1964, that in the event of unemployment Dutch employers were not obliged to discharge foreign workers ahead of Dutch. This was viewed as a concession to employers (interview, The Hague, 1964).

large numbers of foreign workers would today be regarded as a flagrant violation of international agreements and of decent behavior. In addition, the foreign workers would be entitled to unemployment insurance. Instead, the risks are largely borne today by the countries of immigration.

Foreign labor is highly mobile. This means it can transfer readily from firm to firm, occupation to occupation, and region to region within a country and between countries and between abroad and home. As Italian prosperity increased, Switzerland found itself having to go further afield to obtain workers to replace those who went home. And if all the Mediterranean countries were to advance in growth at a rapid rate, the return flow of workers might endanger the countries of immigration. So long as relative economic conditions are the same, a large turnover with a small or no net change is tolerable. When big discontinuous changes occur, the cutting off of new immigration and some acceleration of repatriation could produce a very sharp reduction in labor inputs. Some percentage of the foreign immigrants would remain permanently — 5, 10, 30? The various guesses were discussed in the previous chapter. But a very large decline could take place in a short space of time. This constitutes a risk, the mean probability of which times the probable loss caused by the departure of the workers must be regarded as a cost to offset against the benefits from the inward movement.

West Germany, too, runs an inescapable risk from the presence within its boundaries of the expellees and refugees from East Germany. In the event of reunification, a considerable number of these people may choose to return to their former homes and to reconstitute their lives and businesses outside the confines of West Germany. The risk is doubtlessly low and declines with each passing year. The adjustment of these Germans in West Germany has been easier than that of strangers from a different culture and with a different language, who will remain in much lower proportions. But the risk is positive.

In discussing the possibility of embarrassment through simultaneous return of immigrants, the case of the Irish in Britain may be cited. Here was a large foreign contribution to the British labor force, and large turnover occurred. Net movements were relatively small, however, for gross inward migration took up the places left by gross repatriation. The same has been true in the past, before 1958, of the Algerian contribution to the French labor force.

But it is intellectually dangerous, even if in particular cases it may work out satisfactorily, to regard migration as the result of two large randomly distributed forces or to see the repatriation decision as one which is taken independently by immigrants so that their length of stay follows some normal distribution. The Irish analogy is dangerous because Ireland failed to respond effectively to the stimulus of emigration in rapid economic growth, to narrow the gap between her level of living and that of the British. Irish labor used to go to England on a regular basis: agricultural workers for the harvest, cattle dealers twice a year, and laborers from the beginning of the Industrial Revolution to dig docks and canals, work on railroads, and in factories and mills. In the first 5 months of 1847, however, 300,000 Irish landed in Liverpool, requiring that city to bring in 2,000 troops and swear in 20,000 citizen police to cope with the multitude.[19] In the face of common causes, the decision to move is taken interdependently, and the movements may be large. It must be admitted that the likelihood and the risk are small.

The Limits to Dependence on Foreign Labor

What are the limits to dependence on foreign labor, and are they economic, social, political? Is a halt called to immigration by the interest groups most deeply affected, or is there some national consensus that says, at some point, thus far and no farther? The case has already arisen for Switzerland, which cut down the continued intake of foreign labor when the foreigners reached 30 percent of the labor force (and 15 percent of the total population). It has arisen with respect to colored Commonwealth subjects in the United Kingdom, with the present number some 850,000 out of a total labor force of 25,000,000 (3.4 percent). It arose in the United States with foreign-born at something like 20 percent of the labor force but with the prospect of a very large influx after the interruption caused by World War I. Leadership was taken in the restriction movement by

19. Cecil Woodham-Smith, *The Great Hunger, Ireland, 1845–1849* (New York: Harper & Row, 1962), pp. 270–281.

trade unions, though along inefficient lines. A craft union led the political attack against contract labor, though most of the inward movement was of unskilled labor, recruited by steamships and railroads and not bound by contract.[20] The basic cause of restriction, however, was the widespread fear that immigration was likely to take place at faster rates than could be assimilated or integrated. Hence the restrictions applied first to Chinese, along with contract labor, then to the ill, to paupers, and so on and on. An important but unsuccessful attempt was mounted to make immigration subject to a literacy test. The main force for limitation was "nativism." [21]

If Switzerland with foreigners at 30 percent of the labor force is calling a halt, what about Belgium at 10 percent, France at 9 percent, and Germany at 4.4? [22] I asked the question of numerous people in Germany and found little concern. The 1,500,000 foreign workers envisaged for 1970 out of a labor force of 26,500,000 (5.7 percent) would not be seen as a problem.[23] Stuttgart with 12 percent of its work force foreign might be nearing some sort of limit, but not the artificial fiber industry with 16.1 percent or the metal industry with 13.8 percent in iron and steel casting and 11.5 percent in metal-making generally.[24] Here the limits seem to have been set less by social resistance, though signs of it are not altogether missing, than by the availability of the proper mix of skills (see above, p. 189). In traveling about Germany I found that many people were unwilling even to discuss immigration restriction, although on being pressed they would admit that 30

20. Charlotte Erickson, *American Industry and the European Immigrant, 1860–1885* (Cambridge, Mass.: Harvard University Press, 1957), Pt. III.

21. Maldwyn Allen Jones, *American Immigration* (Chicago: University of Chicago Press, 1960), chap. 9.

22. One should distinguish between old immigrants, who are virtually fully absorbed, and new arrivals. The French and Belgian figures are twice as high as the German but present less serious problems since much of the immigration is old. Another reason, of course, is that much of it is of the readily assimilated Latin peoples. See above, p. 180.

23. EEC, *Economic Development Prospects in the EEC from 1960 to 1970: Report by a Working Party* (Brussels, 1962), p. 25. This report envisaged an increase in foreign labor of 800,000 between 1960 and 1965, and an increase of 400,000 between 1965 and 1970. Since the 1,000,000 figure was crossed in 1964, 1,500,000 makes a reasonable revised estimate for 1970.

24. BAA, *Erfahrungsbericht 1964*, pp. 40–41.

percent of the labor force, as in Switzerland, was too much. Doubling the proportion of foreigners was thought acceptable. There was little intellectual interest in the question of limits for white workers, though some sociological research was being conducted on the problems of colored peoples in Germany despite the fact that their numbers are very small. The social costs and the resistance point may be higher for some communities than for others: it is said that Turin suffers more from the presence of southern migrants than Milan because it is a closed community, with a tradition of turning inward, while Milan, like the Rhineland in Germany, has a long tradition of receptivity to the outside world.

In conclusion, therefore, the short-run economic benefits of intra-European labor migration are positive, though there are social costs. In the intermediate and long run, the economic advantages become less clear, and some social advantages are possible. To rely heavily on foreign labor in one's economy constitutes a positive risk. It does not seem impressive until some considerable percentage of the labor force is foreign. Thirty percent is too high. Ten percent seems acceptable, particularly where there is cultural similarity. To locate the discontinuities more precisely is probably impossible.

CHAPTER XI

Incomes Policy, Active Manpower Policy, and Planning

Substitute for an Elastic Labor Supply?

The importance attaching to an elastic labor supply is seen in the widespread attempts to find substitutes for it. There are three main candidates: one, the most common, is so-called incomes policy, usually a euphemism for wages control; the second, less widely advocated, but strongly urged by the OECD Manpower Division, is "active manpower policy." This covers a wide range of activities including retraining, subsidies to labor transfers, tax concessions, special inducements for entry into the labor force of the old, of women, university students, and other groups, the recruitment of labor abroad, and assistance for all kinds of transfers to increase the numbers of those who make regional, occupational, or international shifts of jobs. A third, not strictly alternative to the first two, is planning. It is perhaps not prejudicial to objective discussion of the first two techniques to characterize incomes policy as price fixing and active manpower policy as holding down price after an increase in demand by manipulating the supply curve of labor. It is dangerous to characterize planning, but at the risk of oversimplification it may be said to project supply, manipulate demand, and leave a gap which can be closed by one means or another. It may be, but is not necessarily, concerned with fixing wage rates.

Incomes Policy

Incomes policy is, as noted, frequently discussed, debated, and urged. Indeed, one unusually defensive mathematical economist, commenting upon a work in pure theory, became sufficiently exasperated to say: "The book will not help us directly in improving the British balance of payments or in formulating an incomes policy; but it is only the vulgar who demand this of every piece of economic writing." [1]

Incomes policy is sometimes thought of as an alternative to devaluation. If a country has two targets — full employment and balance-of-payments equilibrium — it needs two weapons to achieve them simultaneously, according to the theory of economic policy. One weapon is changes in expenditure, which can include both monetary and fiscal devices; the other is some means to regulate the value of wages in international terms. This can take the form of altering the rate of foreign exchange, or, with a fixed rate, it can be incomes policy.[2] If there are three objectives — full employment, balance-of-payments equilibrium, and price stability — three weapons must be used. With a fixed rate, monetary and fiscal policy can be called upon to operate in different directions, along with incomes policy.[3] If they move together as a single expenditure policy, one needs, in addition, exchange-rate policy and incomes policy.

It is all very well to indicate the need to regulate the price of labor. The trick is to do it. One can calculate the appropriate increase in wages permissible without increased prices, by averaging the increase in labor productivity, and establish national "guideposts," as they are called in the United States, or a "guiding light" (in Britain). It may be something quite different to keep separate wage bargains to the stipulated level, especially where increases in productivity are large, or where the claim can be made that wages in an occupation have lagged behind the general movement. The argument as to why wage increases should be limited to the national productivity in lines of above-average increase is well known: if some prices rise, and the average is to be held constant, other prices must fall. In industries with below-average increases in productivity — typically

1. F. Hahn's review of M. Morishima's *Equilibrium, Stability and Growth*, in *Economic Journal*, LXXV (March 1965), 155.

2. Trevor Swan, "Longer-run Problems of the Balance of Payments," in H. W. Arndt and W. M. Corden (eds.), *The Australian Economy: A Book of Readings* (Melbourne: Cheshire, 1963), pp. 384–395.

3. Robert A. Mundell, "The Appropriate Use of Monetary and Fiscal Policy for Internal and External Stability," *Staff Papers*, IX (March 1962), 70–79.

the labor-intensive lines such as services — wages must be raised to the national average to prevent the diversion of workers to other lines. With higher wages and small increases in productivity, prices here must rise. Balance is achieved if, in lines of higher than average productivity, wages rise less than productivity, and prices fall. Elasticities of demand in response to these price changes will bring about quantity shifts from goods and services of high elasticity and higher prices (low productivity) to those of high elasticity and lower prices (high productivity). The difficulties are that if prices are sticky and decline slowly in the highly productive industries, stability is threatened immediately, and even if they ultimately would come down with wages held within the guidelines, transitional profits are likely to be high in the industries of high productivity. This encourages the industries to exceed the guidelines to keep labor happy. In addition, every craft and industry union can muster arguments of impressive weight, though frequently of dubious merit, to show why it at least should receive a substantial increase to close a gap or to restore a traditional differential. When it is decided to halt wage increases after a continuous process of rises, it will be true that many groups — often civil servants (particularly in international agencies), teachers, pensioners, and so on — will have a valid claim for a substantial boost. In Britain teachers received a raise of close to 25 percent, and later postmen one of 20 percent (over 2 years). These big increases in the interest of equity are readily seized upon by other groups as the occasion to resume the escalation process.

Not only is incomes policy difficult to administer, but there are many economists who claim that it is illusory to try. Price fixing is mistaking the substance for the shadow. The way to hold down wages is to hold down demand. With demand at high levels, to interfere with clearing the market through wage bargains is to require a different mechanism for the allocation of labor. If the price system is not used to allocate labor, some direct means must be adopted such as distribution from a central pool or national employment service.[4] Such interference with freedom of contract is usually regarded as repugnant or even intolerable,

4. F. W. Paish and Josselyn Hennessy, *Policy for Incomes?*, Hobart Paper 29 (London: Institute of Economic Affairs, 1964), p. 22.

except possibly in wartime, so that it follows that the way to hold down wages is to restrain demand. In this view there is no such phenomenon as cost-push inflation on which the theory of incomes policy is based. An attempt at raising wages in advance of demand expansion, or without almost immediate confirmation by an increase in demand, would be followed by unemployment. Since cost-push inflation cannot exist, incomes policy has no point.

There is something to this view, but not much. In a well-known article, Paul Samuelson and Robert Solow dispose of the *a priori* belief that wage push is impossible by suggesting that demand-pull inflation implies movements along a given Phillips curve, while cost-push inflation means displacement of the curve itself.[5] Clearly, both are possible. Moreover, a distinguished international group of experts examining the controversy between the cost-push and demand-pull schools concluded: "We believe that wages have generally risen faster than they would have done solely under the influence of demand in a competitive market."[6] Two members of the committee attached reservations to the general recommendation that wage policy is desirable.[7] These reservations applied less to the theory than to the practice, which they believed implies wide interference with wage-setting activity by government with limited chance of success. Neither they nor the majority of the committee, after detailed examination of experience in a number of countries, however, were in doubt as to the existence of pressure on wages from the side of supply.

A significant point made by the OECD experts is that marked differences exist from country to country, both in the degree of wage push and in the response of the labor market to the application of incomes policy.[8] This accords with what has been seen earlier. Dutch labor organizations, for example, have been readier than British to support a national policy of wage restraint, although wage drift and black wages were substantial in Holland under pressure of demand, and incomes policy broke down there in 1963. German and Swiss wage increases were moderate in the

5. See P. A. Samuelson and R. M. Solow, "Analytical Aspects of Anti-Inflation Policy," *American Economic Review*, L (May 1960), 177–194.
6. W. Fellner, M. Gilbert, B. Hansen, R. Kahn, F. Lutz, and P. de Wolff, *The Problem of Rising Prices* (Paris: OECD, 1961), p. 50.
7. *Ibid.*, pp. 63–64.
8. *Ibid.*, p. 55.

face of high demands. While Chancellor Erhard has called business and labor leaders to Bonn to discuss wage policy, no official wage policy has been adopted by that name, and the moderation of the wage demands on the part of labor has been surprising, to Germans as well as to outside observers.[9] So sensitive is German labor to the accusation that their demands might endanger export competitiveness or price stability that the country may be said to have applied incomes policy from below. At the opposite extreme, the British government has had a Council on Prices and Productivity (1957), a Pay-Pause (1961), a National Incomes Council (1962), under the Labour government a declaration of trade-union and employer intent to abide by guidelines (1964), and a Prices and Incomes Review Board (1965), without succeeding in slowing down perceptibly the sharp rise of wage rates in periods of high demand and moderate rises during recession.

In many lines of economic policy, what counts is less the character of the policy than the social, political, and institutional context in which it is applied. Immediately after World War II, it was said that whatever the shortcomings of the disequilibrium system of regulated prices, wages, rationing, priorities, foreign-exchange controls, and allocations of materials and manpower, some countries could operate it better than others. The then-existing discipline of the British, Scandinavians, and Dutch made the system more appropriate to their countries than it would be to Italy, France, or Germany. No country perhaps can run the disequilibrium system effectively over a long time without the pressure of a strong national purpose such as war, reconstruction, or a development spurt; under given circumstances, some countries function more effectively with it than do others. Perhaps no democratic country in the world can match the Dutch record of rent controls with allocation of dwelling space, including the assignment of tenants to house-owners with excess space. In the same way, incomes policy possibly cannot stabilize wages and prices under heavy pressure of demand in any country, but it can do better in some than others. It may be that differences in the social matrix from one country to another are much more important in this matter than differences in the content of incomes policy or the strictly economic skill with which it is applied.

9. *Frankfurter Allgemeine Zeitung,* July 10, 1964.

Indeed, the German experience suggests that differences in labor attitudes and behavior may be more important than whether incomes policy is applied or not.

Much depends upon the circumstances under which wages are regulated. A wage policy cannot be effective except as "part of a coordinated effort to achieve a clearly defined national objective in which the relation between national interests and trade union wage action may be given unambiguous and measurable significance." [10] Price stability and economic growth probably do not qualify as national objectives of this sort. Leiserson found wage policies ineffective in the United Kingdom, Scandinavia, and the Netherlands even before the real pressure on wages in the early 1960's, and he regards the record of Germany and France with no declared wage policies ("wage policies by indirection and default") as more impressive than those of countries which were consciously trying to direct incomes. Black wages, wage drift, upgrading — a host of devices, legal and illegal — exist to frustrate the purposes of wage policy applied under normal conditions by broad directive and moral suasion.

The Labour government's difficulties in translating the declaration on incomes policy of December 1964 into practice in succeeding months led it to threaten to apply mandatory incomes and price policies, which seems to mean giving an enlarged Prices and Incomes Board the power to fix wages and prices, where changes are referred to it, and not merely to express its approval or disapproval. This possibility was anticipated by Messrs. Fellner and Lutz in their reservation in the experts' report on *The Problem of Rising Prices* and was opposed by them. Once governments begin to deal not with averages and trends but with specific wage rates and prices in specific industries, they foresee "political considerations and the usual group pressures." [11] Even if there were no danger of a political solution, it is far from clear that economics is in a position to furnish efficient systems of price and wage determination outside the

10. Mark W. Leiserson, *A Brief Interpretative Survey of Wage-Price Problems in Europe,* Study Paper No. 11 for Consideration of the Joint Economic Committee, 86th Cong., 1st sess. (Washington: Government Printing Office, 1959), p. 55.

11. Fellner *et al., The Problem of Rising Prices,* p. 55.

market process. For a limited time it would be enough to prevent wage and price increases, and perhaps to order price reductions in a few industries of high profits. The trial and error of the market could be replicated by trial and error by the Prices and Incomes Board. After a time, however, there is considerable doubt whether the system could be made to function efficiently, for cumulative creep from the equilibrium solution would necessitate large structural changes, which the authorities would have no way of gauging accurately and which would not be acceptable to the public on a trial-and-error basis.

The purpose of incomes policy is usually given as price stability, most often for balance-of-payments stability. In a few instances, however, and especially in France, the goal is to restore or maintain profit margins to stimulate investment; the aim may even be to relieve pressure on the capital market by providing corporations with internal sources of savings to meet their investment needs.[12] This is wages policy with a vengeance. In the British case, where price stability is the target, wages policy is equated with incomes policy through some explicit or implied restraint on other income shares, including profits—all of which is difficult enough. To roll back wages in order to enlarge profits, however, is sufficiently antithetical to common ideas of social justice that it seems politically excluded.

Active Manpower Policy

A complete or partial alternative to regulation of wages and prices is manpower or labor policy. The Swedish government claims that labor-market policy is *"a necessary element of an economic policy that aims at full employment, stable money and a higher standard of living"* (italics in original). The function of a labor-market policy "can be described as a continuous striving to eliminate unemployment and satisfy the demand for labour by promoting adjustment between sectors of over-supply and sectors of over-demand." While a labor-market policy has many elements, including bringing jobs to workers, "special importance should be given to measures for stimulating adaptation of labour

12. Antonin Basch, *Capital Market of the European Community: Problems of Integration* (Ann Arbor: University of Michigan Bureau of Business Research, 1965), p. 97.

to economic change: a well-informed and efficient placement service, generous facilities for retraining of adults, and financial support to workers willing to move from labour surplus to labour shortage areas, etc." [13]

The ingredients of an active labor policy have been discussed in Chapter VIII. Apart from policies affecting immigration and the birth rate, to which we return presently, they include measures affecting participation rates, mobility, readiness of enterprise to hire and discharge workers, training at the apprentice, adult, and retraining stages, provision of housing, transferability of pensions, and so on. The nature of these measures has also been mentioned and in some cases discussed. Participation rates for women can be affected by tax adjustments to remove the disincentive to work under high marginal tax rates for a wife where the husband has an income. Geographic mobility is stimulated by subsidies for transfers and by realistic rents. Enterprise is encouraged to hire workers by low provision for redundancy benefits upon discharge and encouraged to part with labor by taxes on employment. High unemployment benefits assist by rendering labor more willing to be discharged in the even of slack demand. Subsidies to housing construction encourage workers to move to crowded areas.

But there is considerable question whether this sort of policy can change mobility greatly. The major mobile elements in a labor force are (1) a large natural addition of young people to the labor force; (2) a substantial transfer of surplus labor from the farm to the city; (3) immigration. Short-run policies can do little to affect the natural increase in the population, and there is even doubt whether long-run policies can do so.[14] And many

13. OECD, *Labour Market Policy in Sweden* (Paris, 1963), p. 20. For a recent discussion of worker relocation see the pamphlet prepared by Martin Schnitzer for the Joint Economic Committee, Economic Policies and Practices, Paper No. 8, *Programs for Relocating Workers Used by Governments of Selected Countries*, Joint Economic Committee, 89th Cong., 2d sess. (Washington: Government Printing Office, 1966), treating, in Europe, mainly the United Kingdom, Sweden, and France.

14. There is, for example, debate in France whether the reversal of the interwar demographic experience in France after 1946 was a delayed response to the subsidies of the Family Code of July 1939, or the result of an independent change in tastes. See my *Economic Growth in France and Britain, 1851–1950* (Cambridge, Mass.: Harvard University Press, 1964), chap. 4.

long-run policies for growth or social development, like the extension of the school-leaving age, run contrary to the appropriate short-run policies for labor mobility. Changes in military recruitment have a large impact on youthful entry into the labor force, but these policies, too, are almost invariably decided on other grounds than labor mobility.

Some room for maneuver exists with respect to the farm-to-city movement. A country like Britain, of course, with a very small proportion of its labor force attached to agriculture, can make little use of such room as exists for affecting the transfer of workers from agriculture to industry and services. Other countries, however, can use direct measures such as tightening or relaxing prohibitions against seeking urban employment; they may also use indirect measures such as higher agricultural prices and incomes, which hold labor on the farm, or lower prices and income, which speed up the movement. And the movement can be assisted or discouraged according to whether recruitment, training, provision of housing, and so on are carried on or not. Education may in fact be necessary to qualify rural population for urban living, since in some European countries, perhaps notably France, universal education has been on the books for a long time but honored in the breach rather than the observance in the remoter portions of the country. In the agricultural demonstrations of 1961, for example, one of the complaints of the farmers in the Vendée and Brittany was that they did not have enough education to be able to leave the farm for the city.

While the economic opportunities may exist, constraints may coexist in the political sphere. One would expect Germany, the country of labor shortage *par excellence,* to want lower farm prices and incomes to encourage the movement off the farm into urban occupations. The Christian Democratic Union, however, has a large part of its support among the rural inhabitants and so is obliged to fight in the European Economic Community for higher prices for wheat and other farm products. Political necessity has counterproductive economic consequences. There may also be political limitations on the use of foreign labor — for example, the refusal of the Swiss legislature to ratify the 1964 treaty on foreign workers with Italy, or the defeat of a Labour candidate of cabinet rank in Smethwick because of the color issue. Where immigration is politically acceptable, however, it provides a margin of effective mobility to the labor force which, in the absence of a bulge of new native recruits to the labor force or a heavy movement of educated farm children or adults to the city, can hardly be achieved by active manpower policy.

The point was put strongly by the OECD examiners of Swedish manpower policy. These OECD reviews of manpower and social policies proceed with a statement of policy by the domestic authorities, followed by a report by external examiners who have studied the earlier report and submitted various of the authors to questioning. In the Swedish report, the Dutch and Danish external examiners, both natives of countries which have fairly restrictive attitudes toward foreign immigration, raised the question of whether Sweden should not consider a more active immigration policy.[15] Swedish population growth is slow; moreover, housewives are likely to prefer part-time to full-time work. Other Scandinavians may return to their home countries as incomes there rise. Since working hours are expected to decrease — holidays having just been increased from 3 to 4 weeks and the 45-hour week likely to be opposed by labor influenced by the EEC example — the examiners regarded the normal ingredients of an active labor-market policy (more developed in Sweden perhaps than in any other part of Europe) as insufficient. They recognized that "the problem of a consistent immigration policy, as a long-term measure, may not have found its final solution." But, they said, "it seems that certain problems could be more easily solved by immigration than by internal migration. It could also be stressed that increased migration to Sweden with its high level of productivity would be a contribution to the common growth target of O.E.C.D." [16] The second sentence quoted is an *obiter dictum* so far as this discussion is concerned. The point to be stressed is that elasticity of the labor force may be more easily achieved in economic terms, though not necessarily in political matters, by immigration than by internal migration. An active manpower policy that fails to deal with birth rates, the move-

15. OECD, *Labour Market Policy in Sweden*, p. 53.
16. *Ibid.*, pp. 62, 68.

ment of farm workers to the town, or immigration will still have to cope with a great variety of subjects, but their total effect will be relatively limited.[16a]

Planning

A third alternative to a naturally elastic labor supply may be said to be planning. This presumably goes beyond active manpower policy. By implication, one French authority characterizes active manpower policy as "mere empiricism and pragmatism" which are "not enough." [17] Presumably complete planning would imply a wages policy, as the matrix of factor inputs and goods-and-service outputs implies a set of goods and factor prices. It seems evident from the discussion of French experience, however, that planning in practice does not always involve wages policy, since it is said to require supplementation with incomes policy.[18] What then is planning in the manpower field?

First and foremost, planning in the French context is projection or forecasting. A major ingredient in determining the planned rate of growth is manpower availability. Among the 5 horizontal commissions which operate functionally across the 23 vertical industrial bodies is the Manpower Commission. It has access to the work of demographic experts.[19] In the early stages of the Plan it projects manpower flows in and out of the economy, overall as well as by sectors and by regions, and estimates the possible shifts from sector to sector and region to region. The rate of overall growth is then determined to a considerable extent as a function of the capacity of the economy to provide the requisite manpower of the requisite skill in the requisite place.

There is some question whether these projections of man-

16a. Long after this manuscript was finished, it has been learned that Sweden in fact did experiment with a much more liberal policy of immigration, presumably in 1965, but abandoned it in 1966 because of social problems.

17. Bernard Vrillon, "Active Manpower Policy in France," in OECD International Management Seminar on Active Manpower Policy (Brussels), "Supplement to Final Report," forthcoming, p. 29 of MS.

18. John Hackett and Anne-Marie Hackett, *Economic Planning in France* (Cambridge, Mass.: Harvard University Press, 1963), chap. 17.

19. Haut Comité Consultatif de la Population et de la Famille, *Les Besoins en emplois nouveaux en France par department jusqu'en 1970* (Paris: La documentation française, 1961).

power availability have yet reached perfection. The rate of growth of the Fourth Plan was raised from 5 to 5.5 percent, according to some views because of the prospective return in 1962, the first year of the plan, of the large numbers of Pieds Noirs from Algeria. (Another opinion is that the growth rate was estimated at the very high level of 5.5 percent without any clear idea of the numbers of returning Europeans and was saved by that unexpected event.) When it became clear that repatriation would take place on a large scale, the Fourth Plan foresaw 500,000 returnees in 3 years. As we have seen, there were in fact 800,000 in a few months.[20] Earlier the Third Plan had anticipated a loss of 600,000 workers in agriculture from 1954–1961, an average of 85,000 a year. Though this estimate was criticized as excessive at the time it was made, it was later raised to 110,000. Both figures, however, fell far short of the reality, which was 150,000 a year. The Third Plan projected an increase of 630,000 jobs in industry. Output goals were more than achieved with only 480,000 more workers.[21] The several Plans have provided for maintenance of the high French work-week, which the government has been able to achieve despite the pressure of unions and the reduction of the working week in neighboring Germany. On the question of holidays, the Plan was not so successful, yielding, as noted earlier, to the demand of labor at the government-owned Renault Company.

But French planning is much more than projecting a series of outputs and requisite inputs, which are then handed over to industry and to the labor market to carry out. In the first place, under an "indicative" plan, industry is free to produce what it wants, with or without the guidance of the plan, so that it is necessary to maintain surveillance over the economy and the pressures on it. Secondly, the importance of growth as a target means that the Plan leaves little margin for safety in meeting its input requirements. Margins are shaved, and the labor market is kept under pressure to adjust to the demands of the requirements, rather than limiting requirements to existing availabilities

20. Vrillon, "Active Manpower Policy in France," p. 9 of MS.

21. Claude Vimont, "Occupational Mobility of Manpower," in OECD Joint International Seminar on Geographical and Occupational Mobility of Manpower (Castelfusano), *Supplement to Final Report* (Paris, 1963), p. 16.

in labor. Third, government policy in the manpower field can help adapt labor supplies to planned or actual requirements through programs of education, training, retraining, and the like. Experience with the several Plans has led to more and further steps in what can be called active manpower policy. Under the Second Plan, proposals were made to bring women into the labor market on a part-time basis. The Third Plan had special measures to provide jobs for older people. Organization after organization, with initials like ANIFORMA, FASASA, ANIFRMO, were established in agriculture, industry, and among employers and labor groups to work on retraining. A committee was established to study the staggering of working hours to help adjustment to the city. A large step was taken in December 1963 with the creation of a Fonds National d'Emploi to raise payments to the unemployed and assist redeployment of workers through subsidies for retraining and transfer.[22] This is active manpower policy, and the episodic character of the separate items in it suggests empiricism, which is also characteristic of much else in French planning.

Moreover, the openness of the French economy qualifies a planning solution. On the one hand, access to foreign labor can make up for shortfalls of manpower at least at the unskilled level. It is of some interest that the April 1964 agreement with Algeria provides for the French to specify their needs every 3 months, rather than for 4 years at a time. Recruiting arrangements with Spain, Portugal, and Italy are even more flexible. On the other hand, of course, the competition of other labor markets in Europe leaves France subject to losses of foreign and even French labor, at least along the border as at Karlsruhe, to better jobs, in terms of salaries or amenities, in foreign countries. On this account, the French planning authorities must remain flexible.

The literature on French planning suggests that a major deficiency thus far in practice has been the development of policies for income distribution. This is rather different from incomes policy in the British sense of wage restraint. The latter was finally

22. Laurent Lucas, "France," in OECD International Trade Union Seminar on Active Manpower Policy (Vienna), *Supplement to Final Report* (Paris, n.d. [1965]), pp. 16–26.

added to French planning and active manpower policy in January 1965 when the government established committees of management and labor in the nationalized industries to propose annual wage increases for the government's decision.[23] This measure, like all measures of wage control, has been strongly opposed by French labor. French labor is interested in income distribution, supports the steps to provide better information on the subject, and wants to supplement the economic plan with a social plan favoring the lowest income groups. But while it wants all other decisions in the economy centralized, it does not want centralization of wage decisions, which "destroy their freedom and the raison d'être of the trade unions themselves," turning them into "mere machines for rubber stamping and carrying out decisions." [24]

The broad question of the social distribution of income we leave for Chapter XIII. Here I may conclude by suggesting that planning does not seem to be a substitute for incomes policy or an active manpower policy. These can contribute something, but probably not a great deal, to the elasticity of the labor supply near the level of full employment but less rather than more if they cannot operate on immigration or the movement of labor off the farm.

23. "French Are Wary on Economic Cure," *New York Times,* January 15, 1965.

24. Gabriel Ventejol, "Trade Union Analysis and Appraisal of Programming in France," in OECD International Trade Union Seminar on Economic and Social Programming (Paris), *Supplement to Final Report* (Paris, n.d. [1964?]).

CHAPTER XII

European Growth and the United States Balance of Payments

Europe's running out of labor has important implications for the world economy and especially for the balance of payments of the United States. The consequence in Europe is a change from supergrowth to normal growth: the virtuous circle in which exports led to growth which led to exports is giving way to the more usual mechanism under which expansion turns the balance of payments unfavorable. This has effected profound changes in the current account and basic balance of Europe and the United States. The picture is confused by an overlay of capital movements in both directions caused by imperfections in capital markets and differences in liquidity preferences in the two economies, joined together financially in 1958 for the first time since 1914. It lies beyond the scope of this book to probe deeply into these issues, but it may be useful to provide a sketch of the position to round out the discussion of the labor supply.

European Supergrowth and the United States Basic Balance

In the early period of postwar reconstruction, a substantial dollar shortage was filled by Lend-Lease, the British loan assistance interim, and Marshall Plan aid. High rates of investment and backlogs of consumption in Europe led to high imports and diverted resources from exports. Until about 1950, the balance of payments of Europe was made good by aid.

As the rate of growth picked up after 1950, the dollar shortage was replaced by a surfeit for a number of reasons. Of prime importance was the fact that the growth contained an important element of technical change, which led to import substitution and export expansion. United States dominance in world markets was ended, and even the American market was penetrated in many lines such as automobiles, steel, aircraft. The cost-price relationships appropriate to faster technological change in the United States than in Europe were initially corrected by European devaluations and were subsequently undermined by Europe's closing the technological gap in peacetime goods traded in world markets — though not perhaps in space and some military fields. In addition, rapid growth in Europe attracted American investment in several ways: first, because of the demand for capital financing; second, as a consequence of new European entry into products previously supplied from the United States, many of them highly income-elastic and supported by high growth rates; third, because European events such as the Rome Treaty called United States attention to investment opportunities that may have existed all along but that had lain unnoticed during the period of America's preoccupation with its own industrial reconstruction.

Under normal circumstances, the capital investments by the United States in Europe would have run up against shortages of resources — land and labor — raised costs and prices, diminished profits, and brought about both an import surplus to transfer them and a weakened incentive to sustain them. As it happened, however, the application of the Lewis model sustained profits, and the large technological content of new investment sustained exports (and reduced imports). While Harrod-Domar growth worsens the balance of payments, Abramovitz-Solow growth with a high technological content improves it.[1] The result was that the capital inflow occurred simultaneously with a current-account surplus. Exchange reserves built up.

The End of Supergrowth — the Schumpeterian Phase

When the excess labor ran out, supergrowth stopped and with it the virtuous circle in which exports and growth fed each other. Exports could rise as before, but the process of expanding capacity through investment now led to rising wages and prices. For investment to have a high technological content was not enough in the absence of an available margin of resources. Im-

1. See my *Foreign Trade and the National Economy* (New Haven: Yale University Press, 1962), chap. 11.

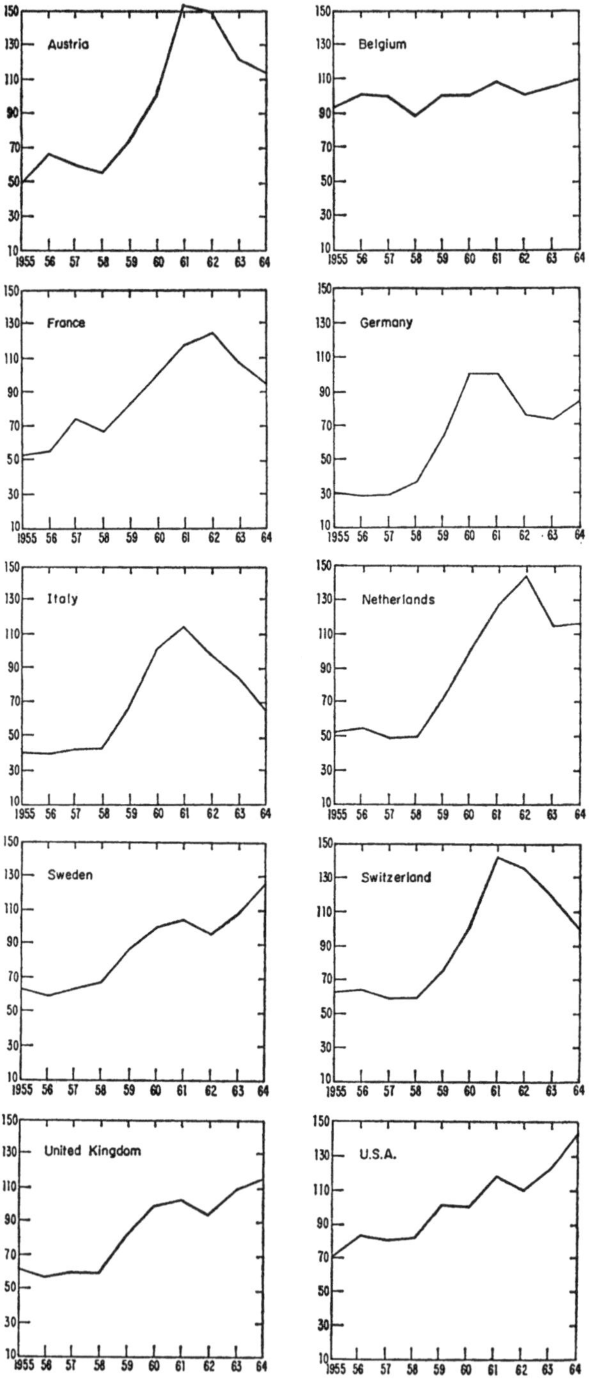
Austria
Belgium
France
Germany
Italy
Netherlands
Sweden
Switzerland
United Kingdom
U.S.A.
150 130 110 90 70 50 30 10
1955 56 57 58 59 60 61 62 63 64

ports increased, and with rising costs, exports became less competitive. Profits declined, as reflected in the record of falling stock prices (see Figure XII-1). Inflationary price increases brought about attempts at restriction in Germany in 1962 and 1965, in France in the fall of 1963, and in Italy and the Netherlands in 1964.

The end of supergrowth did not mean relief for the balance of payments of the United States, however. The trade position of the United States improved, as the Brookings Institution forecast said it would, and for the reason that prices had risen much faster in Europe than in the United States.[2] But the capital account worsened. While the basic balance (current account minus long-term capital outflow) of 17 countries of western Europe as estimated by the Chase Manhattan Bank (shown in Table XII-1) declined in all but one year from 1958 to 1964, it did not turn negative until the last year. Short-term capital inflows were sufficiently large to give these countries increases in official reserves averaging $2.5 billion annually and to bring total reserves to $30 billion.

When profits fall because of a decline in demand, investment declines, and with it rates of interest. When profits fall because of a rise in costs, however, the position is not so clear. Investment may be cut back because of the reduced availability of corporate savings and because, at the higher levels of costs, some investment projects that would have been profitable at lower costs no longer are. But there will also be opportunities to substitute capital for labor, especially when rising costs and falling profits are the result of higher wages. With reduced internal funds, advantage of these increased opportunities can be taken only if firms borrow. Where domestic capital markets have inelastic supplies of funds but markets are joined internationally, the increased demand for funds will spill abroad. Interest rates will rise unless international capital markets are integrated per-

2. See Walter S. Salant *et al., The United States Balance of Payments in 1968* (Washington, D.C.: Brookings Institution, 1963).

Figure XII-1. Course of stock markets in 10 countries, 1955–1964

Source: Organisation for Economic Co-operation and Development, *Main Economic Indicators, Historical Statistics, 1955–64,* Paris, 1966

TABLE XII-1

Aggregate balance of payments for 17 western European countries, 1958–1964
(millions of U.S. dollars)

	1958	1959	1960	1961	1962	1963	1964
Trade balance	−1133	− 547	−2756	−2412	−3989	−4921	−6524
Services (net)	4698	4459	5057	4750	4809	5073	5630
Current account balance	3566	3912	2301	2338	820	152	− 894
Transfer payments (net)	− 76	− 523	− 694	− 789	− 913	− 874	− 945
Long-term capital (net)	− 49	−1405	− 20	− 178	350	1823	1581
Basic balance	3440	1984	1587	1371	257	1101	− 258
Annual increase in official reserves	4086	252	5105	2934	1078	2130	2279

Source: Chase Manhattan Bank *Report on Western Europe,* No. 36 (June-July 1965), p. 4.

fectly. Direct investment is not likely to expand with declining profits, unless foreign firms are in a particularly advantageous position to undertake the labor-substituting, cost-reducing projects. United States direct investment in fact started to fall off in 1963 until the threat of restrictions on capital outflows in 1964 stimulated a sharp increase to place funds abroad while it was still possible.[3] But United States lending to the European capital market in debt form increased substantially. New issues of long-term dollar bonds by Europe in the New York market rose steeply after 1958 and were still climbing in 1963 when the

3. See Chase Manhattan Bank, "U.S. Investment Activity in Europe Slowing Down," *Report on Western Europe,* No. 28 (February-March 1964), p. 4. An undetermined amount of what is recorded as direct investment in the United States balance of payments is actually not investment in plant and equipment but rather an increase in the intercompany credits of United States companies with their subsidiaries abroad, arising from deposits by these subsidiaries in the Euro-dollar market. Where dividends were fated to be added to cash, companies typically postponed remittances to take advantage of the slightly higher rates of interest on time deposits available on Euro-dollar deposits as compared with American time deposits or certificates of deposit. It is accordingly impossible to trace the volume of true direct investment over time. The Chase Manhattan series is based on numbers of new operations of United States companies.

interest-equalization tax (IET) took effect in July. There followed a rapid expansion of long- and short-term bank lending, plus a movement of corporate funds to the Euro-dollar market, which led to the Voluntary Credit Restraint Program (VCRP) of February 1965. Not only was the outflow resisted in the United States; attempts were made in Europe to halt the inflow. The nature of this capital inflow was not thoroughly understood in Europe, or in most places elsewhere for that matter. Some believed that the United States was seeking to take over European productive assets cheaply. The fact that most firms buying European assets chose to borrow in Europe for the purpose, however, suggests that the assets were worth more to the American buyer than to the European seller (hence the sale), less because a given stream of income was capitalized at a lower rate of discount by the American buyer than because American technology was able to produce a larger stream of income with the given assets. This is particularly the case where the United States firm has a technical capacity or a capacity to integrate international operations that is unavailable to a local firm.

A second explanation is that capital movements in direct investment are perverse. If Europe has a surplus and the United States a deficit in the balance of payments, expansionary policies in Europe and deflationary policies in the United States will make investment profitable in the one and unprofitable in the other, thereby stimulating capital movements.[4] This explanation has limited value. The normal expectation is that deflationary policies include higher interest rates and that narrowing the interest-rate gap would attract capital inflows in debt instruments, or at least reduce the outflow. Since direct investment and debt capital moved in the same rather than in opposite directions, it is difficult to attach much importance to this hypothesis. In addition, a "perversity" explanation suffers the fatal flaw that profits have been falling in Europe and rising in the United States since about 1962 when capital movement was close to its height.

A third explanation for the capital movement from the United

4. See James E. Meade, "Exchange-Rate Flexibility" (paper presented to a Symposium on the International Payments Problem, American Enterprise Institute for Public Policy Research, Washington, D.C., 1965), p. 4.

States to Europe is that capitalists were seeking to escape the overvalued dollar and that in direct investment they could get more real assets for a dollar in the undervalued European currencies than they could in the United States with its overvalued dollar.[5] This reasoning has a certain superficial plausibility until it is recognized that the capital outflow to the Euro-dollar market was in dollars. The borrowers may have been interested in going short of dollars — though European banks and individuals lent to the Euro-dollar market as well as borrowed from it. If dollar holders had wished to go short of their currency, they would have loaned to Europe in marks or francs or guilders, and not dollars. There has been lending in European currencies, but the major financial institution of the period was the Euro-dollar market. Nor does overvaluation of the dollar explain the bond market, since European lenders bought a considerable proportion of the dollar bonds that European borrowers sold, and when the New York market was shut down by the IET, the trade was shifted to the foreign dollar-bond market in London.[6] It is conceivable that direct investment was inspired by chronic short positions in dollars and the relative cheapness of fixed assets in Europe as compared with the United States. But the theoretical model which underlies this view is faulty. Firms typically invest by buying flows of income, rather than bundles of assets, and if the bundle of assets is undervalued in a given case, so is the associated stream of income.

A fourth explanation for the movement at long term is that European capital markets are either ridden with monopoly, or

5. See H. S. Houthakker, "Exchange Rate Adjustment," in U.S. Congress Joint Economic Committee, *Factors Affecting the U.S. Balance of Payments*, 87th Cong., 2d sess. (Washington, D.C.: Government Printing Office, 1962), pp. 289–304.

6. See my "European Integration and the Development of a Single Financial Center for Long-Term Capital," *Weltwirtschaftliches Archiv*, XC (July 1963), 189–210. The foreign dollar-bond market proved to be a more flexible instrument of intra-European lending than unit-of-account bonds (supported by Brussels) or the multinational parallel foreign-currency bond issue (promoted by German bankers). See Nathaniel Samuel, "Perspectives on the New York Market: 'Capital Market Aspects'" (remarks before the National Industrial Conference Board, 1964); "Europe's First Bonds: Germany, Conceiver of Parallel Issues, Proves Laggard in Selling the Offering," *New York Times*, July 15, 1965.

dominated by very high liquidity preference, or both. On the first score, suppose that German banks like to maintain control over industrial firms and are prepared to lend at short term but monopolistically charge very high rates for long-term securities and are reluctant to market equity securities. Since banks dominate the sale of securities both by firms and to private investors, they are in position to set rates high for long-term securities. In these circumstances, German firms may find it profitable to borrow in the United States or in the Euro-dollar offshoot of the New York capital market, where rates for intermediate-term borrowing are well below those available in Europe.[7]

Or the spread between short- and long-term rates may be much wider in Europe than in the United States because of higher liquidity preference. After 50 years of war, inflation, capital levy, monetary reforms, and so on, European savers prefer to hold highly liquid assets, typically time deposits, whereas European firms like to consolidate debts, if possible, on something less than an open line of credit at the bank. With more long-term bonds offered than the market is eager to absorb, long- and intermediate-term rates of interest are high in Europe. In these circumstances, it is cheaper to borrow in the Euro-dollar market or the United States. This explanation helps account for the continued rise in European reserves as the trade balance, the current account, and the basic balance all declined from 1958 to 1964; since the European demand for savings was satisfied in the United States, the European supply of savings, held in liquid form, ended up as a claim in dollars. United States funds moving to Europe supplied not only real capital but also the liquidity needed by European savers and the term finance sought by European borrowers.[8]

7. U.S. Congress Joint Economic Committee, *A Description and Analysis of Certain European Capital Markets*, 88th Cong., 2d sess. (Washington, D.C.: Government Printing Office, 1964); see also my "Germany's Persistent Balance-of-Payments Disequilibrium," in R. E. Caves, H. G. Johnson, and P. B. Kenen (eds.), *Trade, Growth and the Balance of Payments: Essays in Honor of Gottfried Haberler* (Chicago: Rand McNally, 1965), pp. 230–248.

8. See my *Balance-of-Payments Deficits and the International Market for Liquidity*, Essays in International Finance No. 46 (Princeton: International Finance Section, 1965).

European observers occasionally counter this reasoning, claiming that the difficulty lies not in excessive demands for liquidity in Europe but in excessive supplies of liquidity in the United States. Monetary expansion by the United States banking system is blamed, and the theory has been propounded by a New York banker that a dollar of money creation in the United States is a dollar of capital exported. It is true that more liquidity exists in the United States than in Europe: larger firms have larger cash flows of profits and depreciation allowances, and a change in company liquidity preferences that has made them shift from demand deposits to time deposits and certificates of deposits has enabled bank credit to be expanded. On the other hand, monetary expansion has been much greater in Europe than in the United States, though money substitutes have perhaps expanded less. It is difficult to make the case that money expansion has been responsible for the capital flow when this expansion is a European rather than a United States phenomenon.

The fifth explanation turns on the change in income distribution. Falling profits and the rising share of wages in national income reduce savings and turn the balance of payments adverse. So long as the incentive to invest is high because of cost-reducing investment possibilities of the kind that Schumpeter believed occurred at the bottom of a depression, more capital is needed. With convertibility and joined capital markets, the capital is provided from abroad. The maintenance of a single capital market among the developed countries makes it impossible for European countries to hold back investment. Interest rates that would rise at home because of reduced savings and a constant or even higher inducement to invest will be held down by capital inflows.

The inflow is sometimes held responsible for the additional investment and the inflation. This is an oversimplified view. The inflation gave rise to the inflow. Moreover, if the inflow is prevented from taking place, as taxes on foreign lending and borrowing and restrictions in both the United States and Europe have sought to achieve, the inflation will continue for a time. Higher rates of interest may fail to cut investment financed by existing cash balances or short-term bank lending. Or the adverse balance of payments on current account could be financed by the repatriation of domestic funds — a capital inflow, but not a foreign one. This occurred in 1964 and 1965 in Switzerland. If banks have only limited short-term capital abroad, the same result can be achieved by a balance-of-payments deficit in which official reserves are drawn down. The beginnings of such a movement were discernible in Germany in the fall of 1965.

The first three explanations for the movement of United States capital to Europe — an attempt to take over European assets cheaply, higher profitability in Europe as a result of monetary policies, and an effort to escape from the overvalued dollar — are not credible. The next two — imperfections of European capital markets, including monopoly and extreme liquidity preference, on the one hand, and reduced savings with sustained investment demand, on the other — are more pervasive. They are not mutually exclusive, but they are of very different importance.

Cost-reducing investments in Europe by Europeans or American firms in the face of declining profits are often associated with big opportunities to reduce costs, typically by substituting capital for labor, and make an important contribution to economic growth in a period of labor shortage. It is wise to encourage them. They are unlikely to continue long in a period of profits squeeze. Much European investment in 1964 and 1965 seemed to be by local governments, such as municipalities, and represented social overhead capital associated, with a lag, with the plant and equipment investments of previous years. Such investment has been large in Switzerland and partly occasioned by immigrants. Action by the British and German governments in the summer of 1965 to reduce local government investments suggests that these lagged expenditures may have been more important in causing the inflation than cost-reducing industrial investment, although figures on which to base judgment will not be available for some time.

The end of supergrowth in Europe and the resultant squeeze on profits as costs rise have required European firms to turn to external sources of funds if they are to sustain investment. This has put pressure on domestic interest rates, and that in turn has led to more intensified liquidity exchange between Europe and the United States. The increase in capital flows from New York to Europe has exceeded the real capital movement transferred through the surplus in the balance of payments, though that has increased, and made United States and European governments believe that the deficit in the United States balance of payments was increasing. On both sides of the Atlantic the response has been to try to cut capital movements further, although the elusive character of money, costless to transport and store and easy to hide, has meant that cutting the capital movement has directed attention successively to the investment bankers (through the IET), the commercial bankers (through the Gore amendment), and the direct investors (through the VCRP) in turn, without eliminating the capital outflow. Such success as the program had by the summer of 1965, however, raised interest rates in Europe, hurt domestic investment then, and slowed down the rate of growth in Italy and France and, prospectively, elsewhere.

It seems unlikely that the rate of investment can long be sustained at high levels in Europe with compressed profits. The Schumpeterian model in which investment responds to opportunities for cost-reduction must ultimately give way to the Keynesian model in which investment responds to positive profits. But if the turning point is inherent in the end of supergrowth, the restrictions on capital movements that tighten European interest rates and restrict capital availability hasten its arrival. Action has been taken in France, Germany, and Italy to improve the functioning of capital markets and, to the extent that this is impossible, to substitute government for private institutions — Italian central-bank purchases of industrial bonds, for example, and French government borrowing to provide long-term funds for private companies such as Citroën. These actions are limited by institutional inhibitions and cannot proceed sufficiently far to enable Europe to achieve something approaching the United States interest-rate structure without gross international capital movements. For the United States to lend long and borrow short because of international trade in liquidity does not lead to a true deficit, if conducted within moderation. Failure to understand this point is what makes the United States and European governments alike desirous of cutting out the capital exchanges, with the inadvertent result of pushing up interest rates in Europe and contributing to the decline or stagnation of private investment.

The Balances of Separate Countries

While Europe's balance of payments as a whole has been steadily worsening since 1959, labor shortages and shifts from capital-widening to capital-deepening investment have led to wide swings in the balances of separate countries. As already noted, the German balance of payments, after worsening in 1961 and 1962, recovered in 1963 as a consequence of the inflationary expansions in Italy and France. The Dutch current account picked up in 1963 as wages soared for the same reason. In 1965 the Italian and French balances improved as the German picture turned adverse.

The Italian and French recoveries of 1965, however, represented something different from the expansion of the earlier decade. The 1963 stabilization plan in France and the 1964 cutback in Italy halted the rise in wages and prices by reducing investment and producing unemployment. Italian labor moved back to the south from northern Italy. French automobile plants cut investment and went on short time. Rather than hold back investment, it became necessary to stimulate it. Both economies shifted from the model where declining profits lead to increased investment, to the one where declining profits discourage expenditure. Rising exports came not from export push with highly competitive prices but from inflationary expansion abroad. Europe shifted from supply-led to demand-led growth.

The change is probably irreversible. Supergrowth from high demand hitting against an elastic supply curve of labor plus a backlog of innovation is probably impossible to resume after the labor supply runs out. Once demand expansion has been halted, cost-reducing investment is much less attractive, and the likelihood is that falling profits will give rise not to more but to less investment. The virtuous circle of positive feedback between exports and growth gives way to the classic mechanism of negative feedback, in which exports lead to inflation which induces the authorities to deflate and brake growth.

There are possibilities of overcoming the block to growth. If Dutch and German investment moves smoothly from capital-widening to capital-deepening and continues the reduction of costs and prices, growth could be sustained. Aside from a continued high birth rate in the Netherlands, capital imports will be required to fill the gap in savings left by lowered profit margins. Restriction of capital exports in the United States or of capital imports in Europe therefore would unfortunately speed the transition from continuous growth at a high level to the normal stop-go mechanism, which Britain has been unable to cast aside.

Or another means of escape from slackening growth may be the substantial increase in entry to the labor force that currently faces France, following the big upsurge in births in 1946 and the shrinkage of military service. France chooses to overcome the deficiencies of her capital market not through the international market for liquidity but by the government route. As already noted, private savings are made available to private industry by lending to the government and by government relending to industrial users.[9] Germany has made more use of this technique than is generally understood, for various German governmental organizations, from the Fund for the Equalization of War Losses to the social-security system, make loans to the mortgage market and to industrial borrowers alike.[10]

A third possible way of returning to supergrowth was pursued by Switzerland for a time but in the end abandoned. This was the importation of foreign labor and foreign capital. The reasons for halting further import of labor were mainly social but may have also included the risk of sudden repatriation in large numbers. The import of capital was stopped for the latter reason, because long-term commitments were being made on the basis of resources from abroad that were nominally short-term in character. As interest rates tightened in Switzerland, however, the Swiss banks brought home their own funds from abroad, so that the short-term inflow supporting long-term investment in housing and social overhead continued.

The voluntary restrictions adopted in the United States in

9. "France Planning Loan to Citroën," *New York Times,* August 26, 1965.

10. See Frederick G. Reuss, *Fiscal Policy for Growth without Inflation: The German Experiment* (Baltimore: Johns Hopkins Press, 1963), chaps. 15, 17; Karl W. Roskamp, *Capital Formation in West Germany* (Detroit: Wayne State University Press, 1965), chap. 4.

February 1965 have had evident impacts in Canada, Japan, Australia, and the United Kingdom. In the rest of Europe, the impact was not so visible. Short-term Euro-dollar rates tightened sharply in the first months as the supply of funds feeding the market from the United States was cut off and substantial amounts were withdrawn. By August of 1965, these rates had declined again. In August, Secretary of the Treasury Fowler said that the restrictions had corrected the balance of payments of the United States, at least briefly, and had had no adverse effect on the rest of the world.[11]

It is hard to believe that a substantial change in the flow of international capital could have limited effects. The observed effect could be explained in a number of ways. (1) Perhaps the anticipatory outflow prior to February 1965 provided the Euro-dollar market with all the funds it could absorb for some time (the immediate tightening of rates was the result of subjective evaluations of the market, rather than fundamental conditions, and could not be sustained). (2) Possibly withdrawals on the part of Americans repatriating capital were made good by additional deposits in the Euro-dollar market by foreign dollar holders, including central banks, and in particular by the Italian change from large-scale indebtedness to the Euro-dollar market in 1964 to a substantial surplus in 1965. This would account for part of the short-term outflow of funds from the United States.[12] (Note the similarity between this result, in which American short-term capital is kept out of Europe only to be replaced by European, and the Swiss attempt to restrict capital inflows only to be defeated by the repatriation of Swiss short-term funds abroad.) (3) Investment in Europe may be rather inelastic with respect

11. "Statement by Honorable Henry H. Fowler, Secretary of the Treasury, on the United States Balance of Payments before the Subcommittee on International Finance of the Senate Banking and Currency Committee" (mimeographed, 1965).

12. Transfers of short-term funds from New York to the Euro-dollar market produce no capital movement to the extent that the Euro-dollar market relends them back to New York. Where this happens, and the funds are subsequently reloaned to non-United States borrowers, the transfer of European funds from New York to the Euro-dollar market at one time would produce a capital outflow from the United States over an extended subsequent period. In the summer of 1965, the scale of the Italian deposits in the Euro-dollar market made it possible for the latter to redeposit funds in New York net.

to higher interest rates, and borrowers shift from the Euro-dollar to the domestic market where rates are high because of monopoly or high liquidity preference without reducing their expenditures significantly.

The restrictions on capital outflows from the United States and Europe will doubtless lower investment in Europe, cut growth, and reduce inflationary price increases. But this would have happened anyway, without the restrictions on capital movements, because of the running out of labor and Europe's inability to maintain growth by means of the Lewis model. Schumpeterian investment, in which rising costs and falling profits lead to increased rather than reduced investment, is a short-run phenomenon by its nature. It was not necessary to limit international capital mobility to bring the price increases of Europe to an end. Supergrowth, Schumpeterian investment, and price inflation are all giving way to normal growth rates averaged out over cycles of expansion and recession, a Keynesian investment function, and much slower price creep. Go-go growth on the Continent is over. The order of the day is stop-go, on the Continent as in Britain.

It seems unlikely that Continental Europe will have expansion periods limited to 15 to 18 months as in Britain. Birth rates are high in France and the Netherlands; there is still some underemployment in German agriculture and in the Mediterranean countries; the Netherlands and Germany have a capacity for labor-saving investment that will prolong expansion from the bottom of recessions. It is too early to say anything about the length of expansion periods before price increases set in or about how long it takes government policy to start revival after it has succeeded in halting inflation and growth. Surely, sufficient experience has been gained to prolong the expansion and shorten the recession. But it seems practically certain that the European experience of the 1950's cannot be duplicated and that of the British will not be.

Joined Capital Markets?

In pure theory, an international capital market that equalized not only the marginal efficiency of capital in Europe and the United States but also the structure of interest rates — apart from a few subsidiary markets like mortgages and savings deposits, which remain imperfectly connected — would improve world welfare.[13] In practice, to join money and capital markets means giving up the use of monetary policy for domestic stabilization and growth and relying more fully on fiscal policy. Interest rates would be changed by small degrees to attract capital to countries with a deficit. But with relatively perfect markets it would be impossible to raise interest rates to suppress inflation in Europe, since United States funds would swamp European money markets, or to lower rates in the United States to maintain expansionary pressure, for fear of capital outflows.[14] With perfectly functioning international capital markets, the need for owned reserves for international liquidity would be much diminished, approaching the 1913 system in which changes in bank rates in England attracted and repelled international funds. But it is by no means clear that the North Atlantic countries are ready to give up the use of monetary policy for domestic purposes. Fiscal policy instruments are not flexible enough, nor are economic analysts or political authorities ready to surrender a weapon of domestic policy.

These matters, as said at the outset of this chapter, are questions to be addressed on a different occasion. Here it is appropriate only to point out that even if it is decided to separate national capital markets, there is difficulty in doing so. "If there is anything international business economists have learned about the character of foreign trade as it has emerged over the Post-War period, it is that foreign trade and investment are integral parts of the same process. Constraints on foreign investment will be reflected in a reduction of exports." [15] And British experience with the lags and leads makes clear that attempts to control

13. Even with joined money and capital markets, interest rates are not equalized everywhere. Observe that mortgage rates and savings-bank deposit interest are higher in California than on the East Coast despite the persistent attempts of the California savings banks to attract funds from eastern depositors.

14. In actuality, it seems to be the case that the United States capital market is so much bigger and broader that changes in its level of interest rates change the level of the whole North Atlantic Community without producing sizable capital flows, while changes in the rates in the separate European countries produce large-scale offsetting capital movements.

15. R. F. Mikesell, "The Voluntary Restraint Program and the International Monetary System" (unpublished paper, 1965).

capital can be defeated through permitted trade movements. It may be a question more of feasible ways than of the desirable way of using monetary policy. A system of imperfect restraints on capital movements while monetary policy is largely used for domestic purposes, with capital leaking at the edges, seems the likely prospect for the near future. In the longer run, the restrictions will break down and have to be abolished in the pursuit of neatness. As the world becomes increasingly interconnected, national policies of economic control will become fewer.

If capital markets are deliberately joined, and if the invasion of European capital monopoly and trading in international liquidity preferences, which remain different in North America and Europe, continues, it seems unlikely that the United States will have a surplus for a long time, as calculated by Walther Lederer or Edward Bernstein. But this, as I have said elsewhere, and as the Brookings Institution insists, is an inappropriate concept of balance-of-payments deficit. The right one is basic balance.

On basic balance, the end of supergrowth means the end of the United States basic deficit. Whether the less important and even misleading Department of Commerce deficit or Bernstein deficits continue turns on whether governments continue their efforts to suppress capital movements. With freedom of capital movements, the "deficit" would probably last for a long time, until liquidity preferences in Europe resembled those of the United States. But these deficits are of limited importance; or would be if they were properly understood.

The most important conclusion of this chapter, however, is that the end of supergrowth for Europe means the adjustment of the basic balance, with rising prices in Europe and the achievement by the United States of a large current-account surplus. The weakness of the dollar in 1958 and 1959 is past.

CHAPTER XIII

Growth, Income Distribution, and Social Justice

The emphasis in this book on the economic aspects of income distribution — and especially its effects on growth and the balance of payments — should not obscure the important social and political dimensions of such distribution. Here is a paradox of social science. Growth is good for welfare, but the increased skewness of income distribution helpful to growth may subvert welfare. The resolution is that the first welfare is economic, the second social. Or it can be put that the welfare of the individual depends partly on his absolute level of living and partly on his relative position. Where growth occurs, even with constant shares, the $3,000-a-year man may object to the $30,000-a-year man receiving absolute increases 10 times greater than his own.

The difficulty can be resolved in some cases in the short run: it is said that Mexico has had the best of all possible worlds in the postwar period with high profits and revolutionary slogans. The paradox resolves itself in the long run when growth or supergrowth slows down to provide an opportunity for more equitable income distribution. It is true that half of Europe with a record of equitable income distribution is today concerned with faster growth — Scandinavia and Britain. It is equally true that parts of Europe that have experienced rapid economic growth are turning attention to the disproportions in income distribution that have been its by-product.

The problem is not new. At an early stage of the postwar period, one British observer characterized German policy as a "savage policy of deflation." In his view, giving up all pretense at controls and the unjust basis of the currency reform (which enabled entrepreneurs and traders to enrich themselves) led "to a co-existence of savage hardship with detestable excesses of luxury." [1] An earlier observer of British nineteenth-century growth found it incredible that economic ideas could so overwhelm social considerations that large numbers of agricultural workers could be uprooted and transferred into urban slums.[2] With the slowing down of growth in the Great Depression, however, more equitable income distribution and attention to problems of social welfare ensued. Similarly, the end of supergrowth on the Continent provides an opportunity for attention to social ends.

German Wealth Policies

While rapid German growth may have been a product largely of technological change plus an elastic labor supply, fiscal policy has played a substantial role. These policies favored skewness of income. Income tax rates were not very progressive, and exemptions were granted for savings. Reinvested profits paid reduced taxes. The number of millionaires in the country increased steadily.[3]

One element in capital formation in Germany was government savings. Karl Roskamp explains that it is wasteful to give broad concessions to private savings and more flexible for government to save and to make capital available to business enterprise as well as to public bodies. With government savings and reinvested profits, savings were largely involuntary.[4]

To obtain some breadth of public participation, the German government adopted policies for spreading stock ownership. The immediate occasion has been the desire of the government to sell off certain large industrial holdings that it happened to own for some reason or other — Preussag in iron and steel, Volkswagen in automobiles, Veba in electricity, Lufthansa in airlines. Special low prices have been made to low-income purchasers of the shares of some companies, as part of a "property for all" policy. Wider sharing of industrial securities is supported by

1. Thomas Balogh, *Dollar Crisis* (Oxford: Blackwell, 1949), p. 26.
2. Karl Polanyi, *The Great Transformation* (New York: Farrar & Rinehart, 1944).
3. "Millionaires in Marks Put at 11,663 in West Germany," *New York Times,* March 12, 1965.
4. Karl Roskamp, *Capital Formation in West Germany* (Detroit: Wayne State University Press, 1965), p. 264.

the Evangelical Church as a healthy social policy designed to increase citizen responsibility, and the Catholic Church even favors forcing employees to save in the form of industrial shares through wage deductions.[5] The specific measures of *Eigentums-politik* (property policy), however, seem designed mainly to widen the capital market for industrial securities and to soak up redundant liquid savings in Germany. German households, which save 12 percent of their income, put them largely into savings accounts and life insurance and increasingly into home ownership. Purchases of shares by the little man is thus regarded as contributing to political stability, on the one hand, and breadth of security markets, on the other. Some loss in corporate savings may be required, since businesses would have to pay higher rates of dividend to make possible a return on shares competitive with interest on other sectors of the capital market. German official policy is still opposed to "excessive tax on incomes" and directed to the promotion of wealth accumulation.[6] The policy of property for all is largely a policy for broadening security ownership without changing a heavily skewed income distribution.

More fundamental discussion of social policy is conducted inside and outside of Germany. The question is raised whether mass prosperity means injustice, and specifically whether the 1951 increase in the turnover tax from 3 to 4 percent should not have been rescinded. Has *Sozialmarktwirtschaft* degenerated into the rule of every man for himself and left Germany with no binding rules of community life, its millionaires hedged against social difficulty, and avoiding taxes, by houses and land bought in Switzerland, Italy, and Spain?[7] Is the inequality of incomes too high a price for economic growth in a country still struggling

5. "Eigentum für ein mündiges Volk, Eine Denkschrift des Rates der Evangelischen Kirke in Deutschland zur Eigentumsbildung," *Frankfurter Allgemeine Zeitung*, April 25, 1962; "Property for All: Germany's Newest Social Revolution," *The Bulletin* (published by the Presse- und Informationsamt der Bundesregierung), February 23, 1965; Günther Behrendt, "Ownership Policy in the Federal Republic of Germany," *The German Economic Review*, III (4th Quarter 1965), 281–289.

6. "Economic Objectives in the Near Future, Minister Schmuecker Points Up Main Issues," *Handelsblatt* (Dusseldorf), July 9, 1965; translated in *German Tribune*, No. 174, July 31, 1965.

7. Hans Herbert Goetz, *Weil alle besser leben wollen: Portraet der deutschen Wirtschaftspolitik* (Dusseldorf: Econ-Verlag, 1963).

to cement its democracy?[8] With prosperity has come a sense of uneasiness.[9] There is no serious class tension or political strife, and all parties are basically agreed on the economic and political system. But it is thought that the economy could be run more equitably. The palliative of *Eigentumspolitik* — wider shareholdings — may be sufficient to dispel the disquiet, or political objectives such as reunification or joining the nuclear club may divert attention from it. With slower growth, however, the question of income distribution is likely to call for more attention.

If a million to a million and a half foreign workers settle in Germany, moreover, a new social problem arises, the dimensions of which have not been considered. If the total levels off at 1½ million workers, but turns over at the average of a 3-year stay, a problem hardly arises. The transient compares his level of living and property holdings, plus his opportunities for housing, education, and so on, with those of people at home rather than with the German populace. If increasing numbers settle, however, a gradual assimilation or integration process must take place. The question of gradualness is crucial. If the process is drawn out over a generation or so, there is likely to be little difficulty. If the guest workers shortly insist, however, that they are Europeans, full members of the family, and entitled to equality of treatment forthwith, the scale of the social adjustment poses difficulties.

Italian Structural Reforms

German prosperity eroded the basic differences between the Christian Democrats and the Socialists, and no Communist party grew up to replace that destroyed under Nazism. The same was not true of Italy. There the demand for social justice was kept alive by a Communist party less aligned with the Soviet Union than engaged in "protest against the injustice, privilege and corruption that taint the 'Italian [economic] miracle.'"[10] Workers who found jobs through unemployment or underemployment in

8. Roskamp, *Capital Formation in West Germany*, p. 266.

9. A similar position is said to exist in Austria, where pride over economic achievements is mixed with doubt over the future, based on mingled economic and political factors. See "Unbehagen in der Wirtschaftliche Grunstimmung Österreich," *Neue Zürcher Zeitung*, August 5, 1964.

10. "Italy Weighs Opening to Left," *New York Times*, November 17, 1963.

agriculture quickly turned attention from progress made to the distance left to go; they and their political representatives attacked industrial monopolies, tax evasion, unequal distribution of agricultural land, poverty remaining in the south, swollen bureaucracies with their waste and graft, the slums of Milan and Turin, the separation of families involved in migration. Radical changes in state and society involving structural reforms were needed before the position would be satisfactory: redistribution of land, nationalization of industry, new taxation on incomes from property, a stepping-up of development plans for the south, and the like.

It was these demands which led to the movement to the Left in Italian government in 1963 and precipitated the flight of capital, the balance-of-payments crisis of early 1964, and the stabilization program. After more than a decade, the end of supergrowth and the advent of inflation precipitated a sharp political debate. The Left blamed the halt in the boom and the downturn on low wages, speculation, and the central government's failure to make agriculture competitive and to streamline distribution. The Right blamed government spending, the rise in wages, nationalization of the electrical industry, and the 15 percent withholding tax on dividends. The basic cause, in my view, was none of these but was the full absorption of labor. The proximate cause was the demand for social justice under rising prosperity.

With the need to halt the inflation and the ensuing slowdown of growth, the opening to the Left lost something in importance. Demand for structural reforms comes second to economic prosperity. Concessions to the financial community helped slightly to revive capital investment. (The nationalization of the electrical industry was not reversed, but the terms of compensation were liberal.) One way of putting it is that full employment is the most important structural reform. When this is satisfied, it is time to move to the next items on the list; when full employment is missing, some compromise of other objectives may be necessary, or progress toward them can be put to one side.

Income Distribution in France

In other countries, incomes policy is largely associated with the price of labor, as we have seen in Chapter XI. In French planning, however, the matter is seen somewhat differently. The Plan says what goods are to be produced; it should also see that incomes are distributed equitably. Planning cannot end the class struggle, of course.[11] But, in the words of the Fourth Plan, it can "adopt certain selective measures benefiting the least favored sections of the population," and it may do more.[12] The two standard books on French planning, by Pierre Bauchet and by John and Anne-Marie Hackett, direct their concluding chapters to the question of whether planning can be used to arrive at a socially agreed distribution of income that is both equitable and efficient.

Little attention is given to the possibility that a plan which attempts to be fully equitable and completely efficient may be overdetermined. If equity is given priority, a plan can surely be efficient within the constraint of a given income distribution. Or for a given rate of growth, if efficiency be put in these terms, it is possible to work out maximum equality of income distribution under a system of competitive pricing for factors of production. But the most efficient and the most equitable may be simultaneously unobtainable, if high profits promote growth and high wages stimulate consumption but fail to provide savings. This dilemma seems not to have been faced squarely in France. A first step was taken in 1962 when it was decided that better information was needed on the distribution of income, and a major investigation was undertaken. Various evident inequities were corrected by raising pensions, lifting minimum wages, and narrowing regional differentials under the Fourth Plan. But the Stabilization Plan of 1963, slowing down the rate of growth, diverted attention from income distribution and returned it to the topic of full employment.

French public opinion is constrained by the monolithic structure of the Fifth Republic and may be diverted from issues of social justice by a national policy of grandeur. At the same time, peasants were restive during the period of rapid growth because of the educational disability under which they labored if they were to leave for the city, and they objected to the purchases of

11. Pierre Bauchet, *Economic Planning: The French Experience* (New York: Praeger, 1964), p. 244.

12. John Hackett and Anne-Marie Hackett, *Economic Planning in France* (Cambridge, Mass.: Harvard University Press, 1963), p. 311.

agricultural land for estates of rich industrialists. Particular segments of the French populace live in peculiarly disadvantageous circumstances, despite the general prosperity. Two million workers are alleged to live miserably in a "proletarian condition." [13] A telling point against the De Gaulle government in the 1965 election campaign was that the administration had neglected France's great numbers of old people, on limited pensions, who had been squeezed by the inflation up to 1963, but whose real incomes had been held down to the lowest level in the stabilization program enacted then. A particularly French passion for justice found expression over the educational system, ostensibly equitable because free but one in which the lack of university places fostered the raising of admission standards by more and more difficult examinations, leading to scandals of examination stealing and grading. But even the clash between equity and growth has been less in evidence after the 1963 stabilization program, with automobile factories going on short time and the rate of growth slowing down. Labor unions and farm groups expressed resentment at government optimism over "autumn upturns" and "the betterment of workers' living standards." [14] Nevertheless, long-range adjustments in distribution of income have been put aside in the interest of short-run expansion.

Leveling of Incomes in Britain

In the United Kingdom, the position is broadly otherwise: growth is slow, but income redistribution has gone much further than on the Continent, apart from the Netherlands and Scandinavia.[15] Taking as a measure the percentage of income that would have to be redistributed among income groups to achieve perfect equality, the inequality index of income in Britain after tax and with social benefits has declined from about 40 before

13. Alain Murcier, "Comment Faire Disparaître la Condition Proletarianne," *Le Monde,* July 11, 1964.

14. "Optimistic Talk Irks Frenchmen," *New York Times,* September 4, 1965.

15. In Sweden, the elimination of poverty and the leveling of incomes have turned attention to growth. See, for example, the Swedish tax reform of the summer of 1964, which raised the turnover tax and lowered income taxes in an effort to stimulate incentives, though it was called "a just and rational distribution of the tax burden" ("Swedish Taxes: Redistributing the Burden," *Economist,* CCXII, August 8, 1964, 573).

World War I to 30 in 1928 and 15 in 1948–49.[16] These data are by no means unambiguous. In a period of rapidly advancing progressive taxation, the income-tax returns of individuals are highly unreliable indicators of equality trends.[17] But the British have a comparatively high standing with regard to social justice and a low one in rates of economic growth, and they are unhappy about it.

The position is simple and clear-cut on neither score. While growth rates are low on the basis of British statistics, the level of living has risen substantially. A citizen returning to the country from India in 1958 after a three-year absence insists that the picture of an exhausted England, divided and stagnant, is untrue. "Britain is rising from the ashes of her Empire more vigorous and dramatic than ever. . . . Prosperity has come to stay. . . . The revolution of comfort has even reached . . . the home. . . . Much of the technological revolution when there is a shift from cotton to 'Terylene' and from wool to plastic-coated furniture does not show in the [national-income] figures."[18] Workers are buying houses (30 percent), cars (32 percent), washing machines (29 percent), and refrigerators (15 percent), as well as the ubiquitous television set (83 percent). In addition, they are acquiring savings.[19]

On the other hand, not everyone believes that income is more equitably distributed in Britain. Professor Richard Titmuss, for example, writes: ". . . There is more than a hint from a number

16. A. M. Cartter, *The Redistribution of Income in Postwar Britain* (New Haven: Yale University Press, 1955), p. 74.

17. John A. Brittain, "Some Neglected Features of Britain's Income Levelling," *American Economic Review*, L (May 1960), 593–603.

18. Taya Zinkin, "Britain's Leap to Prosperity," *Manchester Guardian Weekly*, July 24, 1958, p. 16.

19. Ferdynand Zweig, *The Worker in an Affluent Society: Family Life and Industry* (London: Heinemann, 1961), pp. 8, 104, 125, and chap. 4. The figures on purchases are based on a sample drawn from 5 industrial plants, and where there is a dispersion because of local conditions — in automobiles and house-ownership for example — the figure represents the central tendency, i.e., roughly what is thought would be the median if there were more data. Some considerable part of the prosperity of Britain observed in 1958 and 1959 by Zweig is attributable to the fact that more than half the families studied had 2 breadwinners (216 out of 398) and 16 percent (65 families) had 3 or more (*ibid.*, p. 4). This is an important by-product of full employment neglected in statistics of income per employed worker.

of studies that income inequality has increased since 1949 whilst the ownership of wealth, which is far more highly concentrated in the United Kingdom than in the United States, has probably become still more unequal, and in terms of family ownership, possibly strikingly more unequal in recent years." [20] He believes that capital gains, expense accounts, income and wealth splitting, and a host of other devices developed in the period of steeply progressive income taxes gave Britain, before the tax reforms of 1965, much less equality of income distribution than the world credits her with.

But there is something to it. The picture of the angry young Briton is drawn from literature, not life. Ferdynand Zweig did not find one seriously disaffected young man in 600 industrial workers. Class divisions in economic terms are breaking down, as the working classes move up to middle-class standards of comfort. It is true that class distinctions remain in the factory, though they are breaking down in economic terms outside, and that social cleavages, based on culture and education, remain and may even be intensified. What is remarkable, however, is that among the 300 to whom he put the question directly, Zweig was not able to find one man who thought himself unhappy.[21] The task would not be difficult in France.[22]

Growthmanship

The point of this peroration is the rather banal one that economic growth is not sufficient. It helps to have a rapid rate of expansion and a favorable balance of payments. With brisk demand, a margin of technological innovations to apply, and an elastic labor supply, growth can be sustained and will assist a society in attacking the important problems of community. But the problems of social adjustment can be addressed directly even when growth has slowed down; and they need to be. It is heresy for an economist to say it, but social adjustment is more important than growth. To the extent that growth intensifies social

20. Richard M. Titmuss, *Income Distribution and Social Change: A Study in Criticism* (London: Allen & Unwin, 1962), p. 198.

21. Zweig, *The Worker in an Affluent Society*, pp. 135, 155, 190, 211.

22. See L. A. Vincent, "Niveaux de vie, évolution économique et mécontentement," *Études et Conjuncture*, XIV (February 1959), 143–150.

maladjustment, it becomes growthmanship and is to be abhorred.

The end of European postwar supergrowth is not catastrophic. Efforts to restore it, if the labor supply is inelastic and investment does not readily shift to capital-deepening, may better be applied directly to the important problems of social justice, including, in the forefront, full employment.

Index

Publications Written under the Auspices of the Center for International Affairs, Harvard University

BOOKS

The Soviet Bloc, by Zbigniew K. Brzezinski (jointly with the Russian Research Center), 1960. Harvard University Press. Revised and enlarged edition, 1967.

The Necessity for Choice, by Henry A. Kissinger, 1961. Harper & Bros.

Strategy and Arms Control, by Thomas C. Schelling and Morton H. Halperin, 1961. Twentieth Century Fund.

Rift and Revolt in Hungary, by Ferenc A. Váli, 1961. Harvard University Press.

United States Manufacturing Investment in Brazil, by Lincoln Gordon and Engelbert L. Grommers, 1962. Harvard Business School.

The Economy of Cyprus, by A. J. Meyer, with Simos Vassiliou (jointly with the Center for Middle Eastern Studies), 1962. Harvard University Press.

Entrepreneurs of Lebanon, by Yusif A. Sayigh (jointly with the Center for Middle Eastern Studies), 1962. Harvard University Press.

Communist China 1955–1959: Policy Documents with Analysis, with a Foreword by Robert R. Bowie and John K. Fairbank (jointly with the East Asian Research Center), 1962. Harvard University Press.

In Search of France, by Stanley Hoffmann, Charles P. Kindleberger, Laurence Wylie, Jesse R. Pitts, Jean-Baptiste Duroselle, and François Goguel, 1963. Harvard University Press.

Somali Nationalism, by Saadia Touval, 1963. Harvard University Press.

The Dilemma of Mexico's Development, by Raymond Vernon, 1963. Harvard University Press.

Limited War in the Nuclear Age, by Morton H. Halperin, 1963. John Wiley & Sons.

The Arms Debate, by Robert A. Levine, 1963. Harvard University Press.

Africans on the Land, by Montague Yudelman, 1964. Harvard University Press.

Counterinsurgency Warfare, by David Galula, 1964. Frederick A. Praeger, Inc.

People and Policy in the Middle East, by Max Weston Thornburg, 1964. W. W. Norton & Co.

Shaping the Future, by Robert R. Bowie, 1964. Columbia University Press.

Foreign Aid and Foreign Policy, by Edward S. Mason (jointly with the Council on Foreign Relations), 1964. Harper & Row.

Public Policy and Private Enterprise in Mexico, by M. S. Wionczek, D. H. Shelton, C. P. Blair, and R. Izquierdo; ed. Raymond Vernon, 1964. Harvard University Press.

How Nations Negotiate, by Fred C. Iklé, 1964. Harper & Row.

China and the Bomb, by Morton H. Halperin (jointly with the East Asian Research Center), 1965. Frederick A. Praeger, Inc.

Democracy in Germany, by Fritz Erler (Jodidi Lectures), 1965. Harvard University Press.

The Troubled Partnership, by Henry A. Kissinger (jointly with the Council on Foreign Relations), 1965. McGraw-Hill Book Co.

The Rise of Nationalism in Central Africa, by Robert I. Rotberg, 1965. Harvard University Press.

Pan-Africanism and East African Integration, by Joseph S. Nye, Jr., 1965. Harvard University Press.

Communist China and Arms Control, by Morton H. Halperin and Dwight H. Perkins (jointly with the East Asian Research Center), 1965. Frederick A. Praeger, Inc.

Problems of National Strategy, ed. Henry Kissinger, 1965. Frederick A. Praeger, Inc.

Deterrence before Hiroshima: The Airpower Background of Modern Strategy, by George H. Quester, 1966. John Wiley & Sons.

Containing the Arms Race, by Jeremy J. Stone, 1966. M.I.T. Press.

Germany and the Atlantic Alliance: The Interaction of Strategy and Politics, by James L. Richardson, 1966. Harvard University Press.

Arms and Influence, by Thomas C. Schelling, 1966. Yale University Press.

Political Change in a West African State: A Study of the Modernization Process in Sierra Leone, by Martin L. Kilson, 1966. Harvard University Press.

Planning without Facts: Lessons in Resource Allocation from Nigeria's

Development, by Wolfgang F. Stolper, 1966. Harvard University Press.

Export Instability and Economic Development, by Alasdair I. MacBean, 1966. Harvard University Press.

Foreign Policy and Democratic Politics, by Kenneth N. Waltz (jointly with the Institute of War and Peace Studies, Columbia University), 1967. Little, Brown & Co.

Sino-Soviet Relations and Arms Control, ed. Morton H. Halperin (jointly with the East Asian Research Center), 1967. M.I.T. Press.

Contemporary Military Strategy, by Morton H. Halperin, 1967. Little, Brown & Co.

Africa and United States Policy, by Rupert Emerson, 1967. Prentice-Hall.

Europe's Postwar Growth: The Role of Labor Supply, by Charles P. Kindleberger, 1967. Harvard University Press.

OCCASIONAL PAPERS, PUBLISHED BY THE CENTER FOR INTERNATIONAL AFFAIRS

1. *A Plan for Planning: The Need for a Better Method of Assisting Underdeveloped Countries on Their Economic Policies,* by Gustav F. Papanek, 1961.
2. *The Flow of Resources from Rich to Poor,* by Alan D. Neale, 1961.
3. *Limited War: An Essay on the Development of the Theory and an Annotated Bibliography,* by Morton H. Halperin, 1962.
4. *Reflections on the Failure of the First West Indian Federation,* by Hugh W. Springer, 1962.
5. *On the Interaction of Opposing Forces under Possible Arms Agreements,* by Glenn A. Kent, 1963.
6. *Europe's Northern Cap and the Soviet Union,* by Nils Örvik, 1963.
7. *Civil Administration in the Punjab: An Analysis of a State Government in India,* by E. N. Mangat Rai, 1963.
8. *On the Appropriate Size of a Development Program,* by Edward S. Mason, 1964.
9. *Self-Determination Revisited in the Era of Decolonization,* by Rupert Emerson, 1964.
10. *The Planning and Execution of Economic Development in Southeast Asia,* by Clair Wilcox, 1965.
11. *Pan-Africanism in Action,* by Albert Tevoedjre, 1965.

12. *Is China Turning In?* by Morton H. Halperin, 1965.
13. *Economic Development in India and Pakistan,* by Edward S. Mason, 1966.
14. *The Role of the Military in Recent Turkish Politics,* by Ergun Özbudun, 1966.
15. *Economic Development and Individual Change: A Social-Psychological Study of the Comilla Experiment in Pakistan,* by Howard Schuman, 1967.

Bei Fragen zur Produktsicherheit wenden Sie sich bitte an:
If you have any questions regarding product safety,
please contact:

Walter de Gruyter GmbH
Genthiner Straße 13
10785 Berlin
productsafety@degruyterbrill.com